Controversies in Cr

series editor Victor E. Kappel

MW00574813

Controversies in

Policing

Quint C. Thurman
Texas State University – San Marcos

Andrew Giacomazzi
Boise State University

 **LexisNexis**®

 **anderson publishing**
A member of the LexisNexis Group

Controversies in Policing

Copyright © 2004
Matthew Bender & Company, Inc., a member of the LexisNexis Group

Phone 877-374-2919
Web Site www.lexisnexis.com/anderson/criminaljustice

Thurman, Quint C.
     Controversies in policing / Quint C. Thurman, Andrew Giacomazzi.
       Includes index.
       ISBN 1-58360-552-5 (paperback)

Transferred to Digital Printing 2011

Cover design by Tin Box Studio, Inc.

EDITOR Janice Eccleston
ACQUISITIONS EDITOR Michael C. Braswell

Acknowledgments

The editors of *Controversies in Policing* spent several months developing the outline for this work and then many more working with participating authors to ensure the best possible selections and contributions. Accordingly, there are many people we wish to acknowledge for their help during this lengthy process.

First, we wish to thank our wives, Caryn and Patricia, and our children, for their support and patience during the entire process. Second, we would like to show our appreciation to a stellar group of contributors who, in all cases, provided us with the excellent scholarship that comprises this edition. Not only was it our pleasure to work with them on this project, we learned much from them during the review process about topics that were largely outside our areas of expertise. We greatly appreciate the wisdom they have shared with us and the criminal justice community.

Finally, in the production trenches we want to thank Texas State University's Michele Quinones and Vicki Quintana for their commitment to seeing this project through to the finish; Victor Kappeler for guiding us in the development of the initial project and overseeing the final product; and Janice Eccleston at LexisNexis Matthew Bender for her much appreciated patience and attention to detail during the entire process.

Table of Contents

Introduction to Controversies in Policing

Quint C. Thurman

This book takes its place among several others nearly identical to it in form that Series Editor Victor E. Kappeler has produced for LexisNexis Matthew Bender (formerly Anderson Publishing Co.). Other excellent productions in this series have included *Controversies in Critical Criminology* by Martin D. Schwartz and Suzanne E. Hatty, *Controversies in Criminal Justice Research* by Richard Tewksbury and Elizabeth Ehrhardt Mustaine, *Controversies in White-Collar Crime* by Gary W. Potter, and *Controversies in Victimology* by Laura J. Moriarty. Co-author Andrew Giacomazzi and I are honored to be included as contributors to such a series.

American policing has undergone significant change over time since its first appearance in modern form in the nineteenth century. From its British origins which have long endured—in many respects, worldwide and, in the U.S., to this day—in terms of organization and function, police in this country also have been transformed by social movements and events that have left a uniquely American mark on the public safety agencies that we see in place in the U.S. today.

While we might at this point share with readers a brief history of American policing that would lead us from its origins in this country during the Political Era (roughly 1840 through 1920) through the Professional Era that lasted for the next 50 years until the Community Era, such a historical tour is outside of the scope of the objective of this book. Instead we would refer readers to other sources where this information is available (e.g., see Thurman, Zhao, and Giacomazzi's *Community Policing in a Community Era*, 2001). Suffice it to note that challenging times have led many organizations to adapt and evolve. Such is the case with American policing.

Former Minneapolis Police Chief Anthony Bouza laments in Chapter 1 that it is a sad state of affairs that there indeed are too few controversies in American policing. Mr. Bouza, an author of eight books, is a provocative and eloquent teacher on the state of American policing. Having admired him for many years through several media sources (books, TV, and documentaries), I finally had the opportunity to meet him when I invited him to conduct a lecture at Wichita State University a few years ago. In class and over dinner, I marveled at his intellect and wisdom.

He convinced me that the police have to remain ever vigilant to serving the public (as opposed to just serving themselves). He also reminded me, as an educator, that for learning to occur, teachers must be in the business of provoking thought rather than just entertaining or pleasing their students. In these regards, this book presents controversial topics for consideration that encourage readers to think about what *they* believe ought to be done.

The selections in this book identify several of the existing issues in policing in general that someone ought to do something about and present various viewpoints on what it is that we ought to consider doing. We also attempt to do so against the backdrop of an era of significant change in worldwide security that has caused major changes in the manner in which the U.S. conducts its political, social, and economic affairs.

Since September 11, 2001, the U.S. has experienced widespread public shock, anger, grief, and eventually resignation about the national tragedies that happened on that date. Sociologists could have predicted such responses, and we as a society would have understood it better, if the events of 9/11 had happened elsewhere and on a lesser scale to some other collectivity that had a track record with this sort of thing. Before the events of this date, few Americans would have conceived of such destruction nor would we have ever believed that anyone in the world would have wished us such ill will in the first place.

The events of 9/11 will be recorded in American history as a watershed in the determination of future courses of action in foreign relations, the development of approaches to the threat of international terrorism, and the formulation and application of security measures within U.S. borders. Key among domestic issues beyond the formidable price tag of heightened security, are those issues relating to police powers versus constitutional protections as David Perkins will discuss in Chapter 2 and Victor Kappeler and Karen Miller-Potter will expound upon in Chapter 3. But first we will digress a bit.

The Fear of Crime

If there is something Americans believe they need then they seem willing to find a way to pay for it as the prison construction boom has shown when it was determined that the public had endured too much street crime. How safe do we want to be and how much of our civil liberties we really are willing to give up pose interesting questions. Underpinning this debate is the public's fear of crime.

President Franklin Delano Roosevelt, perhaps the greatest of the U.S. Presidents, reminds us that "the only thing to fear is fear itself." Broadly speaking, Americans don't take kindly to fear and seem all too willing to rise up against a threat against our national interests when we can determine what (or who) the source of threat is and if we can use our military against it. But the challenge of fear attached to phenomena inside our own nation's boundaries is different, if not foreign and perplexing.

Generalized fear associated with crime leads to anxiety for our society because Americans as a group are problem-solvers accustomed to doing something about those things that are cause for concern. Anxiety occurs when we don't know what to do, or don't even know exactly what it is that we should fear. In short, anxiety comes from uncertainty.

Throughout the history of the American criminal justice system the fear of crime mostly has been linked to the fear of street crime at the hands of a stranger. While criminologists will tell us that police officers often are called to deal with situations that ought not to be happening in the first place, most crimes (including the violent ones) are not committed by strangers. Even so, the public continues to be fearful that they will suffer a criminal victimization at the hands of an unknown person. Furthermore, those who tend to be most fearful often tend to have the most unrealistic fears (e.g., citizens who are older, white, and female tend to be the most afraid of criminal victimization).

The fear of crime can be examined according to a continuum of specific threats to those that are less specific in nature. On one end of the spectrum is the fear that we might associate with a direct confrontation with an aggressive assailant as in the case of a robbery or aggravated assault. At the other end is the fear of crime linked to physical decay and disorder made famous in Wilson and Kelling's "Broken Windows" article from 1982. At this end of the continuum, the threat is non-specific but the run-down appearance of a place may signal that the space in question is just a criminal victimization waiting to happen. Awareness of this phenomenon at least partly explains the need for community policing.

The tragic events on September 11 undoubtedly raised citizen appreciation for public safety personnel who risk their lives to protect, serve, and at times even rescue society from dangerous circumstances. September 11 also raised public expectations concerning what should be done in the future to make us safe from new danger that we really never thought possible.

Public expectations concerning the emergence of leadership to help us understand and be assured of an effective course of action principally have been directed at the federal level. In response, the federal government has sent troops to Afghanistan, created a cabinet-level homeland security post, and promised to create a $38 billion homeland security administration which would be the largest federal agency created since the Department of Defense was established in 1947.

But fear on a more personal level is more typically handled locally by public safety agencies hopefully working in cooperation with citizens at the grassroots level. Disturbances that immediately threaten the lives of ordinary citizens like the serial sniper case in the Washington, DC area are going to be reacted to by local men and women in police uniform for they are the first line of defense against violent crime in nearly every community in this country.

Fear Assessment and Reduction

So how do police agencies reduce public fear of crime? Research shows that the reduction of fear is linked to an increase in satisfaction with the police. Citizens who believe that the police in their communities care about their concerns and are responsive to their safety needs are more satisfied with police services and consequently, feel safer than those who are dissatisfied with those law enforcement agents entrusted to protect them. In turn, a public who trusts the police will be more supportive of public safety efforts to make society safer.

An effective police presence is one component of citizen satisfaction. But it matters how the police are distributed and what they do on duty for the police to be perceived as effective. Routine or targeted police patrolling is not a sufficient substitute. Instead, research by Zhao and his colleagues in Chapter 4 shows that a large crime reduction impact is attributable to money spent in communities for the purpose of hiring more police officers to work closely with citizens to identify their crime-related concerns and then work to resolve them. Using community newsletters to contact citizens, establishing victim contact programs, opening police substations, supporting citizens on patrol, and developing crime control programs to reduce disorder are just a few of the approaches that research has shown to be effective at reducing crime, increasing citizen satisfaction with the police, and thereby reducing public fear of crime.

Not every community in the U.S. is alike. Accordingly, not every community has the same risk of incurring the most extreme forms of violent crime or mass violence. Our nation's largest cities like New York, Los Angeles, Washington, and Chicago are at an elevated risk for international terrorism. Medium-sized cities such as Oklahoma City and Omaha in contrast may have concerns that realistically should be geared to the threat of domestic terrorism. Still smaller cities, suburbs, and towns might do well to recognize that mass violence in their communities would be patterned after the kind that was observed in Littleton, Colorado at Columbine High School.

What does all of this mean for citizens, their local public safety agencies, and the fear of crime? Simply this. While we must accept that we live in a different world after 9/11 and we cannot risk complacency where our communities are concerned, we cannot let the fear of violent crime dictate a reduction in the quality of life for the average American nor threaten the freedoms which make this country unique in the world. We can control fear similar to as we have in the past, by working with our local public safety leaders to realistically assess the crimes that might threaten our families, friends, and neighbors and take steps to reduce our risks and enhance our ability to respond to those episodes as they infrequently occur.

Drawing upon the successful strategies of the recent past to reduce crime and the fear of crime seems to suggest a reasonable course for future action. What worked prior to 9/11 in our communities to identify and solve crime-related problems will work now. For example, those places that had embraced community policing would likely find this to be a very practical model for going forward to re-assess the concerns of their citizens and the mechanisms by which citizens may want to join with the police to seek solutions. After all, barking dogs, noisy neighbors, and speeding cars likely will still be high on the list of citizen's concerns in many places. Where mass violence shows up on the priority list in most locales remains to be seen, as does the way in which a community might choose to coordinate a response if they foresee a terrorist event in their community as something that should be of high concern.

Problem-solving and community engagement will continue to be useful tools for getting to better know a community and learning how to develop a more effective response to citizen needs. By contrast, erecting barriers to prevent citizen access, akin to circling the wagons, because policing has gotten more serious, secretive, and tactical in nature cannot be a good adjustment to living in a more dangerous world.

While terrorism has always presented some possibility of occurrence in the U.S., it remains a relatively improbable event at any given time in most U.S communities. As such, most communities should not spend all their time preparing for a worst case scenario that is not likely to occur, at least to the extent that the more persistent and frequently occurring events that directly impact the quality of American life are ignored or allowed to go unchecked. What worked before to fight crime and reduce citizen fear will work in the future.

A word of caution. Most Americans support greater police powers, post-9/11. However, this support will recede over time and the police cannot be burdened with being the thin blue line against the threat of mass violence too. What makes sense is to work even more closely with the public to engage in responsive public safety measures for that will bring us all closer together. If terrorism is the threat, then community engagement and problem-solving may prove useful as the ultimate antidote. But before we get there, we must resolve a number of controversies.

Organization of this Book

The first chapter of this book introduces readers to policing in the context of the events leading up to September 11th. Retired Minneapolis police chief Anthony Bouza shares his views on the controversies facing policing prior to the 9/11 world in which we live today. Following this, David

Perkins, in Chapter 2, confronts the order vs. freedom debate in its most contemporary manifestation—law enforcement in a post-9/11 environment.

Victor Kappeler and Karen Miller-Potter lead off Section II by discussing American policing in the face of domestic and international terrorism. But how do we define terrorism? Who are the terrorists? And what are the ramifications for local and federal police agencies? Chapter 4, by Jihong Zhao and his colleagues, examines the current philosophy of policing in order to assess its utility for controlling crime. Section II concludes with an alternative view of police culture, written by noted author John P. Crank, whose book *Imagining Justice* won the Academy of Criminal Justice Sciences' 2004 Outstanding Book Award.

The next three selections comprise Section III. Here we review operational issues and invite the reader to consider long-standing controversies in policing, set in a contemporary environment. Understanding that the basis for many of the controversies that we face in American policing stem from fears about how to control "the dangerous classes," Chapter 6, by John Liederbach and Robert W. Taylor, deals with the use of deadly force while Andra Katz-Bannister and David Carter write about racial profiling in Chapter 7. Here we are reminded that fears about the criminal element that are perceived by society to be associated with an underclass that is disproportionately nonwhite (as Bouza discussed at the beginning of the book) feed into other controversies that remain problematic for American policing in a post-9/11 world. And in Chapter 8, Donna Hale and Karen Finkenbinder discuss the history of women in policing along with current challenges in a profession dominated by males.

In the fourth and final section of the book, we examine persistent ethical issues in policing that Joycelyn Pollock argues in Chapter 9 will require a re-examination of ethical decisionmaking in law enforcement. Following this, are two common examples where breakdowns in ethical conduct have caused substantial problems for public safety agencies, their employees, and victims of abusive practices. In Chapter 10, John Worrall discusses how the increasing use of civil liability against police excessive use of force underscores the need for clearer law enforcement standards to regulate such behavior.

SECTION I

Setting the Stage—Policing
before and after 9/11

CHAPTER 1

Controversies in Policing before September 11, 2001

Anthony V. Bouza

The very title of this book prompts me to protest that there are, in fact, altogether too few controversies in policing. I believe that most of us glumly accept as fact, bromides fed to us by leaders who rarely bother to think very deeply about issues that ought to lie at the very forefront of our discussions.

In the police world, we wallow in self-pity, make outlandish claims and scorn Socratic intellectual torture that just might lead us to an occasional discovery. For example, we accept the proposition that the press is the enemy—jackals out to unjustly undo us. Could we ignore the value of that institution—arguably our democracy's sturdiest pillar—as a vehicle for informing the people and monitoring the actions of all of us?

Popular opinion is the only real Inspector General capable of examining all aspects of society and exposing wrongs that need righting. It isn't civilian review boards that uncover police wrongdoing and keep cops honest, but the fear of media exposure. Press coverage is a very healthy thing and we ought to embrace it. After all, any police leader thin-skinned enough to be at war with the press is at war with the public he or she serves.

The anti-intellectualism of the police consigns all of us to the ministrations of scholars, criminologists, and sociologists who have the education, training, intellectual rigor, and eloquence to lead us in discussions. Police leaders need to immerse themselves in poetry, Shakespeare, Machiavelli, the Greeks, and other agents of thought so as to inspire critical thinking and deep examination. Consider just a few of the issues worthy of more critical thought.

Street Crime

Over the past decade or so American policing has been enshrouded in a mystery no one seems to understand—that is, a precipitous drop in street crime. Even as police executives rush with the enthusiasm of Pamplona revelers to claim credit for the outcome, no one can really explain the exact origin of this achievement.

Street crime—defined by the Uniformed Code as being comprised of the Part I crimes of murder, rape, aggravated assault, robbery, burglary, larceny-theft, auto theft, and arson—encompasses guns, drugs, and desperation. Consequently, these violent crimes cause fear and the expectation that someone ought to do something about it.

But when crime drops, as has recently happened, this unexpected, mysterious, and welcome development often is accompanied by a chorus of self-congratulatory chiefs' voices describing how their genius led to the result. For awhile, until homeland security came into focus, it looked as if community policing might prove a handy hook on which to hoist the flag of victory, even as a Tower of Babel defined it variously (Wilson, 1982). More typically, though the overall tone of the ridiculously self-aggrandizing claims have centered on the claim of more aggressive police tactics. Can this claim withstand scrutiny? I think not.

A quick, impressionistic look at crime and policing over the past half century or so quickly reveals some fascinating disclosures. The 1950s were a somnolent time in America, characterized by low crime rates, little police activity—except for the periodic scandals appearing like clockwork every score of years—and few initiatives. It was a period of Chicago's O.W. Wilson and his *Police Administration*—a seminal work whose principal premises were to improve management, upgrade technology and the physical plant, and not be overly bothered by either brutality or corruption (Wilson, 1963).

The pulse quickened in the 1960s, stimulated by racial aspirations and the political activism surrounding the Vietnam War. It was a decade of assassinations—JFK's, Malcolm X's, Martin Luther King's, and RFK's—that defined the angst, agony, and activism of the Age. Race riots fueled a rising and alarming level of violence, particularly in core cities. It was a decade that saw the one and only presidential commission to study the effects of street crime and what might be done about it (President's Crime Commission, 1967).

Out of the turmoil of the 1960s grew a dramatically enhanced police aggressiveness. New tactics were developed, such as street crime units, that invented new ways of battling the rising tide of murders, burglaries, muggings, auto thefts, rapes, and such. Police analyzed robbery patterns and stationed well-trained cops in places likely to be hit.

Such strategies were labeled "proactive policing" (i.e., the cops stole the initiative from the street criminals by guiding their actions away from victims and toward the police). Instead of reacting to a crime by investigating it in the aftermath of its occurrence, they intercepted the criminals. This was the Halcyon period of police inventiveness and creativity, and it came at a heavy price, as black leaders assailed the tactics because they largely targeted black males.

Race

And who were the criminals? In the answer lies the central question facing the nation—it can be labeled the Black Experience in America. The creation of an underclass occupied about four centuries and involved large expenditures of energy, treasure, and even lives. It has been a white initiative aimed consistently, and sometimes unconsciously, at the nation's blacks. It began with the first arrival of a slave ship in Jamestown, Virginia in August 1619. This phase concluded with a nation going to the Civil War to resolve the issue.

Slavery gave way to Jim Crowism—a socially and legally sanctioned form of apartheid that lasted about 100 years, mostly in the South. The North used subtler forms of exclusion. As it gave way before the onslaught of the Civil Rights Movement in the early 1960s, a brief blast of hope quickened the pulse of Americans fighting for racial justice.

This transitory moment soon gave way to the latest method of oppression—the wholesale incarceration of black males. By the 1990s, about 1 in 3 were under some form of criminal justice control and almost one-half of America's approximately 2 million jailed prison inmates were black, the total itself a record in an inexorably escalating number of prisoners. This black experience of slavery, exclusion, and imprisonment produced an underclass of impoverished, illiterate, and largely unemployable persons who were consigned to welfare, ghettos, and other dependencies and oppressions (Sentencing Project, 1998).

The Street Criminal

The street criminal was easily identified from the vast populations of prisoners—black, poor, illiterate, unemployable, born to a teenager on welfare with no adult male role models for guidance—other than of the negative variety. Escape into drugs and alcohol proved irreversible options as crime and rioting became expressions of hostility and resistance. Crime was rebellion and the police became an army of occupation in the ghetto.

As the tsunami of crime escalated into terrifying numbers—the number of murders in NYC went from about 1 a day in the 1950s to almost 6 in the 1990s, while the population remained stable—the police accelerated their aggressiveness, targeting recidivists and enormously swelling prison populations. Draconian drug laws mandated sentences and the sharp reduction of parole and probation greatly increased the numbers of nonviolent offenders jailed and geriatrized a population that becomes an increasing health burden for the state long after they ceased being any sort of menace.

Society's approach, through the use of the police, was a foot on the necks of black America that occasionally got dislodged by such appalling incidents as a white cop's shooting of an unarmed black teenager. These dots over the nation's landscape frequently provoked paroxysms of urban looting, burning, and violence. Detroit and Newark were nearly razed by these devastations and the Bronx became a metaphor for urban chaos. Los Angeles, too, would have its share of trouble.

The Price of Black Political Power

Alarmed by the urban destruction, America's power structure gradually concluded that putting a black face on the government might well forestall rioting. This was the true impetus behind the appointment of black chiefs and the election of black mayors, rather than to increase black voting power, because the proportion of black actual voters, among those eligible, has never been high—not to mention the massive disenfranchisement of the many blacks with felony records.

And the ploy largely worked as America's cities all experienced black leadership while riots abated—although never disappeared. But this rise of black political power came with baggage. It was their sons, nephews, brothers, and fathers who languished in the nation's jails and, whatever the legal justification, this cadre of leaders could not help feeling sympathetic to the plight of black males in America.

The Police Retreat

Just as stake-outs were "judge, jury, and executioner," decoys became "entrapment," stings "invitations to burglarize" and other aggressive tactics "racist oppressions." Under this onslaught America's police beat a silent retreat, while never failing to pay rhetorical obeisance to aggressive policing. Indeed, the one area where the energies never flagged, was in drug enforcement, which achieved a black and white consensus as to the desirability of tough measures. Even here, however, the escalation of tragedies makes the alliance tenuous.

One of the unintended consequences of the war on drugs is the sharp increase in nonviolent drug offenders in prison, among an increasingly geriatric population of toothless wonders. Police chiefs never relaxed their tough law-and-order rhetoric, even as they trimmed their enforcement sails and abandoned stake-outs, decoys, and stings. Some of this was replaced by emphasis on low-level "quality of life offenses" like fare beating, pan han-

dling, on—the—street musicians and others. These were part of the bela-
bored issues referred to as the "Broken Windows" syndrome, which requires
no further elaboration.

Crime Declines

Miraculously—just as the levels of crime seemed to be reaching a
frightening crescendo across the nation—the wave moderated. No police
executive marveled at the mystery; rather, they shamelessly paraded a
host of programs responsible for the wonder.

Just as the rising wave enveloped all agencies and cities—even at the
very peak of police activism—the abatement struck the somnolent or
awake with equal force. The chiefs clearly saw the social, racial, and economic forces at work while street crime escalated, but the unexpected
decline prove irresistible to their claims of authorship. The crush of immod-
est claims by the nation's chiefs precluded any rational assessment (or
even a passing examination of explanations for this perplexing development). A rising crime tide that marched inexorably onward from the 1960s
to the 1990s suddenly had receded.

Possible Factors in the Crime Decline

It seems clear that, under the rubric of racist oppression, America had
been able to produce street criminals at a faster rate than even the most ener-
getic police agencies could neutralize. By the time the police arrived, the
criminal was formed and, unless the cops offered themselves as the targets
or otherwise deflected the assault, the crime already had occurred. Most
experiences of the 1960s proved that the police largely were irrelevant to
preventing either crime or to the formation of the criminal offender.

So what might have contributed to a general decrease in crime, albeit
a drop that is likely only to be a temporary one? After all, the underlying
causative factors—racism, poverty and oppression—have not really been
altered. The Census of 2000 clearly showed that our nation's impoverished, excluded, and imprisoned, were still largely black and growing.

It seems pretty clear, in retrospect, that the destabilizing influence of
the crack epidemic in the ghetto—with its destructions of the few fragile
threads holding the black community in tenuous togetherness—had peaked
in the mid-1980s, restoring some social equilibrium. Granted, the gangbuster
prosperity of the 1990s did raise employment levels among the underclass, even though they never approached the conditions attending their
white counterparts. Even welfare reforms might have shifted attitudes as well
as conditions, from disabling dependence to work.

Someday we might learn, for example, that the sharp reduction in welfare caused some impoverished young women to rethink pregnancy as a vehicle for independence. As well, the Million Man March may have been a harbinger of a fundamental shift, among black males, in their attitude toward fatherhood. The point is that these are not areas that receive as much scrutiny as shifts in consumer sentiments that impact the economy. And the shifts, if they exist, may prove transitory in any case.

Nevertheless, crime had declined and if it was not to the credit of police chiefs, then to what? The rise of black political power in the cities indisputably impacted rioting and might have affected criminal behavior. Such unmeasured—and, perhaps, immeasurable—factors as gang activities and membership might have impacted crime levels. Furthermore, consider the rising incidence of abortion. Since the early 1970s, abortion indisputably reduced what has been euphemistically described as the "at-risk male population." One study linked the decimation of the cohort to the decline in street crime, through statistical analysis (Donohue III, 2001).

What seems indisputable is this: a period of police retreat from its most aggressive innovations against street crime (the programs so eloquently extolled by so many police executives) can be consigned to history's rubbish heap. The reality is that the decline in crime remains a mystery. It may be possible, someday, to discern the outlines of the causes of this tectonic shift, but it is not likely to happen without recognizing the existence of the conundrum and a determined and knowing search for the truth (Kerner, 1968). It took 30 years to establish the impact of *Roe v. Wade* on street crime. It may take many years to figure out the other factors in crime's temporary decline.

Challenges Ahead

It is in this search that the true cost of anti-intellectualism is to be found. How are we to develop answers to questions no one dares to ask? Police executives have been cowed by the objections of black leaders, from pursuing really aggressive and legal police tactics (Johnson, 1996). They also have been inhibited from even discussing the issues openly. The police are central to society's safety and well being, yet there is no sense of an inchoate search for the answers.

The controversies in policing focus on such questions as the causes of street crime and its possible cures, even if the answers suggest dramatic shifts in the Shibboleths that guide so much of today's discussions. It is distinctly possible—even probable—that the anguish caused by high levels of criminality in the recent past will return, and then what? The police are very likely to be caught naked in that debate.

So where does this leave American policing in the wake of September 11's awful events? An institution (policing) that has eschewed any role in the meaningful discussion of the issues nearest and dearest to its daily concerns is not likely to contribute meaningfully to a search for answers. And nature abhors a vacuum.

Police activism in the political areas—in terms of monitoring what were then called "subversive activities"—peaked in the mid-1960s, when the general collapse was accelerated by discourses of illegalities by the FBI and unpopular monitoring of anti-Vietnam War peace groups by such organizations as the NYPD's Bureau of Special Services (BOSSI) (Bouza, 1976). A hasty retreat was beaten as intelligence agencies fled the field in disarray. Cointelpro, the FBI's counter-intelligence program, became a poster boy for unacceptably unsavory police monitoring of unpopular groups.

In the fullness of time the FBI would evolve into a miraculously effective investigator of the Mafia, a middling monitor of white-collar crime, a sometimes stumbling inquirer into espionage, and a non-starter into such political crimes as are currently described as terrorism. All the while the FBI stayed in thrall to the spirit of its longtime director, J. Edgar Hoover, bestowing his name on its headquarters even as unsavory disclosures besmirched his reputation and cascaded upon the agency.

Organizational Responses and the Constitution

Organizational habits of secrecy continued to plague the FBI as it failed to share information with the Central Intelligence Agency and other investigative groups. In a mirror image of this insularity the NYPD similarly failed to coordinate or communicate with such sister agencies as the NY Fire Department, with fateful consequences on September 11, 2001.

In the creation of a Department of Homeland Security, we can see the continuation of these baleful trends as no serious thought is even given to the notion of placing the FBI and CIA under its aegis. It seems clear that, after a few pious mouthings about cooperation and coordination, turf jealousies will receive obeisances from bureaucrats anxious to preserve their empires.

As to the threats to civil liberties occasioned by the furor to expand police powers unquestioningly, we need to remember that neither the FBI nor the police were under any constitutional impediment to investigate or interdict the awful events of September 11. That tragedy was an intelligence failure, not a constitutional one.

And let's not forget that the Founding Fathers never intended to deprive us of legal, constitutional methods of self-protection. All of the police tactics described here are perfectly legal, even if they have been abandoned under political pressures. We have only to consider the FBI attack on the Mafia, and the general war on drugs, to see what aggressive policing can look like.

Conclusion

The police world—federal and local—is not keen on Socratic searches for hard truths and this has been its failing. It is most likely to continue to repeat its reassuring, unquestioned bromides to itself while assuring the public of the strengths and wisdom of its programs, even as it performs the sleight of hand of accommodating darker political realities. In this unquestioning environment the hope for real progress is likely to founder on the cruel shoals of complacency, self-congratulation, and Philistinism. American policing must adjust, reform, and re-examine its role in a rapidly changing world. It must continually ask itself the hard questions and not let itself be content with easy answers if it is to meet the challenges of a demanding public over the course of an uncertain future.

Chapter Review Questions

1. In your own words, summarize the article.

2. What are the key elements the author is addressing about controversies in policing?

3. Explain the social changes that occurred from the 1950s through the 1960s that led to the application of more proactive police tactics.

4. What does the author mean by "the black experience"?

5. How has the black experience affected blacks and street crime in America?

6. What political move was initiated to curb urban destruction caused by looting, burning, and violence?

7. The author states that police aggressiveness against one particular type of criminal activity encountered no resistance from both white and black racial fronts. Explain the criminal activity and why it would not have encountered resistance.

8. The author provides several possible explanations for the decline in crime rate. Of those explanations, which, in your opinion, are the most feasible reasons for the decline, and why?

9. Since September 11th, what longstanding organizational problems between the Federal Bureau of Investigations and the Central Intelligence Agency have come to light?

10. What does the author propose criminal justice professionals do to curb the controversies in policing?

CHAPTER 2

The Order vs. Freedom Debate after September 11, 2001

David B. Perkins

Introduction

In his widely acclaimed best seller, "The Road Less Traveled," M. Scott Peck observes the simplest of truths, "Life is difficult" (Peck, 1978). Although much in American life has returned to normal, September 11, 2001 obviously intensified the degree of that difficulty beyond anything that local police administrators ever could have imagined. Much has changed for countless local agencies, and there is ample room for further speculation and prediction as to the directions that local policing will ultimately take in the continuing wake of that tragedy.

This chapter attempts to recognize but a small assortment of potentially provocative issues regarding current and future roles and practices for local police in this country stimulated largely as a result of the threat of terrorism. It begins with a brief look at an immediate dilemma regarding allocation of already scarce local resources, from both financial and personnel standpoints. It then turns to analysis of the nature of terrorism and whether terrorist activity is more appropriately characterized as war or as crime, and how selection between those two optional descriptions affects the roles to be played by local police and their cooperative relationships with others, including federal authorities and the military. The chapter closes with questions concerning the ultimate impact of terrorism on local police and their position in a free society, and how might (or ought) expansion of police authority in the interest of fighting terrorism eventually play out in local police responses to more traditional domestic crime.

Readers are urged to recall the asserted limited nature of this effort. As Michael Gerhardt has so aptly put it, "No one loves a good crisis more than a constitutional law professor. We live for crises. We make our living writing and talking about them!"[2] On the other hand, somebody famous also once said, "I don't have the answers, only the questions." The list of speakers resorting to this phrase in retreat from having overloaded their meager mental capacities is likely to be quite large. Under the circumstances, this writer is assuredly happy to join it.

The Allocation of Scarce Resources

The risk of terrorist activity has forced local law enforcement authorities to "come to attention." When asked the question of what has been the single most significant impact upon local police caused by 9/11, my faculty colleague, Wayman Mullins, simply said, "Since 9/11, a lot of routine situations the local police encounter have become some type of crisis in the minds of a good number of the general public." I took Wayman to be saying that the general public tends toward overreaction to unusual events, and likewise, in looking to its local police for relief from its anxieties, regardless of whether the police do or do not possess the means to help.

There is certainly nothing novel in this mind-set. Expectations landing *primarily upon local law enforcement* to curtail public fears of traditional crimes have existed forever, and notwithstanding 9/11, American communities are still faced largely with highly traditional criminal behaviors. Harvard Law Professor William Stuntz has aptly described these constants:

> The defining characteristic of American criminal law enforcement that most distinguishes it from law enforcement elsewhere . . . is its localism. There are approximately 800,000 police officers in the United States . . . 660,000 of them work for local governments. . . . There are approximately 50,000 federal criminal cases per year. Criminal cases brought by local agencies each year number in the millions (O'Harrow, 2003).

In support of his assessment of the overwhelming differential in local agency-initiated cases relative to federal criminal cases, Professor Stuntz cites data collected by The National Center for State Courts, showing that in 1999 almost 5 million cases were filed in state courts of general or unified jurisdiction, and in excess of 9 million cases were filed in state courts of limited jurisdiction (CBS's, 2003).

In short, city and county police had plenty on their collective platters from a resource management standpoint before the dawning of the 9/11 era. "And to further exacerbate the problem, compared to higher levels of government, local subdivisions have always found it politically more difficult to provide their police with adequate budgets." Stuntz attributes this reality to the difficulty that local governments have always experienced in asking their wealthier residents to redistribute income in the form of disproportionate police protection for poor neighborhoods, and he concludes that, "This is an especially large problem today given the added demands the war on terrorism has placed upon many local police departments" (Mijares et al., 2000)

With the formation of the Office of Homeland Security, the calls for more cooperation between law enforcement agencies at all levels of government have become abundant. Joint efforts have begun. To offer just one example, programs such as the "Matrix" (referred to as a whimsically named system standing for Multistate Anti-terrorism Information Exchange) have been created "to increase and enhance the exchange of sensitive terrorism and other criminal activity information between local, state, and federal law enforcement agencies" (NBC, 2003). The full impact of this new approach, where local police are more actively engaged in operations once reserved primarily, if not exclusively, for federal agencies is still unknown.

The increases in personnel required for what is essentially guard duty, more proactive local investigation and intelligence sharing with federal agencies, and technology upgrading to cope with potentially sophisticated, elusive and highly mobile foes (e.g., communications, transportation, surveillance, weaponry, recordkeeping, etc.) are massive financial realities already here for some local police systems (Mijares, 1993). Also increasing are expenditures for greater and more specialized forms of training for officers as terrorist interdiction becomes more and more the customary and recurring duty patterns of local police. In the interest of brevity, elaboration on the subject of specialized training will be avoided here, other than to point out the existence of both moral and legal imperatives (including civil liability concerns) which seemingly demand them once local police assume these new responsibilities (Mencken, 1983). These demands, nationwide, occur as state governments are also ill-positioned to aid local jurisdictions in that their own financial crises are reputed to be the worst in the past 50 years (Peak, 1996).

Monetary issues aside, it has been observed in the past that as critical incidents unfold, one of the recurring problems for local police administrators is how to effectively deal with these situations without simultaneously depleting the ranks of the patrol force needed to perform traditional police roles (Zhap et al., 2002), including the multitude of simple order maintenance and social service functions that are the true reality of local police operations (Williams, 2002).

A final inquiry offered at this point is that of what looms for established or emerging initiatives in the fields of community and problem-oriented policing? As Congress, the states, and local governments elect to redirect resources to fight terrorism, what impact such a shift will ultimately have upon programs aimed at fostering closer ties between the police and the citizens they serve, and at reduction of the core sources of poverty, social malfunction, and crime, remains to be seen. Local police administrators faced with the public's call for more immediate personal security and peace of mind must seek a balanced line in adoption of police policies aimed at both *short-term gratification <u>and</u> long-range goals.*

The where and how to strike this balance has been the essence of the historical philosophical tension between conventional law and order approaches to policing and the concepts embodied within the community policing movement (Savage, 2002). Not only is that tension undiminished, but it would seem destined for exaggeration by the additional dilution and reallocation of scarce police resources fostered by an age of terror. Coming to a greater understanding of the relative costs and long-term effectiveness of community policing, as compared to conventional approaches, appears to have been a relatively low priority among researchers to date (Savage, 2002). Thus, an intensified commitment to a future research agenda aimed at resolving such inquiries would seem more in order now than at any other time in the history of this debate. And, as will be explored later, how do local police likewise strike an appropriate balance between proactive investigation efforts aimed at potential terrorists, while avoiding claims of selective targeting of particular groups and unreasonable invasions of American privacy?

The Essence of Terrorism: Is It Warfare or Is It Crime?

Was September 11th an act of war or the most heinous crime in our nation's history? If we are at war, it is like none we have ever known. "There is only one standing army . . . ours . . . and no conventional battlefields. Our enemy is furtive, hiding in sinister 'sleeper cells' in our midst" (Feldman, 2002). While the U.S. Attorney General's Office has told members of the American Bar Association that, "We are (indeed) at war, (and) during World War II they weren't asking for a judge's permission before they shot enemy soldiers" (Feldman, 2002:458-461). The American Civil Liberties Union counters that the administration has overused the warfare analogy to justify bullying that bypasses both Congress and the courts (18 U.S.C. Sect. 1835).

How much does it really matter what conceptual niche our reasoning casts terrorism into? Well, it may matter a great deal. As Noah Feldman has so aptly put it, "The selection of such a conceptual framework requires serious re-thinking in light of September 11th, (and) whether we choose the framework of war, the framework of criminal pursuit and prosecution, or some complicated combination of the two will have major ramifications in the spheres of law, politics, and policy" (Bryant, 1995). To extend Feldman's observations into the realm of local policing is to recognize the obvious. The three choices he has identified have both direct and indirect ramifications on the future of local law enforcement planning efforts and actual practices.

No matter the parallels immediately drawn to Pearl Harbor and the natural and at times overwhelmingly patriotic emotions stirred, 9/11 does not fit so neatly within the mold of "warfare" for a number of reasons. To paraphrase Feldman once again, both war and crime involve acts against a state, but a war presents a challenge to a state's sovereignty that is traditionally made by another sovereign state. On the other hand, a crime involves a violation of a specific law of a state on the part of individuals rather than other sovereignties. Also, warfare generally involves no jurisdictional or locational boundaries and is hugely expansive in scale. That is to say the opposing sovereignties attack one another whenever possible, both inside and outside their respective jurisdictional boundaries. They attack one another repeatedly in rapid succession, and they attack in masses (McLaren).

In spite of some Americans' suspicions, to date, verified linkages between the terrorists of 9/11 and another sovereign state do not seem to measure up to Feldman's first identity criterion, that is sovereignty vs. sovereignty. Notwithstanding a few subsequent terrorist acts on foreign soil in which American citizens may have been either the wholly or partially intended targets, fortunately to this point we have not experienced a large series of similar follow-up events either here or abroad. September 11th certainly involved a "massive" attack in the sense of the destructive forces used, the sheer size of the physical targets involved, and the great loss of human life. But, as Feldman further puts it, a "scale" criterion is inherently less susceptible to precise characterization. As extreme as the event was, comparatively speaking the numbers of individual attackers, targets, and even victims involved in 9/11 still do not reach the heights normally associated with true warfare.

The observation that September 11th may not have been so much warfare as a kind of grand criminal activity possessing some war-like characteristics is problematic. Among other things it raises serious questions regarding which of our nation's multitude of potential official responders ought now to be allowed to fight back. Also, from legal, philosophic, and moral standpoints one is likewise forced to reflect upon the old adage about all being fair in love and war. For if what we are dealing with is war, then the rules of engagement are relatively quite relaxed and liberal indeed. But if terrorism is really just the contemporary period's most heinous form of crime, then it should still be clear that in our country the rules of engagement remain considerable more restrictive. And, the restrictions apply in terms of both the selection of our response forces and the specific actions that may be taken by them against terrorists.

USA PATRIOT Acts I (and II) obviously affect and/or call for the further expansion of police powers. The warfare analogy has brought forth other proposals that, if achieved, would undoubtedly impact both local and federal policing significantly. One such proposal is the suggestion that the Posse Comitatus Act be dramatically amended, an initial step that might conceivable lead to its eventual discard (Schmitt, 2002).

During Reconstruction federal military forces were used extensively in the South to keep order and enforce law (Klinger, 2002), a military occupation of the southern states that was characterized as abusive by southern Democrats and which eventually led to passage of the legislation. John

McLaren has observed that amendments to the Act are not a new idea. The last such modifications occurred during another era of perceived crisis to allow the utilization of military manpower and technology, if not to directly enforce the laws, to at least assist domestic law enforcement in President Reagan's War on Drugs (Klinger, 2002:823). Does something ring familiar?

Like the War on Drugs before it, the War on Terror has created a shift in some circles away from concern for the dangers inherent in military enforcement of civilian laws and in favor of expanded use of military resources in domestic law enforcement efforts. According to Eric Schmidt, this shift has been displayed even within the inner circles of the Pentagon, where military officials have historically been reluctant to involve their forces in domestic law enforcement (Klinger, 2002:829).

As alluring as the "terrorism is warfare" analogy may be, if the War on Terror is in reality just another form of the War on Crime, then many liaisons between law enforcement (presumably including local agencies) and the military remain highly susceptible to challenge as violations of the Act. Some cooperative efforts in the nature of indirect support functions and assistance to domestic law enforcement have been accepted from the Act through prior amendments. But, given the fact that courts have already struggled in prior individual PCA cases with where to draw the line in categorizing indirect versus direct forms of military assistance to the police, there are those who apparently believe that the PCA in its current form is an idealistic luxury we can no longer afford.

In one of the earliest post-9/11 commentaries on the perceived necessity for employing a direct military response to foreign terrorists, David Klingler and Dave Grossman called for significant relaxation of PCA restrictions and in effect a specific terrorist exception to the Act (Klinger, 2002:830). Klingler and Grossman seemingly recognize some modest need to continue restraints on the use of the military. They thus propose legislation that would limit direct military involvement "to those situations in which there is *probable cause* to believe that those plotting or engaging in terrorist activity are foreign nationals or American citizens working on behalf of a foreign power" (*Illinois v. Gates*, 1983).

They further suggest that such legislation be crafted to identify a short list of bright line, specific conditions that would presumptively constitute the probable cause necessary to call out the military. For example, they point to such things as use by the perpetrators of military hardware (*Terry v. Ohio*, 1968). They call attention to a specific incident in the City of San Diego a few years ago which involved an individual in possession of a stolen National Guard tank, and offer "That in the current climate it would be imminently reasonable to believe that a tank rolling through an American city is connected to foreign based terrorism" (*Illinois v. Wardlow*, 2000). It seems that in their view this circumstance alone would justify local police in calling upon the military to wipe out the tank. Incidentally, the tank in San Diego proved to have been operated by an escaped mental patient. The question of probable cause, however, has never required certainty in foresight or turned upon what ultimately proved factually accurate in hindsight.

The term *probable cause* has immediate appeal because it traditionally resonates a striking of the appropriate balance between societal security and protection of individual rights. But the difficulty (or the blessing depending upon one's individual point of view) lies in the historic rejection by the courts of bright-line, litmus tests for probable cause that are based upon but one ingredient. Such a notion runs afoul of a significant volume of existing constitutional authority to the contrary. *Illinois v. Gates* (Kushner, 1998) and its progeny have set the test for probable cause in virtually every other context involving searches and seizures as the totality of the circumstances. Again, that's "circumstances" as in plural, not "circumstance" as in singular.

It is true that this standard has been both quantitatively and qualitatively diluted by the courts over time through approval of police conduct in certain specific searches, arrests and temporary investigative detentions based upon only *reasonable suspicion* amounting to less than probable cause (Dinh, 2002). In fact, it would seem that, in the quest to overcome the current restrictions imposed by Posse Comitatus, Klinger and Grossman basically have suggested a standard for military intervention much more the equivalent of reasonable suspicion than of probable cause. And, a reasonable suspicion apparently would in turn be defined under this proposed terrorist model by one factor only.

However, as annoying as it may be to some, even the most dramatic of the above-mentioned diluting cases serve to confirm that the totality of the circumstances or quantitative test still holds at least a modicum of meaningful force within the contexts of both probable cause and reasonable suspicion (USA PATRIOT Act, 2001). While some factors have always been deemed weightier than others in applying that test, its quantitative-oriented remnants would seemingly have to be wiped out entirely before a standard of the sort suggested by Klingler and Grossman can replace them. In short, any further erosion of the totality of the circumstances test would require virtually *exclusive* attention being focused on a *qualitative* analysis of *one particular fact* rather than on a cumulative analysis of multiple facts.

Interestingly, there are others who have recognized that an increasingly qualitative analysis for authorization of government interventions may indeed make sense in the specific context of dealing with suspected terrorists, *if not by the military, then at least by the civilian police.* More will be introduced on this momentarily. Also, should our people fall victim to additional terrorist acts committed inside our nation's boundaries, there are likely to be renewed and even more emphatic outcries in some circles for militarization through modifications or elimination of the Posse Comitatus Act, if not permanently, then at least temporarily. These calls will be especially loud if the triggering events are proved or even suspected to be the works of foreign rather than domestic terrorists. Who knows, then, the precise roles that will be left for local police to play?

But, broader and potentially more critical dilemmas regarding the police function and American freedoms have already been thrust to the fore. These dilemmas existed, in part, before 9/11. They were magnified beyond most of our prior conceptions by 9/11, because the event itself went beyond the imaginings of but a relative few.[3] These are terribly difficult matters, because they involve not only questions of how we control terrorists through the use of our police forces, but how we govern our general population in a just manner after having granted our police (or our military) the power to move effectively against an evil the ultimate dimensions of which we fear are still unknown.

The Rights of American Citizens

It has been said that in the aftermath of September 11, 2001, Americans must select between national and individual senses of security and their critical civil liberties. While people may differ on where to strike the appropriate balance between these two competing interests, it is generally agreed that an expansion of either one of these interests comes at the expense of the other (NBC, 2004). This tension manifests itself for police officers in this country in the quandary of how to deliver to American citizens the product of safety while simultaneously allowing those common traits of freedom that have made our country extraordinary.

Within legal literature, scholarly attention to date seems focused primarily upon the USA PATRIOT Act (Weiss, 2000), together with the specter of racial or religious profiling of Arabs and/or Muslims by federal agencies such as the FBI, CIA, and various other authorities now absorbed within the Office of Homeland Security (Osborne, 2003). Civil rights alarms have risen to the point where a counter movement has emerged in the form of some local governments' reluctance to enforce the Patriot Act, and a growing support by some congressional members in favor of revamped federal statutes more in tune with preserving American privacy interests (a so-called national "Safe Act") (Stunz, 2002).

In a recent article, Jonathan Weiss offers a vintage quote from a 1964 local police academy graduate. "The duties of a modern day officer vary from thief catcher to regulating the best of people" (Pochurek, 1994). One has only to substitute the word terrorist for the word thief to begin an appreciation of the present complexities of American policing. And yet, it seems important to once again remind ourselves that the mainstay of local policing is still more a process of dealing with if not the best of people, then certainly not the terrorist either. It would seem that this reality is at the heart of the above mentioned revolt by a growing number of local cities, towns and counties against certain parts of the USA PATRIOT Act. It is described by some local governmental officials as a re-affirmation of a commitment to the Bill of Rights through the passage of resolutions or local ordinances refusing to cooperate with federal law enforcement under provisions of the Act deemed not in accord with the Constitution (Pochurek, 1994).

In a combination of writings produced both before and after 9/11, Professor Stunz has offered commentaries supporting increased investigative authority in the hands of America's local police forces, at least given the proper circumstances. However, he has likewise recognized one factor, a paradox, within the history of American jurisprudence that in particular gives rise to a wariness to do so.

Stunz contends that indeed the scope of Fourth and Fifth Amendment rights during investigations has historically varied and still ought to vary not only with decreases and increases in overall crime rates, but also with the *nature of the crimes* themselves. He offers examples of these historic realities by observing that crime waves have always produced calls for more law enforcement authority, such as occurred in the 1960s and 1980s. He also points out that, in particular, a nature of the crime criterion developed more than a decade ago when drug dealers were perceived as the most serious problem in our country, and that the courts of the era certainly responded accordingly (Stunz, 2001). One is immediately reminded here of Justice Berger's reputed slip-of-the-tongue dialogue during the argument of a case referring to a so-called "drug exception" to the Fourth Amendment (Stunz, 2001:847). Therefore, Stunz defends the notion that "there is nothing new about, and nothing wrong with, the claim that after September 11th police authority should increase," and he offers extensive reasons for why this should be the case (Stunz, 2001). In this regard, he appears to see great value in a *qualitatively* oriented approach for Fourth Amendment analysis, somewhat like Klinger and Grossman's analysis for proposed amendment of the Posse Comitatus Act.

Ironically, Stunz's misgivings over expansion of police powers are directly related to his observations of the appropriateness of the law's paying greater homage to the extremely serious nature of a particular crime. While he sees historical precedent for this approach and apparently leans personally toward supporting it, he contends that for several reasons Fourth Amendment jurisprudence in its current state also paradoxically displays a distinct and even stronger counter tradition that possesses an inability to distinguish among crimes and criminals (Stunz, 2001:2140-2141).

He offers, for example, the O.J. Simpson case, in which a warrantless search of the Simpson home from societal gain versus social cost perspectives was clearly in favor of the search. In fact, the social gain ought to be viewed as far greater than the net social gain derived from searching a drug dealer's house. Yet, current Fourth Amendment law often handles most cases as the same. In fact they are different, and as Stunz points out, "Reasonableness here, as elsewhere in law requires a balance of gains and losses, benefits and costs. Therefore, given the fair probability of Simpson's guilt, the chances of catching a person who has committed a double murder on balance ought to have made a warrantless search most reasonable" (Stunz, 2001:2132).

On the other hand, in a case such as *Illinois v. Gates* where the police stood only to catch a marijuana dealership, the Supreme Court's creation of a new and more liberal standard for probable cause has since resulted in countless police searches and arrests that arguably are unreasonable based solely on the relatively nonserious nature of the crime (*U.S. v. Arviza*, 2002). Unless majority law shifts away from this impulse to impose a common test regardless of the relative seriousness of crimes, the lowering of Fourth Amendment standards for reasonableness of searches and seizures to accommodate effectiveness in terrorist investigations will in reality lower standards in many other forms of investigations. As Stunz has put it:

> Most constitutional limits on policing are *trans-substantive*—they apply equally to suspected drug dealers (or other criminals) and suspected terrorists. . . . Judges and Justices are likely to think about the effect of their decisions on the fight against terrorism even when the underlying cases involve ordinary sorts of policing. . . . And if the war on terrorism has half the effect on Fourth Amendment law that the war on drugs had, the effect will be large indeed. . . . The natural conclusion is that we will see a loss of individual liberty and privacy (*U.S. v. Arviza*, 2002:2157).

Indicators are present that the trans-substantive leverage of 9/11 is already being witnessed. Following a period of declining crime rates during the 1990's in which various Supreme Court decisions seemed to reflect lesser pressure on the Court to do something about lawlessness (*Whren v. U.S.*, 1996). More recent decisions may mirror a reverse trend. For example, in *U.S. v. Arvizu* (*Atwater v. City of Lago Vista*, 2001) the Court reversed a Ninth Circuit decision and upheld the reasonableness of a temporary investigative stop of a motor vehicle in a drug case. In the course of oral argument of the case, Justice O'Connor was reported to have made a poorly disguised reference to terrorism. . . . "We live in perhaps a more dangerous age today than when this event took place . . . it may be important for us to preserve the *flexibility* of the totality of the circumstances test for reasonableness" (*Atwater v. City of Lago Vista*, 2001:2158-2159). We must understand here that the same flexibility O'Connor was referring to allows police greater leeway by analogy in their other criminal investigations. Prosecutors will cite flexibility granted to police in terrorist scenarios as persuasive, if not outright binding precedents in the imminently vaster sphere of day-to-day cases brought by the nation's local police forces.

The potentially enormous implications of this are displayed in at least two controversial Supreme Court cases involving traffic stops. Thus, Stunz observes that collectively *Whren v. U.S.* (Tyler, 2002) *and Atwater v. City of Lago Vista* (Tyler, 2002:366) deal with the legal authority of officers to

detain, arrest, and search persons in minor crime scenarios, regardless of sub-
jective police motivations to check for more serious crimes. He (as well as
others) views the holdings in these cases to be at the core of the debate over
racial profiling of motorists and pretext stops. He conjectures that these cases,
each of which in its respective way upheld certain classes of detentions and
searches, would not be likely to stand over time but for the ghost of 9/11.
Stunz, therefore, describes this haunting as "the specter of a terrorist who
has violated a traffic law or some immigration rule" (Colb, 1998).

Highly qualitative analysis of Fourth Amendment reasonableness has
raised yet another controversial question. If the police, and in particular the
local police, are indeed to receive the "dividends" associated with flexible
terrorist oriented standards, might there also be appropriate tradeoffs
imposed on them by the law? One such counter proposal that has been
floated is a notion that the police ought to at least then be more mindful of
their manners when conducting their investigations.

At the outset, one might just wish to consider some potentially practical
benefits possibly derived from reflection on police mannerisms. Tom R. Tyler
asserts that the experiences that people have with legal authorities self evidently often involve regulatory encounters. People can resist and seek to
defy legal authorities or they can, as he puts it, "buy into" the decisions of
authorities and voluntarily comply with their directives. However, Tyler
observes:

> Currently police officers and judges typically approach the pub-
> lic from a force or social control orientation. In other words, the
> style that the police bring to their interactions with people is that
> of command and control—they try to dominate people and situ-
> ations by displays of force or the potential use of force. Similarly,
> the courts seek to compel compliance by the threat or use of force,
> including fines and jail time (Colb, 1998:2174-2175).

Tyler thus suggests and empirically supports the premise that authorities should strive to move beyond the exclusive perception that people cooperate with them because of fears of sanctions and recognize that "Citizens
dealing with the police or judges focus on issues of good faith. . . . They seek
to infer the motives of the legal authorities. . . . If they feel the authorities
are acting in good faith, they are more likely to voluntarily defer to their directives. Style may therefore be as important a consideration in these encounters as the underlying justifications for initial contact" (Wood, 2003).

Professor Stunz, for one, has drawn the following conclusions from
Tyler's work. First, citizens possibly view their local police more by their
personal demeanor than by their selection of targets for police attention.
Second, discrimination may be found more in the way local police treat some
suspects after detention than in how the suspects are initially selected. Third,
even if the law could successfully regulate suspect selection (i.e., profiling),
racial distrust in policing would remain significant. Other writers have

touched upon these same themes. He concludes that if Tyler's assertions are accurate, the police have much indeed to gain by looking to mind their manners. Treat suspects with appropriate levels of force and greater dignity during investigatory detentions—receive increased levels of voluntary compliance and officer safety (good things), additional consent searches (good things), and fewer citizen complaints of discrimination (good thing)— all at the same time (Brewer, 1893)!

More directly to the point of highly qualitative analysis of Fourth Amendment reasonableness, relative to officer deportment the *form* in which a detention, arrest or search is cast is likewise an important ingredient in determining the *substance* of a Fourth Amendment violation. And, herein lies the proposed tradeoff with the police. Under this model the more serious the crime giving rise to detention, the less police have to worry that their treatment of detainees will run afoul of the Fourth Amendment. And, vice versa, the less serious the crime giving rise to the detention, the more emphasis the courts ought to place on the factor of police deportment. Therefore, if the police are clearly abusive in the degree of force or disrespect employed in a mere traffic stop, all the drugs they find in the vehicle are subject to the exclusionary rule. If the police want to preserve their abilities to search, given the low gravity of a suspected offense, the least they can do is be civil in the process. Such a rule presumably would translate into increased police civility across the entire and immense range of police-citizen encounters in relatively minor offenses.

There are certainly potential problems with such an approach. First, Stunz has observed that integrating officer demeanor into Fourth Amendment law will not be easy. From case to case, the line between acceptable versus abusive police treatment of suspects can be very hazy, or in other words, ugliness is often in the eye of the beholder. I would personally add here that it would be hard enough just to define the concepts of serious versus nonserious crimes, the other prong of the model's equation. Simply dividing cases between felonies and misdemeanors would seem arbitrary in the search for the standard.

There is no legal litmus test currently available that the courts could resort to in determining if, given the nature of the crime, officer deportment on the whole during the evidence-gathering period was or was not reasonable. Lack of precedents notwithstanding, and while recognizing this definitional problem, Stunz envisions that, over time, judges would be able to develop what he describes as a "common law" of reasonable treatment (Brewer, 1893:281-282). Others, and particularly those who view judges as generally antagonistic toward the police, may not be confident that the new common law of manners would prove to be anything other than an easily abused tactic and means for protecting the guilty.

Conclusion

In closing, it can be restated that our era is by no means unique in the nation's history of conflicts between liberty and security. One has only to review such prior episodes as President Lincoln's suspension of *habeas corpus* during the Civil War, the Espionage Acts of 1917, and President Roosevelt's executive order resulting in the now infamous roundup and detention of Japanese Americans during World War II (Wood, 2003). Long ago, David Brewer offered these words which ring true for such times of national anxiety:

If, as is commonly suggested, a constitution's mandates are proscribed by Philip sober to control Philip drunk, there is likely to be no instance in which Philip is more drunk or less disposed to act responsibly than during a genuine crisis in which authorities are severely tempted to take powers beyond the limits set forth in that constitution (Brewer, 1893:37-47).

Moreover, Michael Gerhardt tells us that when it comes to our particular constitution, we are only just now beginning to understand how it binds our nation. He challenges us to strive for a greater understanding of just how the Constitution, its guaranties and its values are actually translated into action in the real world. He asserts that courts receive too much credit for protecting constitutional rights; that in actual practice most constitutional issues are addressed and implemented in the real world by other players such as legislatures and chief executives (Brewer, 1893:281-282). One could quickly add another group to Gerhart's roster. For reasons primarily associated with sheer volume of citizen contacts, low visibility, and of course discretion, our local police have always had immense practical power to make our constitutional values either meaningful or meaningless. In a time where there exists a general tendency to grant police even greater authority, that reality assumes even more monumental significance (as if that were possible).

This writer once had a graduate student, a former chief of police, who one evening, following a discussion of the law of temporary investigative detentions made a statement to me along these lines. In so many words he said, I'm an *American citizen* as well as an American police officer, and just like my fellow citizens, I ought to carefully weigh just what powers are being asked for and what may likely be granted to the police in *my country*. His observation had a big impact upon this writer at the time, considering the source. It rings now as strongly akin to that of another American who once admonished future generations that those who barter liberty for security may inherit a place where neither liberty nor security long survive (Franklin, 1759). Perhaps it further suggests to our police that in any era in which their power over others becomes enhanced, the principled and at times self-restrained manner in which they exercise that power may prove to be the truest measure of their patriotism.

Chapter Review Questions

1. In your own words, summarize this chapter, identifying the key elements the author is trying to convey.

2. How have the publics expectations of law enforcement changed since September 11th? In this age of terrorism, how have financial strains affected law enforcement at local and federal levels?

3. How has the fight against terrorism affected local law enforcement in their communities?

4. Early on in this chapter the author poses the question, "Was September 11th an act of war or the most heinous crime in our nation's history?" Given what you have learned from this chapter, how would you answer this question?

5. Explain the origins of the Posse Comitatus Act and the role it plays today in American Society?

6. Since 9/11, political movements such as the Patriot Act, the Safe Act and the expansion of police powers have citizens and politicians debating over the extent to which our civil liberties can be violated to ensure our safety. Considering what you have learned from the chapter, what is your position on the matter?

7. What does the author mean by the term *trans-substantive* and how has it affected the criminal justice system from policing to the courts?

8. The author asks, "If the police, and in particular the local police, are indeed to receive the "dividends" associated with flexible terrorist oriented standards, might there also be appropriate tradeoffs imposed on them by the law?" Why or why not?

9. Identify some problems with integrating officer demeanor into the Fourth Amendment.

10. Find a recent instance where there question as to whether there was an excessive use of police powers. Taking what you've learned from this chapter, pick a stance and argue for or against expanding police powers.

SECTION II

The Role of the Police
in a Democratic Society

CHAPTER 3

Policing in the Age of Terrorism

Victor E. Kappeler
Karen S. Miller-Potter

Introduction

The movement toward globalization and the rediscovery of terrorism as a social problem are two interrelated forces that promise to forge the development of American policing well into the twenty-first century. The governmental response to terrorism requires changes in policing, even at the local level. Globalization marks a change in the economic system, which also requires modifications in policing. Major changes in the economic conditions of all societies are coupled with transformations in institutions of social control. As formal agents of social control, the police have consistently adapted to comply with major changes in economic conditions. Shifts in the modes of production, the circulation of capital, and the techniques of generating capital all affect the foci and practices of police institutions.

The more rapid and drastic an economic change, the more radical the transformation in a society's social control institutions. When societies undergo rapid change in economic conditions, it is referred to as a revolution. Scholars generally recognize three major economic revolutions: the agricultural, industrial, and the technological/information. Less frequently discussed, however, are the accompanying transformations that occur in social control institutions like the police. When a society undergoes an economic revolution there also is a tendency to realign the constellation of social control to better fit the emerging economy.

Background

American policing institution has historically followed the circulation of capital and has been closely linked to the economic engine of society. In this context, 'capital' refers to the unity of production and money. It is the accumulation of goods and/or wealth used for the production of more goods (Marx, 2000). Shifts in the modes of production or in the manner in which capital is generated witness changes in police practice, language, and tactics. The police modify their appearances (Manning, 1999) to bring the institution more in line with changing economic and social conditions. The agricultural, industrial, and technological economic revolutions each resulted in a significant shift in several dimensions of police and society. With each revolution a change has occurred in the police and public's geographic orientation, the enforcement of emerging norms, the groups targeted for control, and the methods of knowledge acquisition.

American policing now is shifting in response to a new revolution. Globalization offers different ways of generating and new locations for circulating capital. A successful capitalist economic system must expand to produce more capital (Marx, 2000) and the current trend toward globalization is to this end. The international growth of capitalism expands the consumer base and increases the surplus labor population. This facilitates wider profit margins and reproduces more capital. Successful globalization requires relatively open borders, free trade, and accommodating importation laws. The policing of terrorism is antithetical to these requirements. The convergence of globalization and the construction of terrorism as a social problem are leading to a metamorphosis in contemporary policing. As with all historical economic revolutions the police, as agents of social control, must redefine who is dangerous as well as their geographic orientations. Before discussing the contemporary economic revolution, it is necessary to understand the police institution's role in responding to and facilitating historical revolutions.

Policing Revolutions and Revolutions in Policing: Targets and Force

The police have historically served as an institution that distributed concrete force (Bittner, 1970) to maintain and promote control, rather than reduce any real danger to the public. As major economic shifts occurred, public safety has realigned its attention to accommodate the emerging economic order. From the slave patrols, forerunners of many modern police departments, who tracked down the economic engines of an agrarian society to the platoons of urban officers charged with controlling the organized labor movements, riots, and strikes of the industrial revolution, police have played a key role in promoting economic order by distributing force. Historically, police attention and force were directed at societal members thought to be "dangerous classes" (Shelden, 2001). Specific attention was usually paid to individuals thought to present an immediate threat to an existing or emerging moral and economic order. In the Anglo-American legal tradition, those deemed as dangerous and in need of formal state control have overwhelmingly been members of the lower classes (Manning, 1999a). While policing traditionally acted to promote order among the poor, its attention ebbed and flowed with popular and political conceptions of dangerousness.

In part, during these periods and because of the ambiguous nature of criminal law and political interests, police relied on crude signifiers to distinguish dangerous people and activities. The distribution of force, as Bittner (1972) remarked, was situationally applied based on individual officers understandings of situation and necessity. This method of distributing force led police to adopt crude signifiers to trigger action. In policing, these signifiers were fundamental to traditional enforcement practices and were often described as "suspicious activity." However, police action still was primarily directed at individuals, situations, and activities based on concrete signifiers of dangerousness. Those deemed as members of a dangerous class were under more police scrutiny and the behaviors and activities of these people were often formally labeled criminal. Criminalizing behaviors facilitated the formal control of dangerous groups. For example, during the agricultural revolution the targets of police attention and force were runaway or curfew violating slaves. It is difficult to imagine in contemporary society that an adult could be severely punished for running away. However, during the agricultural revolution, slaves were not only a dangerous class but the primary source of labor and any attempt at individuality or freedom among this group was criminalized. During the industrial revolution union organizers, striking workers, rioters, or people associated with labor movements were deemed a dangerous class, which led to the criminalization of many behaviors associated with labor organizing. During both economic revolutions, police tactics were similarly crude and were situationally directed at groups rather than individuals. Modifications in police application and distribution of force did little to alter the signifiers of which groups were in need of state control.

More recent economic shifts and political movements offered the police an opportunity to refine their tactics and modify their targets. In the 1960s the police targeted groups of a different character. As a result of the Vietnam War protests and the Civil Rights Movement, police targets had an overt political dimension. What began with slaves and then labor organizers had changed to students and civil rights protesters. Police attention was focused on political dissidents, the new dangerous class. The distribution of force, however, remained relatively unchanged with advances in its application merely reflecting better organization. The police relied heavily on riot squads and saturation patrols in an attempt to control the activities of this dangerous class. In addition to the traditional means of applying force, other techniques had become available. These new mechanisms for the application of force reflected simple first generation technologies like pepper foggers and riot gear. Regardless of the techniques utilized and the groups designated as dangerous, police have historically maintained order through the use of force. It is not an overstatement to say that, for the first 200 years of American history, police administered order from the ends of nightsticks with the recipients of that order being those individuals thought to constitute a threat to the political-economic order.

Policing Revolutions and Revolutions in Policing: Geographic Orientation

The geographic orientation of both the police and society has followed a similar economic pattern. The limited technology, communication, transportation and trade of the agricultural revolution focused police and public attention on very localized concerns. During pre-modern times, the absence of communication and transportation technologies ensured that citizens rarely summoned the police to address social problems and that police had a limited ability to project force and control. Merely contacting the police could require an entire day's horse ride to a county seat to summon the sheriff. Accordingly, most conflicts were handled by informal methods in private rather than public forums. Likewise, labor and economic development were very localized. With the emergence of the industrial revolution, the advent of the car and telephone and the creation of factories, the geographic focus of both the police and society expanded and assumed a regional gaze. Labor could organize, communicate and protest conditions in larger groups and information could spread more rapidly. This led to social revolts in numbers and sizes not previously experienced. The police responded by broadening their geographic orientation.

The technological advances that allowed dangerous groups to be more organized also allowed citizens to summon the police for less significant conflicts. This led to issues formerly viewed as private problems to come to the attention of the state. These issues were transformed into public concerns that could be addressed by the police. While police power was still primarily concentrated in larger cities that served as the hub for the circulation of capital, police began to project power on a more regional basis. The regional focus of police agencies was primarily facilitated by the emergence of state police organizations. The development of the railroad system, the interstate transportation system, and the population flight from the cities all marked a dramatic shift in the circulation of capital from the inner cities to more distant locations. Policing followed suit with the creation of municipal police forces in these more distant locations. The development of these agencies greatly enhanced the state's ability to project social control and force over a larger geographic area. At this time, the inner cities that were once the hubs of economic activities were mostly abandoned by both capital and police attention. As the regional focus grew, the attention paid to inner cities increasingly involved a reactive and containment strategy. By the end of the industrial revolution police and public attention had become national rather than rural and localized.

At the close of the twentieth century, police tactics and the signifiers of those in need of state control changed considerably. Urban space once again became a lucrative place of investment. Often under the rhetoric of urban renewal, businesses and the more affluent began to reclaim urban space and a gentrification of American cities became desirable. Abandoned warehouses, railroad stations, and riverfront properties that once marked the locations of capital were reclaimed in large numbers. Policing, more than at any period of history, began refocusing on urban space and paying attention to more abstract and symbolic threats as capital began to flow back into cities. Federally supported programs like "weed and seed" become the metaphors for state sponsored seizure of these new locations for business and development. These efforts, however, amounted to little more than the use of police power to dislodge the poor and manage signs of disorder in an effort to attract and protect investment capital. Although the recipients of overt police force remained relatively the same, the manner in which police distributed force and the nature of that force underwent substantial change. Refinements in the distribution of force were advanced with media crime talk, police disorder speech, and an emerging criminology of place (see, Sherman, Gartin & Buerger, 1989). The net effect of this was a shift in policing from the politically reactive distributors of overt force to the proactive managers of symbolic violence.

The targets of police control shifted from crude signifiers based on race, class, or political activity to abstractions affixed symbolically and scientifically identified as "hot-spots," "third-parties" "safety zones" and "problem places." Location based on the movement of capital rather than race, class, and criminality became the new signifiers for police distribution of force. Police work was redefined in terms of fear of crime, low-level drug dealing, and a host of other quality-of-life "crimes" (Bratton, 1995). This refocus occurred because these quality-of-life issues threatened the circulation of capital. Urban areas once abandoned by investment and contained as "red light districts" or "skid row areas," became the center of police attention when these areas became attractive to capital investors. Inner cities, railroad yards, and riverfront properties are once again viewed as valuable due to their ability to produce capital. After being abandoned and policed as "skid rows" (Bittner, 1967) for decades, these areas became the focus of police attention because they become valuable as locations for capital investment.

The reclaiming of these areas is occurring under the language of urban renewal and revitalization often expressed in political phrases like "weed and seed." Behaviors and activities traditionally ignored suddenly became police concerns. For example, juveniles on the streets at night, music blaring from car stereos, graffiti artists' sprawling murals, panhandlers obstructing merchant doorways, and a lack of civility by skateboarders were quickly deemed problematic. In this transformation, abstractions far removed from any underlying criminality or actual danger replaced strikes, riots, political protest, and serious crime as focal concerns of the police. This transformation marked a significant change in that it moved the focus of police from individuals to places and from criminality to the ordering of a wider range of social behaviors that matched the circulation of capital. Individual-based suspicion (Skolnick, 1966), the cornerstone of police action, was being replaced by surveillance and the control of populations and places said to threaten or defy the new rationality of place, purpose, and capital. The change in the geographic orientation of the police and the focus on place rather than individuals was coupled with transformations in the police use of force and in where definitions of danger originate.

Policing in the Late Twentieth Century

Three general themes emerge in considering the nature of police and society in the late twentieth century. First, policing facilitates economic shifts in society, often following the movement of capital into locations of value and leaving less lucrative locations and populations free to police themselves. Second, police force is influenced and transformed by available forms of technology and innovations in their application. Third, there was a shift from social elites and political officials to the police as those responsible for defining danger and the need for order. As society grows more complex in terms of social arrangements and technological innovations, the police also exhibit innovations in response to social change and its core function. In essence, the police became more capable of both facilitating economic control and broadened their core function to include symbolic violence while expanding the targets of their violence by abstraction.

Recent decades have seen the police begin to use symbolic violence and hyper-efficient applications of traditional force. Police began the symbolic occupation of public and problem spaces through the intrusion of service agencies, institutions, and private as well as residential space. These intrusions were made in an effort to further order society and often utilized symbolic violence. Recent years have witnessed the proliferation of police use of force specialists in terms of paramilitary units (Kraska & Kappeler, 1997) as well as the adoption of more abstract forms of symbolic violence. These symbolic forms of violence include coercive third-party policing, the use of collateral social control agents for actual or simulated surveillance, and the creation of false notions of community will for the purpose of manipulating public expectations (Kappeler & Kraska, 1998). In short, the police are fast becoming the managers of the abstract symbols of disorder, crime and control.

Traditionally, a clear distinction between formal and informal social control practices is observable, particularly when considering the police institution. It was possible to argue quite effectively that police represent society's most formal institutions of control and had only a distant effect on influencing, organizing and managing informal social controls. Police historically had little organized interaction with service agencies and when this interaction occurred, it was usually in response to requests from these agencies. Police were primarily reactive and had their attention directed by legal, economic and political institutions. Today, one of the most dramatic changes in the American police institution is its emergence as an organizer, manager and generator of an array of complex formal and informal social controls. The police are no longer clearly distinct from service agencies and informal social controls that emerge from social movements and cultural sentiments. They now inform and direct an increasingly complex and interrelated system of control and actively seek to promote an ideology of crime control through external agencies and institutions.

This phenomenon represents a fundamental change in the alignment of social control in a post-industrial society. Policing, traditionally a reactive institution, began emerging as a proactive institution that not only administered the law through the distribution of overt force, but also generated and directed an array of social control efforts. Many of these efforts entail the manipulation of the signs and symbols of disorder, crime and crime control. In this repositioning of the police, the institution transplants its crime control ideology into the fabric of agencies and social institutions. Rather than being directed by social institutions the police have effectively made inroads into the institutions of education, law, economics, and family. These institutions were historically insulated from crime control co-optation. Police incursions into social institutions have been coupled with an increased use of enforcement tactics unthinkable a few decades ago. The incursions into social institutions and the increased use of some enforcement tactics are the culmination of the roles of policing during the historical economic revolutions. They also, however, will greatly facilitate the changing role of policing in the contemporary economic revolution.

Globalization, Terrorism and Policing

Social and economic revolutions should not be seen as clearly distinct or as having a marked beginning or end. The effects of the agricultural and industrial revolutions still linger and influence both the police and society. Police still address rural and urban concerns, they respond to protests, riots, strikes, and labor disputes, and they still use force as their core response to social problems. Police will always manage their appearances and will be active constructors of the symbols underlying our conceptions of disorder, crime and crime control. There are, however, emerging social changes that promise to further transform the police institution well into the twenty-first century.

Many scholars mark the demise of the industrial revolution by the rise of a service and information economy. It is often argued that the reduction in the manufacturing industry is being replaced with the provision of services, investment banking, the management and sale of information, and the rise of computer and Internet technologies as the new economy. This assertion, however, fails to recognize that the emerging economic revolution has merely dislodged the location of the production associated with the industrial revolution to developing nations, not replaced it. At the same time there has been a tremendous growth in international and global trade. The American economy is fast transforming from a production-based economy to an economy based on the control and distribution of world capital (Harvey, 1989). While the emergence of computer, information and Internet technologies have enabled this transformation, the circulation of capital has become global. Where the agricultural revolution saw capital circulate in local venues and the industrial revolution experienced capital circulation at the national level the current revolution is witnessing capital being controlled on a global scale (Harvey, 1989). Perhaps a better metaphor for the new economy may be globalization, rather than service and information.

Globalization is one of the dominant social themes of the twenty-first century. Not unlike the agricultural or industrial revolution, globalization is a concept that captures the current state of social and economic circumstances. While there are various definitions and ways to think about globalization the term generally connotes an increasing worldwide integration of social, cultural, and economic systems especially, markets for goods, services, labor, and capital (Appadurai, 1990). The changes in the economic, social, cultural, and temporal boundaries are facilitated by technologies (Lash & Urry, 1987; 1994). In the economic sphere it is a rise in the influence of large multi-national corporations (MNC), an emerging world economy, and more frequent intervention into domestic policies of nations by international institutions like the International Monetary Fund (IMF), World Trade Organization (WTO), and the World Bank (WB). Collectively, these economic changes are seen as creating a global financial system. In this framework, the United States is fast becoming a producer of capital rather than a producer of goods and services. By controlling the distribution of capital to developing nations, the engine of the industrial revolution is being relocated to developing nations. The American economy is more dependent on the generation of capital through the extraction of profit from foreign rather than domestic labor and making developing nations debtor states. In essence, the American economy is increasingly a controller of production rather than a nation of producers.

Figure 1
Structure of Major Social Revolutions

Pre-modern	**Agricultural Revolution**
• Human and Animals	–Slave Patrols
• Religion	–Morals
• Local/tribal	–Commodities
Modern	**Industrial Revolution**
• Machines	–Strike Breakers
• Science	–Riots
• National	–Contraband
Postmodern	**Information Revolution**
–Data and Cyber-Commerce	–Internet
–Signs	–Terrorism
–Global	–Economic

In the social and cultural spheres, globalization denotes a process by which groups that are socially and geographically distinct become more interconnected. This is facilitated by greater travel, immigration, communication, and the exchange of information. The exportation and importation of goods, the norming of cultural beliefs and practices, and the eradication of social and cultural practices that inhibit globalization all act to reduce cultural diversity. At the same time cultural difference and resistance to globalization are seen as barriers that need to be removed in order to create a risk-free opportunity for economic expansion.

The creation of a risk-free environment for this new economic revolution requires a transformation in formal mechanisms of social control. This means that there must be changes in who is defined as dangerous, the dominant ideology must be exported, and laws must be conducive to the economic system. More importantly, globalization requires an ability to project force on a global scale. The focus of social control institutions must be realigned to better fit the emerging economic order. Police must change their focus to those places where capital now circulates and those people deemed to be threatening to the emerging economy. Terrorism and terrorists are quickly becoming the new targets of formal agents of social control.

Terrorism has been rediscovered as a unifying construction of dangerousness that inhibits globalization. This situation arose long before the terrorist incident of 9/11. Both the current and former directors of the FBI attempted to expand the designation of 'terrorist' to groups that seek political, economic and social change (see, Freeh, May 10, 2001). The very definition of terrorism is problematic. In its most simplistic sense terrorism means the threat or intentional use of violence that is directed at civilians for the purpose of achieving an objective. The use of terrorism is thought to instill shock and fear in such proportions that it creates conditions by which social change occurs. The concept of terrorism must, however, be distinguished from that of revolutionary or guerrilla warfare, as they are not forms of terrorism. While they seek political changes and use violence to that end, revolutionary and guerrilla warfare do not necessarily target civilians to achieve their objectives. In this sense revolutionaries as well as governments can become terrorists when they use violence to achieve objectives, if that violence is directed at civilians. It is important to understand that acts of terrorism can be committed by individuals, groups, or even governments.

What constitutes terrorism or a terrorist is being reconstructed due to globalization. This reconstruction has recently become highly politicized and is increasingly being defined in economic terms. For example the former director of the FBI attempted to extend the scope of terrorism to groups that are clearly outside the classical definition. Louis Freed made the following remarks in a speech on terrorism well before the attacks of 9/11:

> "Anarchists and extreme socialist groups—many of which, such as the Workers' World Party, Reclaim the Streets, and Carnival Against Capitalism—have an international presence and, at times, also represent a potential threat in the United States. For example, anarchists, operating individually and in groups, caused much of the damage during the 1999 World Trade Organization ministerial meeting in Seattle" (Freeh, May 10, 2001).

Consider how Attorney General John Ashcroft, the nation's top law enforcement official, constructs the history of federal law enforcement activities:

> We build on their heritage, the men and women who were the "trust busters" of the 20th century, who safeguarded our nation's internal security from fascists and communists; who declared a legal war on organized crime—the mafia bosses and corrupt political machines; and who crusaded for every American's equality and civil rights. Their victories built the foundation upon which we now stand (Ashcroft, November 8, 2001).

It is apparent that what each of these groups have in common is a demonstrated resistance to both free-market capitalism and globalization. In similar fashion law enforcement is now using rhetoric to gain unrestricted access to the new methods of transferring and circulating capital in a global economy. Claims made about cyber-stalkers, identity theft, child pornography and internet fraud have replaced the traditional concerns about street crime and even the "quality of life" and "weed and seed" language of just a decade or so ago. Urban space, street crime, and community policing as formal police focal concerns have been dislodged with talk of global terrorism, domestic surveillance, Internet crime, international trade in humans, narco-terrorists, and coordination of international law enforcement activities. Law enforcement is beginning to shift its attention to globalization protesters, who resist the changing economic order regardless of their violent or peaceful nature.

The reassessment of targets of social control is impacting the policing institution on many levels. Arguably, the most important shift relates to the federalization of municipal police agencies. What was traditionally defined as local or state policing is assuming a mandate that was historically reserved for federal agencies. Municipal police are devoting more of their attention and resources to securing the conduits of capital. Whether they are controlling the nation's borders, the Internet, seaports, or enforcing immigration laws, municipal agencies are assuming a more federalized agenda. They are experiencing greater centralization, a loss of jurisdictional integrity and local political control. Antiterrorism hyper-rhetoric is also being used to sustain and expand specialized use of force groups like SWAT teams, crowd control units, and rapidly deployed military units. Local police are beginning to play a greater role in domestic surveillance and are becoming the eyes and ears of Federal enforcement agencies. The new emphasis by local police on the enforcement of immigration laws is an example of this phenomenon.

The federalization of municipal agencies is leading to an internationalization of federal law enforcement. Federal agencies are increasingly training the police of foreign nations and protecting capital on a global scale, while leaving domestic crimes like bank robbery, white-collar crime, and civil rights enforcement to local police. Federal law enforcement also is focusing more on intelligence gathering and protecting the interest of capital in foreign nations. Historically, these were the duties of the CIA, but this mandate is being assumed my many federal agencies in light of the global expansion of capital. Consider a few of the changes that are coming about in both local and federal law enforcement because of the globalization movement.

Figure 2
Shifts in the Role and Functions of U.S. Police

Federal Law Police Focus
> Decline in Civil Rights enforcement
> Decline in traditional domestic crime investigation
> Increased dependence on local information
> Increased international investigation
> Increase in international police training
> Increased collection and analysis of intelligence data

Municipal Police Focus
> Increased watchman/security oriented
> Security of infrastructure rather than businesses
> Reemergence of Bomb Squads and Hazard Materials Units
> Reduction in drug enforcement
> Increased role in immigration law enforcement
> Increased domestic surveillance
> Decline in community policing orientation
> Renewed emphasis on crowd control

These changes are likely to continue into the next decade, though modifications will occur because the political focus on terrorism stands in stark contrast to the forces of globalization. It is more likely that the changes occurring in federal law enforcement will remain for an extended period of time, whereas the shifts in local policing may be short-lived.

Conclusion

A primary role of police in a capitalist society is the protection of capital. As capitalism has expanded throughout history, the demands on the police institution have changed. The geographic areas, individuals, and behaviors policed during each economic revolution have revolved around threats to the expansion of capital. The fact that a new economic revolution is underway is leading to a shift in American policing. Its geographic focus, the individuals, and the behaviors policed are changing. For example, profiling of the 1990s largely involved seeking drug law violators among minority males (Cole, 1999). That is changing to a focus on the identification of possible terrorists among Middle-Eastern males. The policing of terrorism and the rhetoric of this agenda are leading to a federalization of municipal police agencies and an internationalization of federal agencies. Local and state law enforcement organizations are increasingly funded by federal sources while simultaneously experiencing a reduction in local and state monies. They are increasingly trained and provided equipment designed to fight the anti-terrorism cause. Historically, international crime was of little interest to American policing, but this is changing. Globalization, especially the expansion of capital, is the driving force in the new international interest of the American police institution.

The newly identified targets of social control and the expanded geographic focus are based on the identification of the groups and regions most threatening to the expansion of capital. Like the labor organizers of the industrial revolution, terrorist groups threaten the emerging economic ordering of society. The threat comes not from the terrorist acts, but the policing of those acts. Globalization and true policing of terrorism are diametrically opposed. Globalization and the expansion of capitalism require accommodating importation laws and the free flow of goods, people and information across political boarders. A true attempt to limit terrorist activities demands secure borders and strict importation laws. True policing of terrorism not only requires a search of passengers boarding aircraft, but it demands a search of cargo. It requires knowledge of international corporations and the reexamination of nation states deemed as friendly. Successful economic globalization demands the opposite.

The expansion of capitalism calls for expeditious importation and exportation, which equates with limited inspection of cargo. It requires that the practices of international corporations go unchecked, which allows the use of sweatshops and lack of labor standards to continue unabated. Most importantly, it requires that the activities of nation states be examined only to the degree that they impede or encourage economic expansion. In short, the competing agendas of globalization and the policing of terrorism cannot coexist. Eventually, the demands of economic globalization will prevail and terrorism will be normalized. That does not mean that enforcement efforts will stop, in fact, quite the opposite is likely to occur. Terrorism will be the excuse for the use of force on a global scale. In truth, however, the force applied in the name of antiterrorism efforts will facilitate the expansion of capitalism. If history is any indicator, the conceptions of who is dangerous, the geographic areas that are deemed dangerous, and the force applied by the police institution will be modified as a result of the globalization of capitalism. Corporate and business interest will conflict with the hyper-rhetoric of terrorism. Eventually, national security, safety and law enforcement practices and focuses will succumb to these interests.

Chapter Review Questions

1. In your own words summarize the chapter.

2. We have established that police have reassigned their focus in accordance with the pressing issues of the moment, (i.e., slaves, labor groups, civil rights activists, and college students). Where are their energies focused now, and why?

3. How have technological advances affected the geographical orientation of policing?

4. What do the authors mean when they discuss the reclaiming of areas under the "language of urban renewal and revitalization"?

5. "At the close of the twentieth century, police tactics and the signifiers of those in need of state control changed considerably." Their efforts were focused away from crude signifiers like race and class, to locations. Why did this change occur?

6. What does the author mean by symbolic violence?

7. In terms of formal and informal control, compare and contrast the traditional roles of policing and their current authority.

8. How are cultural differences and resistance seen as a threat to globalization?

9. Briefly explain the difference between terrorism and guerilla warfare. How do governments become involved in terrorist acts?

10. How has the reassessment of targets of social control impacted the policing institution?

CHAPTER 4

Community Policing:
Is it Soft on Crime?

Jihong Zhao
Matthew C. Scheider
Quint C. Thurman

Introduction

Community Oriented Policing (COP) has become the dominant theme of contemporary police reform in America. But along with its widespread implementation has come criticisms in a variety of forms, including the claim that this approach is soft on crime. This chapter examines this and related issues that address the value of community policing in the twenty-first century.

Since the 1990s, community policing has undergone waves of change characterized by widespread acceptance and adaptation among law enforcement agencies (Greene 2000; Zhao, Lovrich & Thurman, 1999; Eck & Rosenbaum, 1994; Hickman & Reaves, 2001). One of the key events facilitating the willingness to embrace community policing practice during the 1990s was the strong endorsement of the Federal government marked by the passage of the Violent Crime Control and Law Enforcement Act in 1994. The statute reflected "an investment of more than $30 billion over six years" (NIJ, 1997). This has been the largest domestic anti-crime legislation in the nation's history. In addition, this bill contained provisions for subsidizing the hiring of an additional 100,000 police officers who are engaged in community policing activities. In order to implement this program, the U.S. Department of Justice established the Office of Community Oriented Policing Services (the COPS Office) which coordinates and supervises community policing programs, and provides training for local law enforcement agencies. Since 1994, the COPS Office has invested $10.6 billion through a variety of grants to more than 12,000 law enforcement agencies across the nation to advance community policing.

41

To some degree, COP also has caught the attention of the mass media. Television stations and newspapers published numerous stories regarding community policing in the 1990s. Politicians in city governments typically have embraced the prospect of community policing—improving police/community relations and reducing social disorder (e.g., New York, Silverman, 1999; Chicago, Hartnet & Skogan, 1997; Seattle & Lyons 2002). Furthermore, most scholars tend to agree that community policing is the most recent significant reform in American policing (for a review, see Greene, 2000).

Despite all the attention COP has received, it would be a mistake to believe that the popularity of COP is equal to its effectiveness. While scholars and practitioners agree that COP has been widely implemented in U.S. cities to varying degrees of success, there is little agreement regarding the outcomes of innovative COP programs and strategies. This partly is because program implementation does not automatically translate into program effectiveness. But perhaps the most stinging criticism is that COP is soft on crime.

This chapter addresses the issue of whether or not COP is soft on crime. We do this by first describing how community policing differs from a more traditional, bureaucratic approach to policing. Following this and recognizing there is a lack of "hard evidence" to suggest that COP is effective at reducing crime, we present findings from a national study that we recently conducted, that speaks to the issue of the effect of COP on crime. Here we examine the impact of federal funding for COP on local crime rates.

Traditional Policing and Its Effectiveness

The era between the early 1900s and the 1970s is known as the professional era of policing, which focused almost exclusively on crime control (Kelling & Moore, 1998). As such, numbers of crime incidents were at the center of measuring police performance and effectiveness (Thurman, Zhao & Giacomazzi, 2001). Measuring trends in crime became possible in the early 1930s with the inception of the Uniform Crime Reporting system (UCR), which to this day provides information on the eight most serious types of crimes—known as Part I Offenses: murder, rape, robbery, aggravated assault, burglary, larceny, motor vehicle theft, and arson. Today, more than 16,000 city, county, and state police department (90% of all eligible agencies) regularly report local crime incidents to the FBI. Crime rates (the number of incidents per 100,000 residents) make it easier for law enforcement agencies to track crime rates and compare them over time and even across jurisdictions.

For the first 30 years, police departments benefited significantly from the use of the UCR crime rates as a measure of effectiveness, and for a number of reasons. First, a focus on crime control gave American police the professional status as "crime fighters" (Walker, 1977). Second, two operational strategies gained importance: preventive patrol and criminal investigation. Police departments viewed these strategies as two pillars supporting crime control as the most crucial function of the police. Finally, centralization and rule driven organizational structures were created to ensure the goal of crime control. In his seminal book, *Police Administration*, O.W. Wilson (1950) outlined the ideal type of police organization, typifying a chain of command and limited span of control.

In the 1970s and 1980s, several factors contributed to the questioning of the use of crime rates as a primary indicator of police effectiveness. The first factor concerned the change in crime rates that took place in the mid-1960s. Police departments across the nation appeared incapable of responding to rising rates of crime, particularly violent crime (Thurman et al., 2001). In a span of 26 years (from 1965 to 1990), the rate for violent crimes (murder, robbery, rape, and aggravated assault) increased approximately 240 percent, from approximately 2,000 incidents per 100,000 citizens in 1965 to almost 7,000 per 100,000 in 1991. Though the number of arrests significantly increased between 1960 and 1980, and police budgets increased substantially by 20 percent during the same period, crime rates continued to rise. In addition, clearance rates (the number crimes solved by arrest) continued to decline (Thurman et al., 2001:107).

Second, the public's fear of crime also appeared to be on the rise. Paralleling increasing crime rates, a substantial number of Americans felt that crime rates in their own areas also had risen too high. Accordingly, nearly half (40%) of the Americans asked about crime between 1966 and 1978 reported feeling uneasy about their safety. This perception was exacerbated by widespread media coverage of crime, which often occupied the front page of local newspapers and was a dominant theme on the national television news (Thurman et al., 2001). Increasing public fear of violent crime raised questions about police effectiveness, and departments were relatively unprepared to deal with such issues.

Furthermore, police-community relations were deteriorating, particularly between police and minority groups, stemming from broad social changes during 1960s and 1970s. By the 1970s, middle-class, white families began to migrate to the suburbs in order to escape high crime rates and avoid paying high city taxes. As a result, minority populations in large cities continued to rise, and the role of urban police departments became primarily "hard-line" enforcers of law, which created distrust on both sides. In addition, a considerable number of minority residents were poor or unemployed thus resulting in a diminishing tax base from which to draw on to pay for public safety (Wilson, 1986).

Not surprisingly, these factors forced American police to search for alternative measures of their effectiveness during the 1980s and 1990s. Failing to achieve the goal of crime control, newer issues needed to be addressed, such as reducing fear of crime and improving police-community relationships. Two options were available for American police at that time: (1) to further narrow their organizational goals similar to what had been done at the turn of twentieth century, or (2) to expand organizational goals in order to exercise greater control over the external environment, similar to the early days of police history. Because the first option was not feasible, COP became an inviting alternative for police agencies during the late 1970s and 1980s. However, there existed an inherent problem with the second choice: the more complicated an organization's goals, the less likely that the agency will be able to develop precise measures of organizational effectiveness.

Community-Oriented Policing and the Expansion of Measures of Effectiveness

The expansion of police organizational goals is the defining feature of COP. Police agencies are now expected to pay attention to social disorder, fear of crime, crime itself, and police-community relationships, as well as a host of new services that fall within the COP model. The rationale for this shifting focus of police work is that if these other community elements are not maintained—especially social disorder—then law and order in a community may deteriorate. According to Wilson and Kelling (1982), disruptions in social order can breed serious crime incidents.

COP also emphasizes that the process by which police choose to maintain social order is important. While it is possible to maintain social order through very authoritarian measures such as intensive police crackdowns, the COP philosophy emphasizes that building police community relationships produces more effective, long term solutions to problems and can greatly enhance police legitimacy and trust. Consistent with this expansion of organizational goals, numerous innovative programs have been implemented (fear reduction, promotion of police-community partnerships, and zero tolerance policing).

Today it seems as if virtually any new program or strategy can be labeled COP, even if it appears to fit better a traditional law enforcement approach. Thus, the question "Is Community Policing Soft on Crime" is a difficult one to answer. Because COP still emphasizes the need for the police to respond to calls for service and arrest offenders, it is no softer on crime than the more traditional response oriented measures which characterized the professional era of policing. Rather than being soft on crime, COP emphasizes being "smarter" on crime and views arrest powers as simply one tool in a police officer's toolkit.

The broad nature of the COP philosophy can be seen in the various attempts to define it. For example, in his review of COP literature, Greene (2000) identified three styles of COP, including community policing (e.g., community building through crime prevention and proactive crime control), problem-oriented policing (e.g., problem focused), and zero-tolerance policing (addressing specific order problems in neighborhoods, primarily through enforcement). Similarly, Cordner (1997) suggested that COP has four essential elements (philosophical, strategic, operational, and managerial). Finally, the U.S. Department of Justice, COPS Office presents a model of COP focusing on three core elements of community policing: organizational, tactical, and external (COPS Office Web Site).

A major advantage—and disadvantage—of broad definitions of community policing is that virtually anyone can claim that their activities fall under the rubric of COP. As a result, this makes COP a very popular police reform. On the other hand, these broad definitions make assessments of the overall effectiveness of COP rather difficult, if not impossible. For example, in his case study of New York City in the 1990s, Silverman (1999) found that COMPSTAT had made a significant contribution to the unprecedented drop in the violent crime rate after taking into consideration demographic changes. However, it is interesting to note that other cities (e.g., San Diego) which did not have COMPSTAT programs also experienced a similar drop in violent crime rates during the 1990s. Does this mean that other innovative programs are at work in crime reduction in these cities?

Alpert and Moore (2000) argue that the evaluation of COP effectiveness should include the following components: (1) police-related and intergovernmental activities that improve the social fabric of the community, (2) projects with the assistance of private industry that improve informal and formal social control in the community, (3) indicators of fear of crime, and (4) victimization and police service programs that help promote community sprit in those neighborhoods where none previously existed.

Recent research shows that increased contact with citizens can improve police-community relationships. Similarly, in their review of 26 projects on police fear reduction between 1973 and 2000, Zhao, Scheider, and Thurman (2002) found that if programs were implemented successfully, they seemed to produce significant drops in residents' fear of crime, which led to increases in their satisfaction with local police departments. In the past 15 years, there have been a number of edited books on the effectiveness of COP programs implemented across the country, several major review articles (e.g., Greene, 2000; Cordner, 1997), and numerous evaluations published by the COPS Office and academic journals. Overall, these sources have reported various degrees of success regarding COP programs and strategies across multiple outcomes.

But Is COP Soft on Crime? A Recent Study on COPS Office Funding

Despite the emphasis on multiple outcomes in determining the success (or failure) of COP, Bittner (1972) has forcefully argued that no matter what kind of functions police may play, the bottom line for police work is a focus on law enforcement activities. As such, the primary test of police effectiveness is the reduction of local crime rates. This goal is consistent with the argument made in the "Broken Windows" theory (Wilson & Kelling, 1982). Most of the attention has focused on the potential spiral relationship between social disorder and crime. Consequently, police need to expand their functions and work with local residents on crime prevention activities. The theory also implies that the containment of social disorder also means ultimately lower crime rates in communities.

Due to the wide variation of COP implementation at different times, a true test of COP across the nation is simply not feasible. Accordingly, a few years ago, we decided to conduct a limited test of the effectiveness of COP by examining the relationship between COPS Office funded activities and crime. In so doing we examined local crime rates between 1994 and 2000, a period during which COP was particularly popular. While this test spoke more to the effectiveness of the COPS Office than it did to community policing techniques specifically, it is relevant here because the primary mission of the COPS Office remains the advancement of community policing.

Three Categories of COPS Grants

Title I of the Crime Act, known as the "Public Safety Partnership and Community Policing Act of 1994," authorized the use of $8.8 billion to fund local law enforcement agencies in the fight against crime through the enhancement of community policing capabilities. To carry out this task, the U.S. Department of Justice created a new agency—the Office of Community Oriented Policing Services (COPS Office)—to administer and supervise new grant programs resulting from the act (Roth & Ryan, 2000). From 1994 to 2003, the COPS Office invested $10.6 billion to advance community policing nationwide. The grants funded by the COPS Office can be grouped into three categories.

First, *hiring grants* are designed to directly assist local law enforcement in the deployment of additional community police officers. While the Universal Hiring Program (UHP) has become the primary and best known initiative, smaller precursor hiring programs included PHASE 1, the Accelerated Hiring, Education, and Deployment Program (AHEAD), the Funding Accelerated for Smaller Towns Program (FAST), and the Police Hiring Supplement Program (PHS). To date, the COPS Office has awarded approximately $5.5 billion in hiring grants to law enforcement agencies.

The *MORE grant program* (Making Officer Redeployment Effective) represents a second award category. MORE grants provide funding for law enforcement agencies to acquire new technology and to add civilian personnel in order to increase officer effectiveness and efficiency. Civilians are hired to perform administrative and support tasks previously performed by officers. To date, COPS has awarded approximately $1.3 billion in MORE grants.

Innovative grants comprise the third group of awards offered by the COPS Office.[1] Innovative grants fund specialized programs targeted at specific jurisdictions and/or categories of crime and social disorder. The Distressed Neighborhoods Grant Program is one example of an innovative grant program targeted at specific jurisdictions. This program provided funds for eighteen jurisdictions that were identified by the COPS Office as having some of the most significant public order and economic challenges in the nation. Cities were directed to analyze various sources of neighborhood level data in order to concentrate community police officers into a relatively small number of high problem areas within their city. Innovative grants typically represent the most competitively determined awards, although some awards result from targeted solicitations by the COPS Office. To date, COPS has awarded approximately $661 million in innovative grants.

Data Collection for the COPS Funding Study

A full description of the data collection techniques and variables for our 2002 study is beyond the scope of this particular work, but is detailed elsewhere (see Zhao, Scheider & Thurman, 2002). Here, we briefly review the context of the study and the main variables used to determine whether COPS Office funding made a difference in crime rates.

Two dependent variables were used in our study, which were derived from UCR data. Consistent with the UCR format, the violent crime rate reflected the sum of the incidences of four crimes (murder, rape, robbery, and aggravated assault) divided by each city's population and multiplied by 100,000. Similarly, the property crime rate reflected the sum of the incidences per 100,000 for three crimes—burglary, larceny, and auto theft.

Additionally, three independent variables were used in our study to represent the type of award made (hiring grant, innovative grant, or MORE grant). The total amount of each type of grant funding received by a city in each calendar year (1994-1999) was divided by the city's population so that the total for each type of grant program was standardized to indicate the dollar amount received per year, per resident for each city. In addition, the total dollar amount of COPS funding was adjusted to 1994 dollars, using the Consumer Price Index.

There were three additional specifications for the independent variables. First, the three COPS grant independent variables (hiring grants, MORE grants, and innovative grants) were lagged by one year when their impact on crime was analyzed. This one-year lag provided implementation time to hire officers, procure technology, and initiate innovative programs. This one year lag was based on internal COPS Office tracking systems that indicated on average that it takes 12 months to hire, train, and deploy an officer from the award start date.[2] Accordingly, data concerning COPS Office funding coincided with grants awarded from 1994-1999 and UCR crime data were included for 1995-2000. Second, because hiring grants are intended to hire officers over a three-year period, hiring grants awarded to police departments were allocated over that period in a declining rate according to the following factors: 38 percent for the first year, 34 percent for the second year, and 28 percent for the third year.[3]

It also should be pointed out that, although MORE grants are designed as one-year grants, agencies typically took a longer period of time in order to procure the technology, make it operational, and train officers in its use. Therefore, the technology portion of the MORE grants was spread out over a period of three years to compensate for this fact according to the following allocation: 36 percent for the first year, 36 percent for the second year, and 28 percent for the third year.[4] In addition, analysis of COPS Office tracking systems (COPS Count) indicated that civilians were typically hired within one year of the grant. Thus, the MORE funding variable used in this study was calculated for the first year as the sum of the civilian portion of the grant plus 36 percent of the technology portion of the grant. In the second year, 36 percent of the technology portion of the grant was used, with the remaining 28 percent of the technology portion allocated to the final year.

Our study also employed a number of control variables, including the 1994 crime rate, which allowed for the analysis to be standardized to examine the change in crime rates since 1994. This also allowed us to focus on the period after the creation of the COPS Office.

In addition, six other control variables, designed to account for the socioeconomic health of communities, also were included in the study. Social disorganization theory developed by Shaw and McKay provides a theoretical framework for the inclusion of these variables in this analysis (for a discussion and testing of social disorganization theory see Shaw & McKay, 1972; Bursik, 1988; Sampson, 1985; Sampson & Groves, 1989). Social disorganization theorists argue that unique socioeconomic characteristics of communities are closely associated with local crime problems.

According to Osgood and Chambers (2000), there are three primary socioeconomic dimensions that merit empirical scrutiny. The first dimension is community heterogeneity. In this study, heterogeneity was represented by the percentage of minority residents and percent male in a community. The second dimension is a community's socioeconomic status, measured here by five variables: the level of unemployment, percentage of single parent households, percentage of young people between the ages of 15 to 24, percentage of home ownership and per capita income. The final dimension we controlled for was community mobility as indicated by the percentage of people having lived at the same address since 1985.

Can COP Affect Crime Rates?

As might be expected, our data showed that on average the property crime rate per 100,000 population (5,263) is much higher than the violent crime rate (821) in the cities we studied. Similarly, hiring grant programs were the largest programs funded by the COPS Office with a mean of $2.23 per person during the six-year period, followed by MORE grants ($0.42) and innovative grants ($0.79). The demographic variables showed that the six-year average of unemployment in the sample was 4.78 percent. About one-third of the residents living in these cities identified themselves as minority (39.74%), and single parent households comprised 12.11 percent of the population. The percentage of young people was 15.12. In addition, 55.92 percent of the residents were homeowners, about one-half of the residents (50.71%) lived at the same address.

Results from the multivariate analysis of violent and property crime rates suggested that both hiring grants and innovative grants have had a significant effect on crime reduction in this group, after controlling for previous crime rates (the 1994 crime rate), demographic variables, and unobserved systematic variation. The explained variance of the model predicting the violent crime rate was 89 percent, indicating that the independent and control variables were able to explain a very high percentage of variance in the model; similarly, the explained variance for the property crime rate model was 87 percent.

Our analyses indicated that an increase of one dollar in grant funding spent for hiring purposes resulted in a corresponding decline of 5.49 violent crime incidents per 100,000 residents. A dollar increase for hiring community police officers contributed to a decline of 25.22 property crime incidents per 100,000 in the population. Similarly, regarding innovative grant programs, a one dollar increase in innovative grant funding contributed to 5.31 fewer violent crime incidents per 100,000 in the population and 20.65 property crime incidents per 100,000 in the population between 1995 and 2000. MORE grants did not have an effect on violent crime rates in these cities, but did decrease property crime rates by 21.47 per 100,000 in the population.

The effects of demographic variables on violent and property crime rates in the two models were similar. For example, the percentage of single parent households and mobility were positively associated with violent crime rates, while the percentage of home owners were negatively correlated with violent crime rates. Similar patterns of effects of demographic variables were found in the analysis of property crime rates.

Conclusion

This chapter attempts to answer the question, "Is COP soft on crime?" We went about this by first focusing on the popularity of community policing programs that have enjoyed wide acceptance by politicians and police professionals across the nation. We emphasized that community policing has earned a place in the history of American policing. However, there has been lack of consensus regarding the effectiveness of community policing. Because COP is a loosely defined concept, there are a wide variety of programs and strategies implemented by police agencies nationwide. These programs and strategies vary from victim contact program, foot patrol, zero-tolerance policing, to Total Quality Management. In fact, virtually any program that is different from a traditional, reactive response and random patrol can be labeled as a form of community policing.

One advantage of this broad definition is that COP can more easily rally supporters. The disadvantage is that this variation in implementation makes it extremely difficult to evaluate the effectiveness of COP. Moreover, despite the broadening of police responsibilities, to a great extent, the main focus of police work remains producing reductions in local crime rates. COP philosophies emphasize that this should be accomplished through fair and collaborative processes. Controlling social disorder and promoting police-community partnerships are very valuable processes by which to accomplish this objective, but we must ask: can these activities reduce crime? There are numerous reports regarding COP programs that demonstrate that COP can produce declines at the individual city level. However, critics point out that similar programs have often not produced similar reductions in crime at other locations and times. This lack of "hard evidence" regarding crime reduction has been a "soft" spot in COP research.

The second part of this chapter reviewed a relationship between COP and crime reduction in America from a unique perspective: the effect that COPS Office funding has had on local crime rates (also see Zhao, Scheider & Thurman, 2002). This study did not directly address the issue of whether or not COP per se has produced reductions in crime, but rather allowed for the examination of the effect on crime that a large scale Federal program may have whose specific mandate is to advance community policing nationwide. Our study of the relationship between COPS funding and crime rates enabled us to compare the rate of crime drop within groups (individual cities across 7 years) and between groups (different cities with different amounts of funding by year and by city across 7 years). Therefore, the results can be considered as the contribution of COPS grants on the crime drop over 2,300 cities with populations greater than 10,000.

Our findings indicate that overall, the amount of COPS funding has significantly impacted the drop in crime in U.S. cities with populations greater than 10,000. In particular, hiring and innovative grants have had significant effects on violent and property crime rates in these cities. Again, although this evidence does not speak directly to the issue of the effectiveness of community policing on crime, it does provide some support for the argument that community policing programs, in their variety of manifestations, can have an attributable impact on crime.

In conclusion, we believe that it is fair to say that COP is no softer on crime than traditional policing measures because many of those same measures (responding to calls for service, arresting offenders, sting operations, crackdowns etc.) are encompassed within COP philosophies. The difference is that COP attempts to determine when these measures will be most effective and apply them accordingly. It also attempts to widen the array of responses and proactive crime prevention measures open to police. Today, police departments are developing and implementing an even wider array of strategies and programs under the umbrella of community policing to proactively address crime and social disorder issues. COP increases the number of options available to the police in dealing with crime and social disorder issues to include among others, collaborative problem solving, partnerships with community and other government entities, empowering officers to develop solutions to geographically specific crime problems, using technology to enhance information exchange and problem analysis etc. Expanding the tools available to the police to prevent and respond to crime and disorder problems does not result in softer policing, but rather, smarter policing.

Endnotes

[1]   In this analysis, the following COPS programs are categorized as innovative grant programs 311, Advancing Community Policing Program, Organizational Change Demonstration Centers, Methamphetamine Initiative, Distressed Neighborhoods Program, Community Policing to Combat Domestic Violence, Anti-Gang Initiative, Problem-Solving Partnerships, Youth Firearms Violence Initiative, Integrity Initiative, and the School Based Partnerships Program.

[2]   This is based on an analysis conducted by the COPS Office of its yearly "COPS Count" data, an annual survey of all of its hiring grants.

[3]   These numbers are based on COPS Office recommendations regarding how agencies spend money over the three-year period. The adjusted allocation of COPS hiring grant over a three-year period is used for panel data analysis.

[4]   This allocation method was based on an analysis of the average actual spending patterns of police departments who have received COPS MORE grants. The adjusted allocation of COPS MORE grant over a three-year period is used for panel data analysis.

Chapter Review Questions

1. Discuss the reasons for the emergence of community oriented policing as the dominant model of policing in America today.

2. What do the authors mean when they say "it would be a mistake to believe that the popularity of COP is equal to its effectiveness?"

3. How did the UCR affect performance measures for policing during the professional era (early 1900s to 1970)?

4. Why does the ambiguous nature of COP, as implemented, make determining its effectiveness particularly problematic?

5. How does the "Broken Windows" theory relate to COP?

6. What is the COPS Office? What is its mission?

7. Discuss the three general types of funding offered by the COPS Office. For each type of funding program, discuss its implications for the advancement of COP.

8. Describe the main variables used in the COPS Office funding study conducted by the authors of this chapter.

9. What were the main findings of the COPS Office study?

10. Based on the findings of the COPS Office study, is COP soft on crime? Why or why not?

CHAPTER 5

Police Culture in a Changing Multicultural Environment

John P. Crank

Introduction

This chapter addresses the question of whether police culture is an impediment to reform. It is a question that is frequently asked, and itself deserves consideration. The question is addressed reflexively, as an inquiry into perspectives that would suppose a relationship between culture and reform. The inquiry, I argue, emerges from a standpoint, locating culture in the tension between someone's notion of negative police attributes and administrative reform. Culture, however, exists in the eye of the beholder; it emerges from observations and interpretations of a group's behavior. This chapter consequently is about the standpoints that enable us to think about police culture and how they predispose us to think about it in particular ways.

Culture as a Bad Witch

> Dorothy has been whisked by a tornado from her home in Kansas to the Land of Oz, a place of fantasy and magic. Her arrival in Oz is violent—her house falls on a witch, crushing her. The good witch of the North arrives and gives the bad witch's ruby slippers to Dorothy. From that point forward, Dorothy's concern with Oz focuses on one end—she must somehow find the Wizard, so that she might get home again. The remaining evil witch will seek to enslave her, preventing forever her return home. Dorothy sets off on her quest.

Police culture is not so much a field of study as it is an accusation. For those who are dissatisfied with police service, or who fail to see their vision of police behavior or organizational activity take hold, police culture is the chief villain. Whether it is a police officer in Los Angeles involved in drugs and violence against suspects, the FBI denounced for failing to follow so-called "911" leads, or officers in New Jersey using racial profiling strategies to make routine stops, culture is culpable. It is the dark force of the police, the hidden unity that protects officers from oversight, and the evil within. Culture is like Dorothy's bad witch—it is an evil that will resist one's efforts and that one must overcome. And it is a "hidden" evil, and obstacle full of unknown and obscure power.

The negative concept of police culture works, according to Waddington (1999:293), because of its "condemnatory potential." It is located in the notion that the police are to blame for the "injustices perpetrated in the name of the criminal justice system." It is a view of police culture that reflects a civil libertarian concern about police and due process of law (Reiner, 1985). That is, it is concerned, not with analyzing police behavior, or understanding it, but with reforming it.

In Los Angeles, a study commissioned by the police officer's union found that the culture of the Los Angeles Police Department was to blame for corruption. The author of the report observed that "The board of Inquiry (into corruption) fails to recognize that the central problem in the Los Angeles Police Department is its culture." The solution? A return to community policing, a stronger civilian police commission, and a system in which people can more easily complain about alleged police misconduct. The findings, summed by the civil rights attorney who assisted in the review, was, "It's the culture, stupid" (CNN.Com, 2000).

This aspect of police culture is the enemy within. It is virulent and perverts the oath of office. It thrives on greed, prizing loyalty to ones corrupt colleague above loyalty to police service. Its weapons are those of the standover merchant and it depends on group loyalty, a tradition of mateship and peer group pressure. Those who subscribe to it hold little fear of being exposed (Wood, 1996:45; in Shanahan, 2000:1).

Albittron (1999) summarizes the literature that has emerged both from professional and from academic circles as follows:

> Indeed, the "police subculture" is often depicted as an occupational and organizational environment that fosters highly questionable and singular codes of deviance, secrecy, silence, and cynicism, as well as such "pathological" personality dispositions as suspiciousness, insularity, brutality, authoritarianism, ultraconservatism, bigotry, and racism . . . the police subculture has been persistently analyzed and stigmatized as the most potent obstacle to progressive reform in policing (Albittron, 1999:163).

This literature presents an image of police culture as a metaphorical container of evil spirits. Its contents include such diverse elements as insularity, brutality, civil rights violations, peer group pressure, authoritarianism, peer loyalty, and corruption. It is from this "culture is a container of evil spirits" way of thinking that police culture is seen as the primary impediment to the good of agency reform.

The "culture is a container of evil spirits" way of thinking is only one of many ways to think about police culture. There are ways of thinking about it that have a good conception of culture, or that are simply neutral. To sort through these conceptions, this chapter takes a reflexive look at police culture. Of interest herein in that conceptions emerge from someone's worldview, someone who has an idea of what good policing is and how culture affects that idea. When we think about culture in this way, we recognize that conceptions of police culture are a consequence of the way an observer looks at police work. The conception is inseparable from the observer, a property of the way the observer considers the world of the police. The concept of culture is determined by someone's standpoint, which is itself determined by his/her life experiences. It is not necessarily a property of the police.

Once we think about culture as a property of an individual's standpoint, the study of culture is transformed. We open several doors that make the study of culture muddy and complex—issues of value neutrality, objective social science, the relationship between the observer and the observed, and the problem of evaluating the relative merits of different notions of police culture—all of which need to be carefully considered and perhaps abandoned. This chapter explores the muddy complexity created by locating police culture within standpoints.

> Oh what a strange land Oz is, brimming with good and bad magic, people transformed into strange beasts, yellow-brick paths that lead to illusory goals, and fallible witches who melt in water and get crushed by houses. Dorothy is received as a sorceress. Through her travels, she is pulled into the life of Oz. Her standpoint is clear—go home to see Aunt Em again, yet her standpoint merges with those of her traveling companions, the Scarecrow, the Lion, and the Tin Man, who each seek goals symbolic of personal growth and are destined to become rules of Oz's strange inhabitants.

From Culture as "Object" to Culture as "Standpoint"

The study of culture is complicated. Culture is not some "object" like a rock that, discounting the eon's-long effects of entropy on its nuclear energy, will continue to exist independently of our observations of it. Culture exists because we imagine it to exist. Culture has the property of intentionality. By intentionality, I mean that things take meaning because we create meaning for them. They do not exist without the assigned meaning. Shweder (1991) discusses at length the word "weed," as an intentional term (see Crank, 2002). All of the meanings associated with the word weed have to do with human judgments of value applied to plants. In the world of political phenomena, the word "flag" is similarly intentional—its meanings are wholly determined by our intent. The meanings associated with flag—patriotism, First Amendment rights, loyalty, cultural history, for example, are created by our language and superimposed on the object of our interest.

Culture has the same property. It is an intentional term for social phenomena. There is no independent, objective thing called culture. Through what Searle (1998) calls "collective intentionality" we construct shared meanings, which are embodied in a terminology of social phenomena. These meanings tend to carry all sorts of moral and ethical prescriptions. So if culture is not an objective property of the thing we are trying to explain or study, what then is it?

Standpoint

When someone becomes interested in police culture, his/her interest derives from a standpoint. The term standpoint derives from "standpoint epistemology." Epistemology refers to how we know whether something is real. Standpoint epistemologies particularly challenge the way the social sciences represent the world. Theorists have challenged the notion that there is a single view from which an overriding version of the world can be written (Denzin, 1997). The notion of a positivist science, in which there is a correspondence between the way we see the world and its actual reality, is Eurocentric and serves the interest of ruling elite, particularly white males.

Standpoint theory emerged in feminist perspective. Feminist standpoint "begin(s) from the perspective of women's experiences—experiences shaped by a gender-based division of labor that has excluded women from the public sphere (Denzin, 1997:55). Standpoints can be "hybridized" to the extent that individuals are members of diverse subaltern groups. Anzaldua (1987), for example, explores the nature of her identity as a Tejana, white, woman who is lesbian and locates that identity in the borderlands of her upbringing between Texas and Mexico (see Denzin, 1997:82-85). Indeed, hybridization is integral to standpoint; hybridization recognizes the legitimacy of different standpoints and the complexity of social status, locating value in the ability to comprehend the extent of diversity in the surrounding world.

The central point of standpoint theory is that the world around us can only be understood from the "point of view of the historically and culturally situated individual" (Denzin, 1987:87). Standpoint epistemologies have been largely developed by subaltern groups seeking a voice to legitimate their cultures, traditions, and worldviews. However, the central issues in standpoint—that the world experiences of the observer determine to a large extent the way in which knowledge about the social world is received, experience, and what it means—is a general principle that applies to all groups that share an identity of purpose or meaning.

Standpoints gain their force because they represent the collective wisdom of particular groups. Of central importance in the recognition of standpoint is that it is reflexive. It requires that, when we look at views of police culture, we consider the cultural dispositions of the groups that are interested in police culture. People develop an engaged perspective by considering the diversity of standpoints available (Lorber, 1998). The value of standpoint is twofold. First, it links social knowledge with the breadth of our knowledge about different groups in the world. And second, it allows us to sort through much of the literature on culture so that we can understand why it is important to the person who writes about it.

Standpoint refers to the nexus of a person's status identities, how those identities lead to particular kinds of life experiences, and how those experiences legitimize their view of the world. By *the study of standpoint*, I mean that we look at how a person's perceptions of the social world around them is mediated through their cultural understandings. The social world I am interested in is police culture. A person's standpoint predisposes their view of police culture, as it determines their reason for being interested in police culture, it constrains the outcomes they select to associate with culture, and it is shaped by the language or vocabulary used to describe police culture.

Imagine an interested observer of the police, perhaps a former line officer personally committed to an ethic of police professionalism. This observer has studied the police in an academic environment and has become familiar with the idea of culture. This observer, then, carries out a research project, using a survey questionnaire to assess officers attitudes about due process, crime control, corruption, and community policing. Reviewing the literature, she finds that culture is a characteristic of what is called "informal organization," which is defined as a way of short-circuiting formal organizational processes in order to accomplish tasks in an overly bureaucratic job. However, she also finds that it enables the police to avoid effective administrative oversight. Her conclusion is that she has "discovered" a great deal about local police culture and can provide a set of recommendations regarding ways to improve oversight and improve the department's "ethical climate."

Let us think about this work. The observer has carried out typical social science research, and has "objectified" her work with coding schemes, measures, data reduction strategies, measures of significance, and acquired data that enabled her to draw conclusions about her work. The fruit of her endeavors is a work on police culture combined with a set of recommendations aimed at ethical development. Like Dorothy in Oz, she has entered an "enchanted" arena of social activity, one whose meanings and con-structions of reality are unknown and emergent. She has imposed a notion of social order over this unfolding social setting. The social order enables her to take a position about it and to deal with the problems of police cul-ture to make the police a more ethical occupation.

The term "culture" cannot, however, be understood only as something the observer discovered through social science research. It is a term she used to overlay police behaviors she disagreed with and that she thought needed eth-ical control. The concept of culture she used does not exist independently of the discourse she shares with like-minded others. All of the meanings asso-ciated with the term are meanings provided by the observer and her partic-ipating cohort. This notion of culture may become institutionalized over time, with a widely accepted definition, set of attributes, and accepted set of research modalities. However, that it is institutionalized does not mean that it is not still a property of the observer. It is an institutionalized standpoint, a view carried by a group, embedded in a way of thinking and legitimized by the group's world experiences. Additional research will increase the insti-tutionalization of the concept, but not its truth-value. It is still a standpoint.

Standpoints and Rationalities

Standpoints can be located in different intellectual traditions on the police, each with their own rationalities. In the example above, a norma-tive rationality guided the standpoint (see Figure 1). The recognition of dif-ferent rational traditions means that, when we operate from different standpoints, the way in which we form the linkage between motive, action, and outcome may be fundamentally different. MacIntyre (1988) conceived of traditions and rationalities broadly. Assessing the nature of justice, he argued that the meaning of justice is embedded within rational discourse. Rationality is meant as the "intellectual and social tradition in which it (an inquiry) is embodied (MacIntyre, 1988:8). Doctrines, theses, and argu-ments all have to be understood within historical context.[1]

A review of the literature on police culture suggests the presence of "ratio-nal traditions," in which particular standpoints on police culture emerge from identifiable traditions, each with their own vocabularies and languages of inquiry. Four of the traditions contain a conception of good policing and locate culture in that conception of policing. Only one of the traditions does not articulate a notion of good policing, but has instead developed a notion of good inquiry. Each tradition includes a *worldview* in which the police are of interest. It also contains a conception of what constitutes good policing (*outcomes*), how good policing is achieved (*orienting values*), and how cul-ture is associated with that conception (*conception of police culture*). Tra-ditions also have their important *language or vocabulary* for describing police work and culture. Each of these is discussed below.

Worldview. A worldview, also known as ideology when used with regard to political discourse, refers to the general beliefs and predispositions that make the social and physical world meaningful to someone. To be pertinent to this discussion, the police must be somehow pertinent to the worldview.

Outcomes. Outcomes represent the observer's conception of the good (or bad) ends produced by policing. For example, an observer who is studying deviance and police sexual behavior may derive his/her view from a perspective distrustful of unsupervised police authority, and in which close formal administrative and civilian oversight are good end and signify good relations between police and a citizen populace. The dependent variables selected for analysis state a great deal about the standpoint one has regarding culture. In this chapter, the outcomes I am interested in are recommendations, embedded in each standpoint, for police reform. These recommendations carry the recommender's notions of what good policing should "look like."

Orienting Values. Orienting values are the values or meanings that mobilize an interest in police culture. These associate policing with even broader worldviews in which an image of policing is located. They are called orienting values because they are seen as disposing the observer toward a particular way of generally thinking about the police. This view provides the meanings within which a conception of police culture emerges.

Conception of Police Culture. The conception of police culture emerges in a broader notion of what constitutes policing generally and, from most perspectives, the relationship between idealized or "good" policing and policing as it is actually practiced. In the opening section of this chapter, police culture was presented in a highly negative way, one that was consistently in disagreement with the way the various authors thought police work should be conducted. A reformer, for example, might be interested in police culture as a source of resistance to reform. An ethnographer could be interested because it represents something different, whose characteristics are unknown. And an attorney might view police culture as a screen behind which police circumvent due process.

Language/Vocabulary. Words are the basic categories of information through which we organize our social environment. Language, when associated with standpoint, does not simply map the world "out there." In the world of social construction, language makes the exterior world possible. Language, consequently, is never value neutral. To the contrary, when we select a vocabulary, we are engaged in the act of assigning meaning and value to our lives (DiCristina, 1995). The vocabulary we impose in the world around us is comprised of the words that most "meaningfully" describe it. Each police culture standpoint carries a terminology that is not value neutral. To the contrary, the terms used to describe police culture are values-drenched. They carry the central meanings that make culture an object of interest.

Police Culture Standpoints

Six standpoints on police culture are presented below. As standpoints, they are constructions of what I think are the dominant rationalities that have dealt with police culture, and that summarize prevalent views about the police. These standpoints are summarized in Figure 1.

The Normative or "Police Professionalism" Standpoint

The normative standpoint refers to the behavior and organization of the police as a traditional element of the criminal justice system. Normative approaches to the police are concerned with efficiency and effectiveness. These do not tend to look for explanations of the police as a dependent variable, but instead consider how the police can better do what they do. In academic research, the normative standpoint is about the application of scientific principles to the study of crime and crime prevention police strategies and tactics.

In organizational practice the normative standpoint was embodied in the police professionalism movement. The movement emerged in response to the nineteenth century municipal corruption, and represented reformers commitment to control of the police. This standpoint is about the application of scientific or "rational bureaucratic" principles of management to administration, personnel issues, organizational design, management, and community relations.

Normatively, police culture is seen as inefficient, created by weak organizational oversight. Some reform advocates have argued that the absence of formal policy may result in the creation of informal street policy with unknown consequences. An informal organizational structure also creates the opportunity for negative outcomes, particularly cynicism, violence, and corruption (Scheingold, 1984). One of the issues in the literature written from this standpoint is cynicism. Police, it is suggested, became cynical from the constant exposure to rafts and illegal behavior. Cynical officers, in turn, are highly vulnerable to all kinds of corruption (Niederhoffer, 1969).

The solution to the problem of culture is greater rigor in the control of police discretion, more training, and more thorough policy review. Oversight is the key to potential problems created by culture (Delattre, 1996:103). This perspective is similarly described in the following passage, advocating the training and hiring of the officers under the Police Corps, a federal program aimed at providing scholarships to college students who volunteer for 4 years of police service:

Figure 4

Culture and Standpoint

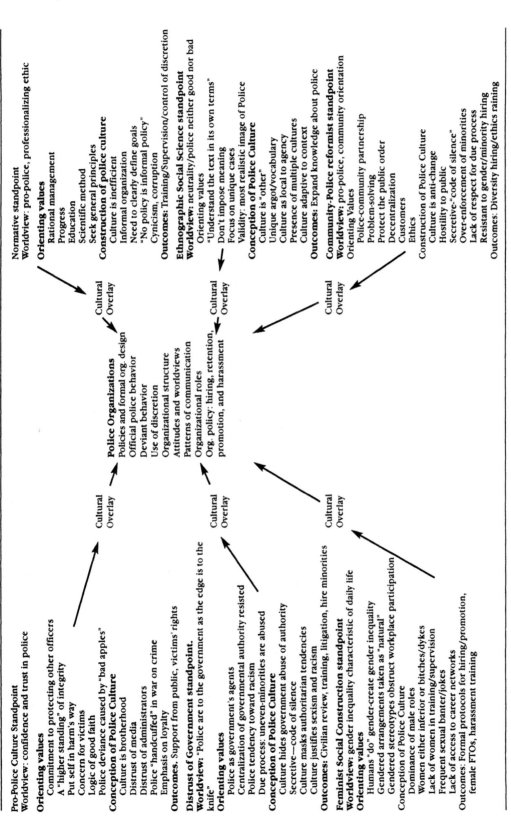

... a good argument can be made that the idealism of the Police Corps graduates will invigorate the cynical and alienating atmosphere of many quad rooms. This could counter the depressing police subculture which breeds burnout, corruption, and brutality among police veterans (Carlisle, 1995:68).

Community Police Reform Standpoints

This standpoint is represented by many reformers who view the police positively and think that culture is a problem that hinders otherwise good police work. The central theme in this standpoint is that police should make and tend supportive relationships with the people in their jurisdiction. Community police reform has emerged in response to problems associated with the police professionalism standpoint and the belief in the 1960s that then popular police practices alienated minority constituencies (Crank & Langworthy, 1997). The language of this standpoint is partnership, problem solving, decentralization, and customer service (Ritti & Silver, 2002). This terminology is about different aspects related to making and tending relationship. For example, decentralization is concerned with broadening community access to the police. Problem solving is concerned with dealing with underlying problems faced by citizens. And social science surveys enable the police to obtain public commentary unfiltered by media.

The reform standpoint characterizes police culture as an obstacle to police reform. Culture is a gloss for all the elements of policing that are "anticommunity involvement." Hence, reformers are concerned with police secrecy, which is seen as a mask for avoidance of due process and behaviors hostile to citizens. Behind the "blue shield," as reformers fear, is a great deal of resistance to gender and minorities, and a lack of respect for multicultural differences. The solution, for reformers, is to limit the influence of "traditional" police culture, usually through greater citizen oversight, training practices, and broad hiring practices aimed at women and minorities.

Carlson (2002:26) describes a notion of culture consistent with this view. He notes that police culture is an "invisible style, or a way of doing business that in many ways is more powerful than the rules and regulations of the police department." It has the effects of "shaping, driving, and sustaining the group's choices and actions." According to Carlson (2002), it can be a force for both good and bad. One of its goods is its emphasis on loyalty in a dangerous occupational setting. Unquestioned loyalty in the form of assistance in dangerous situations is central to policing. However, it can become excessive, as when loyalty becomes covering up or lying for another officer. In this case, the "blue shield" enables illegal and ignoble behavior to continue and even prosper.

Officers are protected by a code of silence, behind which police hide behavior that may be discriminatory, brutal, or illegal. The code of silence emerges as a principle obstacle to departments wishing to instill community policing. In his discussion of the "seven veils," Carlson (2002) describes the relationship between culture, the code of silence, and abuse against minority citizens, presented in Figure 2.

Figure 2
The Seven Veils of Policing

Carlson described the seven veils as a revered metaphor. Salome, of biblical history, did the dance of the seven veils, uncovering a layer of skin with the removal of each veil. Assimilation into the culture of the police occurs with the addition of veils, each addition increasing the distance between the Police and the public.

1. The first veil is when an officer separates himself from those who commit acts of violence: He or she is one of the "good guys," and they are the "bad guys."

2. The second veil falls into place when the officer recognizes that he or she is also different from people who commit relatively benign infractions, for example speeding violations.

3. The third veil: An officer concludes that non-police citizens are clearly different from him and therefore among his "other" group.

4. The fourth veil: Everyone above the rank of sergeant has lost touch with the realities of the street.

5. The fifth veil: The only real police work is done on the officers' shift. Everyone else is wasting time or is not getting the job done.

6. The sixth veil: The only person the officer can trust is his partner.

7. The seventh veil. Sometimes his partner cannot be completely trusted.

The seven veils, Carlson suggested, contributed to the well-publicized beating of Rodney King by members of the Los Angeles Police Department. The secretive, insular world of the police prohibited anyone from stepping forward to take responsibility for the beating and obstructed efforts to investigate the beating. In that secretive climate, the actions of a few officers are hidden by the small sins of the many, who fear that they, in turn, will be investigated.

Distrust of Government Standpoint

This standpoint includes those who distrust the police, who are troubled by the reach of police authority, and who view police culture as a "shield" for non-democratic and authoritarian police practices. Distrust does not focus so much on police as individuals but on police as agents of government, and individualizing explanations of police behavior are generally not a part of this standpoint. But "Big Brother" government is not to be trusted, particularly in the area of justice practice. Bayley's famous dictum "The police are to the government as the edge is to the knife" typifies this view.[2] This dictum summarizes what many see as a central problem of democracy—maintaining order while preserving democratic values.

The distrust of government standpoint is similar to the community policing standpoint in that it views the failure to address minority and gender concerns as among the principle problems facing contemporary police. It differs in that it does not view illegal and unethical behavior as an excess of police culture, but as a consequence of it. According to this standpoint, police culture is one of the mechanisms used by the police to repress civil rights and to act in discriminatory or brutal ways. Culture enhances the ability of the police to act with impunity against a citizen populace. Without adequate organizational, legal, and civil controls, the natural tendency of the police will be to expand authoritarian tendencies.

Kappeler, Sluder, and Alpert (1998:110), for example, state that culture "provide(s) officers with a shared cognitive framework from which to view the world, people, and situations." However, it does more. "The subculture facilitates deviance by providing its members with the beliefs, values, definitions, and manners of expression necessary to depart from acceptable behavior." Of interest to Kappeler, Sluder, and Alpert is how culture facilitates unlawful behavior and norm violation. This is a sharp critique of the "bad apple" theory of police deviance, according to which officers commit crimes because bad officers were inadvertently hired. Through culturally learned strategies to neutralize deviance, officers learn to justify police brutality, act in discriminatory ways, and become involved in drug-related corruption.

Pro-Police Standpoint

The pro-police standpoint is located in ideas of police contribution to society. It is a worldview grounded in a traditional morality, in which the police perform a central community role in protecting citizens, aiding victims of crime, finding programs for young people, and holding troublemakers responsible for their behavior. It is grounded in the language of officer safety, personal responsibility, and dealing with bad guys and assholes (Crank, 2004; see Ragonese, 1991). Key to the underlying rationality is a logic of good faith—belief that fellow officers do the right thing, and do it for morally right reasons. The logic of good faith is so strong that it justifies a great deal of police secrecy, which reflects officers' beliefs that they should protect each other in the face of legal and personal controversy.

The term "police culture" is infrequently used in this literature, but a variety of similar terms have currency. One such term is "brotherhood," similar to culture but differing with its emphasis on in-group loyalty. The brotherhood refers to line officers, and is distinguished from citizens and administrators, neither of whom are trusted. Baker (1985) describes the brotherhood as follows:

> The real reason most police officers socialize exclusively with
> other police officers is that they just don't trust the people they
> police—which is everybody who is not a cop. . . . The "us versus
> them" attitude also applies within the ranks of the police them-
> selves . . . They are the brass, concerned only with their careers,
> not with the welfare of the cop on the street (Baker, 1985:211).

The worst harm that an officer can do to another officer, Baker observes, is to become a member of the Internal Affairs division. "Actively trying to hurt a member of the brotherhood," Baker (1985:212) observes is simply unthinkable to many cops.

Crank (2003) argues that police culture is, in part, a product of conflicts with other community groups. From the pro-police standpoint, one can see many elements in conflict with the other views. The antipathy of line officers toward administrators and a sharp distrust of internal affairs are elements of culture in conflict with the "police professionalism" and "distrust of government" standpoints. Ideological conflicts between police officers with other elements of society, particularly the press, the courts, academics, and administrators in their own organization, have been widely noted (Crank, 1998; Kappeler, Blumberg & Potter, 1993).

One is hard-pressed to find in the social science literature a supportive review of police culture even among those writers who hold police in favorable review. An exception to this is a consideration of police culture as characteristic of a learning organization (Shanahan, 2000). However, a set of pro-cultural factors is no difficult to extrapolate from the available literature. Figure 3 presents 10 police pro-police cultural factors.

Ethnographic Standpoint

Ethnography is a form of inquiry, historically associated with the field of anthropology, whose purpose it is to identify the underlying cultural "reality" of some social group. It is a method for the study of the "other"—groups whose social dynamics seem different and whose social meanings are unknown. Ethnography has historically imagined itself as a grand enterprise that could develop a broad knowledge about the world's cultures. Current perspectives on ethnography take a more limited perspective, recognizing that the inquiry into social "knowledge" is itself biased by the predispositions and cultural understandings of the observer.

Ethnography creates a narrative of a culture, which is a story with its own meanings and sense of history. In a sense ethnography creates the identity of the group it studies. The narrative process that creates an ethnography can be understood as a standpoint. The colorful phrase "understanding the text in its own terms," borrowed from Gadamer (Johnson, 2000), describes the importance of capturing the meanings of ethnographies, including their location in historical time and space. Gadamer presents the interpreter with a challenge to try to understand the text as it was meant to be understood by the original author. Denzin (1997) describes the ethnographic process as "locating the social inside the text." Only in this way—through the active interpretation of the text, which is itself an interpretation of a "culture"—can we extend our existing knowledge of culture into new realms. This interpretive notion of culture analysis is central to ethnography and has been integral to contemporary explorations into cultural analysis (see Geertz, 1983).

Figure 3
The Construction of Culture from a Pro-Police Culture Standpoint

1. The culture enables police recruits to learn about police work.

2. The culture enables recruits to adapt to a punitive occupational setting.

3. The culture provides a basic set of assumptions, metaphors, and classifications that enable officers to recognize the signs of genuine danger in seemingly innocuous situations.

4. The culture preserves elements of a complex legal notion of individualism consistent with a democratic heritage, characterized in terms of a legal responsibility not to cause felonious harm to others.

5. The culture fosters a sense of responsibility for the protection of local communities, manifested in terms of responsibility for one's beat.

6. Because officers tend to be drawn locally, the values that characterize police culture tend to reproduce local community culture.

7. Culture enables officers to adapt to a complex occupational environment characterized by conflicting legal expectations and diverse constituencies, while being continually observed by a highly intrusive media.

8. Culture provides a core occupational identity to assist officer during periods of personal grief and professional tragedy.

9. Culture provides a set of stories and occupational gambits that enable adaptation to an unpredictable occupational setting.

10. Culture is a tool-kit that informs and gives substantive meaning to police discretion, providing ways of thinking and acting regarding coercion and law enforcement in concrete circumstances.

The posture of ethnography is that culture is "other." Lacking reformist language and terminology, it is neither positive nor negative toward police culture. Ethnographic approaches to police culture tend to look for distinguishing characteristics of its uniqueness. Manning's writings on the police (see particularly Manning, 1997) contain many good descriptions of social construction of reality and are insightful into cultural factors that provide the police with their particular identity. Kraska's (1997) study of paramilitary attitudes of police officers captures an important development in contempo-

rary themes of police culture. The focus of cultural study may be on the identification of meanings embedded in language. VanMannen's study "The Asshole" (1987) is the classic example of ethnographic focus on language.

Ethnography has tended to find heterogeny in police culture. By heterogeny, I mean that culture does not lend itself to simple formulas, but tends
to become complex and highly variable. For example, Barker (1999:33), in
her ethnography of the Los Angeles Police Department, notes that:

> After focusing on homogeneity and conformity I kept finding
> counterexamples—officers who simple did not fit the patterns I
> had so carefully extracted from the data. Often they seemed the
> opposite. . . . Actually, I was learning that officers in different
> phases of their career have different views, behave differently and
> emphasize very different issues than do officers in other phases
> of their careers.

As a standpoint, ethnography carries predispositive values. The finding
of heterogeny in police culture is not surprising because the nature of the
ethnographic process is to seek out that which uniquely identifies local culture. Also, by focusing on the other, it tends to overlook that which is shared
with the observer. It tends to view itself as reality based, yet, like other standpoints, its narratives are molded by the worldviews of the observers. And
ethnography is seldom a mere cataloging of social "facts." Narratives tend
to become moral plays, fusing the meanings and values of the observed and
the observer into a narrative text, which affirms local cultural identity.

Feminist Social Construction Standpoint

The specification of a feminist rational tradition and standpoint is difficult, not for its absence, but because there are many articulated feminisms
(Lorber, 1998). Feminism can be thought of as an umbrella term covering
a range of perspectives concerned with gender inequality. In police practice, gender inequality cuts across a broad swath of issues. The linkage of
inequality and culture has been described in terms of the absence of roles
for women in the traditionally high gendered police occupational environment (Martin, 1980, 1997). A feminist standpoint focuses on how gendered differences are culturally reproduced, and how gendered cultural
dynamics inhibit the participation of women in policing.

One kind of feminism is called "social construction feminism" (Lorber,
1998). Social construction is the idea that humans are active participants
in their culture. This is an interactionist notion of culture, according to which
culture is under constant and active creation by its participants. Because gendered relationships are ubiquitous to our cultural heritage, we tend to act
in ways that reinforce gender differences. In a word, we do gender (West
& Zimmerman, 1998).

By doing gender, West and Zimmerman (1998) state that we tend to actively organize our daily lives in a way that expresses gender. We interpret our social arrangements as a part of the natural order of things, the inevitable consequence of historical development. Social differences become re-interpreted as biological distinctiveness and legitimate the existing arrangement of things.

Martin (1980) discusses how social constructionism results in a highly gendered police environment. Women hired into police work often find that there is no existing social role into which they can fit. The workplace is so highly gendered that the status of police and woman is contradictory. Women could become police WOMEN, with an emphasis on the role of women, but women who took such roles did not tend to stay in policing. By accepting a female role, women were protected. They were also treated as if they were weak and unsuitable for the rough-and-tumble of police work. Or women could become POLICE women, abandoning their gender and emphasizing their toughness, aggressiveness, and emotional detachment. Women who played to the police part of their role were often labeled bitches or dykes.

In an "update" on women in policing, Martin (1997) noted that women continue to face a variety of cultural barriers, a view echoed by Hale and Wyland (1999). Language keeps women officers "in their place" by constantly referring to them as ladies or girls (Martin, 1997:2). If women do not conform to stereotypes they become whores and bitches. Frequent sexual jokes characterize women as objects of desire, not work companions. Women, in turn, avoid interactions that might suggest availability. These factors excluded women from career-promoting networks, contributed to harassment, and accented work-related stressors such as denial of information, acceptance as officers, and back up protection during vehicle stops (Morash & Haarr, 1995).

Parsons and Jesilow (2001) observed that women are denied the fruits of cultural participation:

> To be accepted into the law enforcement world, women must exhibit behaviors and language that are consistent with the belief system: they must, in the vernacular, "walk the walk and talk the talk." They may, however, initially lack the inside knowledge, the trade secrets which can be helpful in getting approval . . . They had no women as role models to teach them how to do their job (Parsons & Jesilow, 2001:129).

This also is a social constructionism view, in that it looks at the absence of role models to assist entry into the culture. Recommendations for organizational reform focus on hiring, promotion, and retention issues, and on workplace harassment. Because barriers to women are often rooted in informal organizational processes, women must be protected through the establishment of formal organizational protocols. The recruitment of women into policing is central, but should be accompanied by female recruiters, advertisements with women displayed as police officers, special workshops with a focus on work stressors, in-service training on ethics, and discussion and training concerning harassment. And opportunities for the promotion of women should be institutionalized (Hale & Wyland, 1999),

Issues and Discussion

Four issues are associated with the model of standpoint and culture presented in Figure 1. First, how do we go from standpoint to culture? That is, assuming that we begin with a standpoint about policing, how do we arrive at a useful conception of police culture? Second, is there a way to decide or to think about which is the "best" theory of police culture? Third, what are the implications of standpoint for value neutrality? And fourth, is culture an area of study—or an act of social science creation?

From Standpoint to Culture

Figure 1 displays arrows from each standpoint, passing through a "cultural overlay" and proceeding to the center box titled "police organization." This indicates that the notion of culture is a product of the standpoint, not a property of the police themselves. In other words, notions of police culture merge within and sustained by rational traditions. The standpoints infuse a notion of culture with meaning, and they are the meanings of those who carry the standpoint. Writings on police culture tell us more about the people who study police culture than they do about the police. By studying cultural narratives reflexively, we further our understanding of the different constituencies with which the police interact.

This is the central point in the model of standpoint presented in Figure 1—that police culture attains meaning and value in the eye of the beholder. In this sense, police culture is a "test" whose story will never be complete, but will continue to develop according to the insight and predispositions of the observer.

The "Best" Standpoint of Police Culture

Standpoint implies relativity. The notion of standpoint is very frustrating for anyone who would like to know how to get an accurate view of police culture. "Just tell me," a student might wearily ask, "which is the best?"

The question *Which standpoint is best?* is particularly acute when elements of one standpoint conflict with elements of another. For example, the community police reform standpoint views culture as an obstacle to police-community relations, and sees the hiring of women and minorities as one way to deal with the problem of culture. On the other hand, the pro-police standpoint views personnel procedures as a threat to department traditions (Barker 1999:209).

Any effort to find the best standpoint comes up against an insurmountable problem. There is not an exterior "truth-based" view from which to select among contending standpoints. Once we grant that perspectives on culture are historically situated, we have moved out of the realm of truth-claims. Warnke (1993) describes this as a reductionistic problem. To decide which is the best perspective of culture, we have to develop a new perspective or theory. But how, then do we know that this new theory is right? We need a new theory, ad infinitum.

Value Neutrality

Standpoint has implications for value neutrality. Many social scientists claim value neutrality in their work. By value neutrality, they suggest that, though the object of their research might have been driven by personal interest, the use of rigid methodological procedures based on notions of validity and reliability protected them from the charge that the outcome is in some way biased.

The problem with this argument is that it suggests that, if the researcher does not in some way bias their work, it is value neutral. This is an extraordinarily narrow notion of value neutrality that fails to account for standpoint or any of its elements, reflects a social science standpoint—that humans are independent, rational creators who make judgments based on rational calculi of known outcomes. The problem with this view is that it fails to recognize the implications of intentionality. By this I mean that the selection of descriptive vocabulary, the rationality used to knot the language into meaning, the methodology used to frame the question of interest, and the outcomes studied require value judgments and carry predispositions whether recognized or not. Put differently, police culture can never be studied from a value-neutral perspective. Its conception and meaning will always be from a standpoint, and the elements of standpoint preclude value neutrality (Crank, 2002; see DiCristina, 1995).

Is Police Culture An Area of Study or a Social Science Creation?

Academic criminal justice can be traced to police training and education in the early twentieth century (Morn, 1995). In the late 1960s, departments of criminal justice began a process of dramatic proliferation in academic settings. These programs were spurred by the twin influences of the Law Enforcement Assistance Administration and the community college movement of the 1960s. These twin influences imparted a particular quality to criminal justice programs that continues into the current era—criminal justice has been service-oriented and organized around community outreach.

Criminal justice degree programs have recruited students primarily from future criminal justice employees, most of whom were police officers. Instructors, on the other hand, have been mostly brought in from its parent discipline of sociology. For several decades, future and in-service police officer have learned about the concept of culture as it applies to elements of the criminal justice system. This educational practice has introduced the logic and way of thinking about anthropology's "root metaphor," culture, in local terms of criminal justice practice. Criminal justice instructors, in other words, are actively involved in the creation and dissemination of a notion of police culture. And their police students learn to think about their occupation in a way that includes a notion of police culture. It is probably more accurate to think about police culture as a social science creation for two reasons: (1) instructors speak the language of culture, and (2) educated police take positions in organizations that they have been taught to view in part as cultural entities. For this reason, we can talk about a pro-police standpoint, carried by officers, in which the vocabulary and content of police culture is emerging.

Conclusion

Culture is always understood from a standpoint, but the standpoint may not be obvious. The predispositions and bias of early English anthropologists in the study of African social organization led to an equivalence of culture, social stability, and village that we now recognize was selective and, in some ways, highly misleading. The essence of standpoint is that it appears to be the "truth" from the point of the observer. It is the fruit of a collective wisdom, together with its rationality, its focus of interest, and its meaningful language.

Once we understand the issue of standpoint, we see that there really is no such thing as police culture itself. Culture is a container metaphor in which we place areas of police action and organization that are important to our particular interests (see Lakoff & Johnson, 1992).

That culture emerges and takes its meanings from a standpoint does not mean it should be abandoned as too relative to be of utility or interest. Knowing that standpoints are relative, if we wish to organize our thoughts systematically, we may find culture to be useful. And we must make decisions based on that choice. To abandon the topic of culture because it is too intangible to deal with is itself a standpoint. And such a way of thinking is in many ways unsatisfactory. The same concerns about standpoint and relativity can be made about crime, justice, and all the important social constructions to which we assign value and meaning. Yet, the world around us acts on those words as if they were hard truths. And being human is in large degree about how we find and act on meaning in our lives. For most people, "dropping out" is not an option.

> What was Dorothy's standpoint? It seems that she is as perplexing as standpoint—there are 2 of her! There is the 1930 Dorothy in the movie titled *The Wizard of Oz*. She wandered through the countryside, saw strange things, and met new people, but learned little from it. She was an involuntary observer in an enchanted land she desired only to leave. But in the end it turned out to be only a dream from which she woke up safely, protectively cocooned by her friends, shielded from the disturbing otherness of Oz. How sad.

And there is Baum's (1900) Dorothy, for whom Oz was no dream. And there was no waking up at the end, but a mystical journey home instead. The ruby slippers that made the journey possible were lost in the great deserts surrounding Oz. But in later books, Dorothy returned to settle in Oz, and brought Auntie Em with her! This Dorothy, as Salman Rushdie observed, adventured on the road of life, leaving behind her grey monochrome existence to Kansas, not to return the same person.

Rushdie's observations on Dorothy are inspiration for the standpoint herein offered. Recognizing that there is no escape from my standpoints on police culture, I end this chapter acknowledging my own. Of the various standpoints, ethnography sets as a condition that I seek ways of thinking about the world around me that are inconsistent with my own. As Denzin (1997:250) noted, ethnography is the most worldly of all our interpretive practices.

The study of culture, properly carried out, can be a journey for which there is no conclusion, and no Kansas to return to and reclaim innocence. The study of culture requires that we deal with and understand people that we may think are different, perhaps bad, or whose morals we find incomprehensible. As we study culture, our knowledge of people expands. A part of us becomes other. Culture is "re-enchanted" as we discover that current collective definitions of the social world around us are an inadequate and sometimes incorrect gauge of its breadth (see Wallerstein, 1996). Dorothy feared the witches—yet, they enabled her to return home. She feared the enchantments of Oz. But they saved her in the end.

Endnotes

[1]   "Rationality itself, whether theoretical or practical, is a concept with a history: indeed, because there are a diversity of traditions of inquires, with histories, there are, so it turns out, rationalities rather than rationality, just as it turns out that there are justices rather than justice" (MacIntyre, 1988:9).

[2]   Opening quote, in Chevigny, 1995.

Chapter Review Questions

1. In your own words, briefly summarize the article.

2. What does the author mean when he refers to the "condemnatory potential" of police culture?

3. Define and explain "standpoint epistemology."

4. How is the concept of "standpoint epistemology" relevant to the study of police culture?

5. Explain the emergence of standpoint theory and its central issues (hybridization, identity, force, etc.).

6. Identify and explain, in your own words, four identifiable traditions.

7. What is an "institutionalized standpoint?" How do "institutionalized standpoints" come about?

8. What is the significance of the ethnographic standpoint of police culture?

9. The author of this chapter suggests that writings on police culture tell us more about the people who study police culture than they do about the police. What does this mean? Do you agree?

10. What is your position on police culture? From where do you believe your perspective derives?

SECTION III

Operational Issues in Policing

CHAPTER 6

Police Use of Deadly Force

John Liederbach
Robert W. Taylor

Introduction

On July 9, 1990 Leonard Barnett, an African-American robbery suspect, led Indianapolis police on a lengthy car chase that culminated in Barnett wrecking his vehicle and injuring himself. According to police accounts, Barnett—suffering from a broken leg—had quickly moved from the crashed vehicle and returned in an apparent attempt to retrieve a weapon. Indianapolis police officer Scott Haslar shot and killed Barnett as he moved about the vehicle. No weapon was recovered from Barnett or from his automobile. Officer Haslar was awarded the police department's medal of honor for his "heroic handling" of the armed robbery incident, and he was subsequently promoted to sergeant (Human Rights Watch, 1998; *UPI*, 1991). While Officer Haslar's actions earned him departmental praise and commendations, the fatal shots produced markedly different reactions within the city's minority community. Some expressed outrage over the shooting of an unarmed, seriously wounded suspect and the department's "insensitivity" in awarding such behavior. Eight months after Barnett's death, the department issued an apology through the media, indicating that the awards should not have been given (Human Rights Watch, 1998).

Whether one views the Barnett case as an example of appropriate, even heroic, police work or as a tragic illustration of an unjustified police shooting, the opposing reactions of the police and minority community in Indianapolis clearly highlight the degree to which the deadly force issue can impact relations between the police and members of the public. As policing scholars have long observed, the use of force (or threat thereof) is central to the legitimate functioning of police in a democracy (Bittner, 1970; Klockars, 1995; Reiss, 1971). Bittner (1970) neatly summarizes this line of reasoning by defining the police as having the ability to use situationally justified force in society. This definition recognizes the importance of coercive force, which includes everything from simple verbal commands to the firing of a weapon, in supplying police the tools necessary to meet their occupational mandate. In this regard, the justified use of deadly force—however messy the consequences may be—can serve to legitimize the police role in society.

When the public perceives that police use of deadly force is unnecessarily brutal or unjustified, the resulting acrimony can create a rift between the police and the community that is difficult to mend. For example, the shooting death of 19-year-old Timothy Thomas by a Cincinnati police officer in April 2001 touched off three days of rioting in the city (Vela, 2001). Thomas, who was unarmed and fled from a police pursuit stemming from numerous misdemeanor and traffic warrants, was the fifteenth young African-American male shot and killed by Cincinnati police over a five-year span. While most of these deaths were the result of justified levels of force, the community reaction to the Thomas case revealed how troubled the relationship between the city and its police force had become, and it served as a lightning rod that eventually ignited longstanding public dissatisfaction relating to more generalized civic concerns such as job creation and economic opportunity (*Cincinnati Enquirer*, 2001).

The primary issues concerning the police use of deadly force arise from these emotionally charged scenarios, and the importance of the debate reveals an often tenuous balancing act in which society attempts to control the powers that it has given to police. Although society grants the police the sole right to use deadly force, we also maintain the right to regulate officer discretion in order to ensure that force is used legitimately—to, in effect, police the police. Over the course of the past 30 years, extensive legal and administrative restrictions have been erected through state and federal codes, U.S. Supreme Court decisions, and departmental rules and regulations. Do we now have adequate restrictions on the police use of deadly force as a result of these legal and organizational safe guards? If so, have these restrictions been used in such a way as to maximize their benefits?

This chapter addresses these issues by examining the existing legal and organizational restrictions on the use of deadly force by police officers. In addition, the chapter will provide an overview of recently developed less-than-lethal (LTL) technologies, which may increasingly provide police alternatives to deadly weaponry. In order to offer a more salient context to these analyses, we initially present a brief summary of what is known regarding the use of deadly force by police officers, including how often it is employed and the factors that have been found to influence its occurrence. More importantly, these findings will also be used to inform the subsequent discussion regarding the appropriateness and effectiveness of the various mechanisms that are intended to control the use of deadly force.

When and Why Do They Shoot?

Despite the substantial media attention that inevitably follows deadly force cases and the significance attached to these events by policing scholars, empirical research has consistently shown that police officers rarely use coercive force in practice (Adams 1999; Garner & Maxwell, 1999; Sykes & Brent, 1980). Findings from studies using a variety of research methodologies, including observational data, victim surveys, and police officer "use of force" reports, conclude that less than 20 percent of all arrests involve *any* type of physical force, let alone lethal or deadly force, on the part of the officer (Adams, 1999; Sykes & Brent, 1980).

As a consequence, the use of deadly force is an exceedingly rare occurrence. Officer surveys suggest that somewhere between one and two officers per 1,000 shoot at civilians each year, and firearms are used in only 0.2 percent of all arrest situations (Pate & Friddell, 1993; Adams, 1999). These cases most commonly arise in public locations within high-crime areas. Victims of deadly force are often suspects in armed robbery crimes or "man with a gun" dispatches. They disproportionately involve young, African-American suspects who are armed (Geller & Scott, 1992).

Given these general descriptions, researchers have attempted to identify the relative influence of a variety of factors on the use of deadly force, including the individual characteristics of officers involved in shootings (Binder, Scharf & Galvin, 1982; Blumberg, 1981), community-level variables (Sherman & Langworthy, 1979; Langworthy, 1986), and the race of suspects shot by police (Blumberg, 1989; Fyfe, 1981). This line of research has primarily emphasized the direct relationship between the level of "situational risk" faced by an officer and the decision to use deadly force. Situational risk refers to the immediate scenario within which police must decide whether or not to shoot. Did the suspect assault the police? Was the suspect armed? Did the suspect shoot at police? These situational factors appear to explain the use of deadly force more directly than other variables.

For example, research findings have attributed the disproportionate shooting of black suspects by police officers in several cities to disproportionate situational risks—black suspects were more likely to be armed and to shoot at police (Fyfe, 1981; Blumberg, 1989). Likewise, African-American officers have been found to use deadly force at higher rates than do white officers, however, African-American officers appear to use deadly force more often simply because they tend to reside and/or patrol in communities that generate more situations that involve immediate situational risk to the officer (Fyfe, 1981; Blumberg, 1989). Finally, the relationship between larger community variables, such as homicide rates, and the individual officer's decision to employ deadly force, has proven difficult to determine because these community factors may directly impact the level of situational risk an officer experiences on the street (Langworthy & Sherman, 1979; Langworthy, 1986).

These research findings provide a framework for evaluating the adequacy and effectiveness of existing restrictions on the police use of deadly force. We know that these restrictions will only apply in a small percentage of arrest situations. On the rare occasion that deadly force is used, the situational risks involved in dealing with armed and dangerous suspects often create exigent circumstances in which police shoot non-electively and with little use of discretion. These "shoot or die" scenarios are largely out of the control of police administrators and legal code restrictions, and they provide for the legitimate use of deadly force against dangerous suspects. What is the most effective way to influence the split-second decision to shoot?

Controlling the Use of Deadly Force

Prior to the 1960s, police officers had little guidance in the appropriate use of deadly force. Individual police departments varied widely in their policies concerning the firing of weapons, and written restrictions were often non-existent. The absence of any clearly defined policies in many departments could be at least partially attributed to a general resistance on the part of police administrators to address the issue definitively (Fyfe, 1988). Negative perceptions within the law enforcement community regarding the viability of controlling the use of deadly force were driven by concerns about officer safety and the ability of police to fight crime effectively (Fyfe, 1988). Could the police continue to protect citizens and apprehend dangerous suspects with their hands tied by new regulations?

The issue remained largely dormant until political and social upheavals propelled the subject to prominence. By the late 1960s, many urban police departments faced increasing public and political criticism in the aftermath of large-scale urban riots. Police attempts to control the unrest through coercive—sometimes lethal—force were captured and broadcast by the national news media. Charges of police brutality and the excessive use of force against protesters signaled the need for change, and eventually led to the creation of a President's Commission (1967) aimed at addressing the issue.

The ensuing decades brought about the development and application of increasing legal and organizational restrictions designed to control the use of deadly force by police. They include the use of existing state criminal codes, Supreme Court decisions, civil liability laws, and organizationally derived guidelines and procedures. But do these adequately control the use of deadly force by police?

State Criminal Codes

Most states provide guidelines for the police use of force in existing criminal codes. While these codes vary from state to state in their complexity and terminology, they generally contain definitions of "justified" levels of force within which police can legally operate. The level of force used to complete an arrest or otherwise protect public safety must be commensurate with the crime being committed and proportionally related to its necessity (Klockars, 1995; Cheh, 1995). Thus, police officers who use "excessive" levels of force resulting in the unnecessary maiming or killing of citizens may be criminally prosecuted for a range of offenses including homicide, manslaughter, and assault with a deadly weapon. In this way, the application of severe criminal penalties against officers who unjustifiably use deadly force would serve as an expression of public condemnation, and reinforce the ideal that police may not act above the law in the dispatch of their duties (Cheh, 1995).

The issue of whether or not existing criminal statutes should be expanded in order to effectively control the use of deadly force appears largely moot because these laws already prohibit any level of force that is over that which is necessary to complete an arrest or protect public safety. Simply put, police officers who have been found to use deadly force in a capricious or excessive manner can be defined as "criminals" much as any ordinary citizen would be. The question at hand is to what extent can criminal prosecutions control the abuse of deadly force by police?

The utility of using the criminal law as a tool to control the use of deadly force appears to be limited by both practical and philosophical considerations. The practical reality is that police officers are almost never prosecuted in criminal court for actions taken while on duty, including the questionable use of deadly force (Cheh, 1995; Hubler, 1991; Klockars, 1995; Kobler, 1975; Petrillo, 1990). While comprehensive statistics on the number of criminal prosecutions against police officers do not exist, research suggests that criminal prosecutions are initiated in approximately one of every 500 cases involving police shootings (Human Rights Watch, 1995; Kobler, 1975).

There are several obstacles to initiating criminal prosecutions against police officers in response to even the most egregious cases of excessive force (Human Rights Watch, 1995). First, local prosecutors are reluctant to file criminal charges against police officers, primarily because prosecutors traditionally must maintain close working relationships with them in order to successfully prosecute other cases. These close relationships, which invariably aid the state in securing convictions against ordinary defendants, create a conflict of interest that impedes criminal prosecutions against cops who may use unjustified deadly force. Second, criminal prosecutions are not initiated because these cases are especially difficult to win. Juries are reluctant to define police actions as "criminal" offenses, given the dangerous nature of police duties and their status as authority figures. Finally, some prosecutors claim that they lack information relating to possible cases of excessive force because there are no mechanisms requiring an exchange of information from police internal affairs units to the prosecutor's office. Potential cases of excessive use of force simply "wash out" of the system before reaching the prosecutors office (Human Rights Watch, 1995:87).

In light of these limitations, some observers have suggested strategies that could increase the frequency of criminal cases against officers who abuse their power, thereby strengthening the deterrent value of criminal penalties in the control of excessive force. For example, they propose the creation of special prosecutorial offices at the state level that would be given the responsibility to prosecute police accused of criminal conduct (Human Rights Watch, 1995). These offices would not suffer from the same conflict of interest that local prosecutors experience because they would be removed from the day-to-day prosecution of ordinary cases.

Presumably, such changes could make criminal prosecutions more frequent, however, philosophical issues remain as to whether or not the criminal law *should* be used against police accused of using excessive deadly force given the typical nature of these situations. As outlined previously, officers are often forced to make split-second decisions concerning whether to use deadly force based on their assessment of situational risk. In cases where officers use deadly force under the mistaken presumption that it is warranted, the criminal law provides no alternative other than "guilty" or "innocent." As a result, the criminal sanction may only be appropriate in cases where officers willfully shoot innocent civilians (Cheh, 1995). While isolated prosecutions of rogue cops serve to garner headlines, the effectiveness of prosecutions in preventing the more typical cases involving officer negligence or recklessness appears to be severely limited.

The Supreme Court and "Fleeing Felons"

The United States Supreme Court was largely silent concerning the use of deadly force by police throughout much of the twentieth century. The court had deferred constitutional questions arising in these cases to existing state codes and English common law traditions, some of which dated back several centuries. The court began voicing opinions on the subject in order to rectify inconsistencies among state laws concerning whether, and under what conditions, police could fire on fleeing felony suspects. A minority of states continued to recognize the common law "fleeing felon" rule, which allowed the use of deadly force against all fleeing felons in order to subdue them (Zalman & Siegel, 1991). Cognizant of the need to clarify these state level disparities, the court began to review fleeing felon cases on Fourth Amendment grounds (Samaha, 2002). Justices argued that the amount of force used to affect an arrest, especially in the case of lethal force, is clearly a search and seizure issue that falls within the scope of Fourth Amendment protections.

In *Tennessee v. Garner* (1985), the court heard arguments regarding the death of an unarmed, 15-year-old suspect shot by Memphis police as he fled a burglary scene. The court ruled that existing statutes allowing the unrestrained use of deadly force against fleeing felons was unconstitutional. The decision struck down existing fleeing felon statutes and limited the use of deadly force against fleeing felons to those situations where there was probable cause to believe that the suspect had or would inflict serious bodily injury on the officer or others (*Tennesse v. Garner* 1985).

The court articulated additional constitutional standards in *Graham v. Conner* (1989). The decision resulted in the application of the "objective reasonableness" test in cases arising from claims of excessive use of force by police. Consistent with the ruling in *Garner*, the court defined *all* excessive force claims in terms of Fourth Amendment protections, ruling that the extent to which use of force is reasonable must be judged using the perspective of a reasonable officer on the scene (*Graham v. Conner* 1989). The decision recognizes the need to evaluate police actions in light of the circumstances that confront police, which are at times stressful and uncertain (*Graham v. Conner* 1989).

The profound scope of these decisions and their relative notoriety within law enforcement circles suggests that the Supreme Court has played a major role in determining limits on the use of deadly force by police. This view has been questioned, however, by researchers who cite the fact that most states had abandoned the fleeing felon doctrine in favor of more restrictive codes by the time *Garner* was decided in 1985 (Fyfe, 1988). So too, many police agencies had already constructed internal policies restricting the use of deadly force because they recognized the perils of civil liability and the reality that large damage awards were likely in cases where officers shot felony suspects who were clearly unarmed and posed little immediate danger (Fyfe, 1988). Other evidence regarding the impact of *Garner* indicates that these conclusions may be overstated. For example, cases of police shooting at fleeing felons have declined since the *Garner* decision, and many departments have implemented restrictive policies *in excess* of what *Garner* requires (Tennenbaum, 1994).

From a larger perspective, the ability of the Supreme Court to provide continual preventative controls on the abuse of deadly force by police appears to be marginal given the court's inherently reactive nature and the equilibrium already provided by the *Garner* decision. The fleeing felon rule was a vestige of an earlier era when the criminal law proscribed death for most felony convictions (Zalman & Siegel 1991). That was no longer the case by 1985, and the court rightfully acted to rectify inconsistencies in state codes. It appears that the Supreme Court has already fulfilled its mission in this area by using its constitutional clout to strike down an outdated rule that had clearly outlived its usefulness.

Civil Liability

We leave it to our colleague, John L. Worrall, in Chapter 10, to extensively review issues of civil liability. However, here we briefly review civil law remedies as potential control of police use of force. Since its earliest days in chancery courts, civil law has recognized that people in the conduct of their daily affairs have certain rights, responsibilities, and obligations. Breaches of those rights, responsibilities and obligations, whether through negligence or malice, are *torts*—or civil wrongs against another, which must be answered for in civil court. The injured party initiates the lawsuit and in most cases, seeks an award of monetary damages. Examples of tort actions that are commonly brought against police officers and their departments are allegations of criminal violations such as assault and battery (police brutality), invasion of privacy (through illegal search and seizure) and negligence that usually arises during incidents involving police use of deadly force (Barrineau, 1987). There are three general categories of torts that cover most of the suits brought against police officers for use of deadly force, including negligence torts, intentional torts, and constitutional torts (Swanson, Territo & Taylor, 2001).

Our society imposes a duty on individuals to conduct their affairs in a manner that does not subject others to an unreasonable risk of harm. This responsibility also applies to the police. If an officer's conduct creates a danger recognizable as such by a reasonable person in like circumstances, the officer will be held accountable to others injured as a result of his or her conduct. In *negligence torts*, defendant police officers will not be liable unless they foresaw, or should have anticipated, that their acts or omissions would result in injury or death to another. The key in negligence suits is "reasonableness." Was the conduct or action reasonable in the eyes of the court? Was the action within the policy and guidelines of the agency? In use of deadly force incidents, the key question is often whether or not the action represented the last option for the officer, or whether or not the action was taken as a result of an imminent threat to life.

An *intentional tort* is the voluntary commission of an act that to a substantial certainty will injure another person. It does not have to be negligently done to be actionable. Therefore, an intentional tort amounts to a voluntary act, such as an assault or false arrest. In use of deadly force incidents, these tort cases may be accompanied by formal criminal prosecutions for crimes such as criminally negligent homicide or even murder.

Constitutional Torts arising from Title 42, U.S. Code Section 1983 provide another avenue of control. The duty to recognize and uphold the constitutional rights, privileges, and immunities of others is imposed on police officers by statute, and violation of these guarantees may result in a specific type of civil suit. This law, passed by Congress in the aftermath of the Civil War and commonly referred to as the Civil Rights Act of 1871, was designed to secure the civil rights of the recently emancipated slaves. The

Reconstruction era was filled with many abuses by local law enforcement officials, who often posed as "night riders" or even fully dressed Ku Klux Klan members to terrorize former slaves. The Civil Rights Act of 1871 was specifically designed to stop this type of collusion between local police and clearly outrageous and illegal hate groups. The Act prohibits depriving any person of rights, privileges, or immunities guaranteed by the Constitution without due process of law.

After 90 years of relative inactivity, Section 1983 was resuscitated by the U.S. Supreme Court in the landmark case *Monroe v. Pape* (1961). The Court concluded that when a police officer is alleged to have acted improperly (e.g., conducting an illegal search), the officer could be sued in federal court on the grounds that he or she deprived the suspect of his or her constitutional protections against unreasonable search and seizures contained in the Fourth Amendment. Cases involving police use of deadly force, however, most often fall within the "life and liberty" clauses of the Bill of Rights or the due process clause of the Fourteenth Amendment. Under Section 1983, not only is the individual officer liable, but also the governmental unit or department in which he or she works. The common law theory of *respondent superior* poses significant responsibilities on federal, state, and local police agencies. Essentially, police administrators and trainers are ultimately responsible for the actions of their subordinates and trainees. The courts affirmed these principles in *Peer v. City of Newark* (1961) and *Popow v. Margate* (1979). In the Peer case, the court specifically held that a police department had a duty to properly train its officers, particularly in the safe and responsible use of firearms. Failure to do so places the department liable to the injured party. In more recent cases, the Court has limited and refined the use of inadequate police training as a basis for Section 1983 actions. The Court has held that inadequate police training may form the basis for a civil rights claim when it can be shown that there was deliberate indifference to the rights of those persons who come into contact with the police and where this indifference amounts to policy or custom (*City of Canton v. Harris*, 1989).

Individual citizens have a clear constitutional right to be free from excessive use of force when they are being arrested (*Tennessee v. Garner*, 1985; *Colston v. Barnhart*, 1997). Use of excessive force by the police constitutes a violation of either the Fourth or the Fourteenth Amendment, depending upon the party's status at the time of the claim (*Riggs v. City of Pearland*, 1997). The party must show that he or she (1) suffered some injury, (2) resulting from force clearly in excess of the force needed, and (3) such excessiveness is objectively unreasonable (*Heitshmidt v. City of Houston*, 1998; *Spann v. Rainey*, 1993; and *Garza v. United States*, 1995). The legal test pinning liability hinges on two issues. First, is the law governing the officer's conduct clearly established? Second, could a reasonable officer have believed that his or her conduct was lawful? In use of deadly force cases, the matter of law is relatively straightforward. However, it is the plaintiff's burden to demonstrate that no reasonable officer could have thought his/her actions were lawful. The question of whether a right is clearly established boils down to determining whether the police officer had "fair warning" that certain conduct violates a constitutional right (*King v. Chide*, 1992; *Snyder v. Trepagnier*, 1998; and *United State v. Lanier*, 1997). The ultimate issue, of course, is whether or not the officer's acts or actions were objectively reasonable as a matter of law.

In light of these developments, it is clear that the role of the civil courts in controlling the police use of deadly force has been large. Legal decisions have worked to expand the scope of liability. Today, local units of government can be made liable for the conduct of individual police officers. Likewise, chiefs of police, sheriffs, and mid-level supervisors can be held *personally* liable for the conduct of their subordinates. And of course, the individual officer can be directly sued for specific actions taken in violation of policy and law, and for non-purposeful actions amounting to negligence. The dramatic rise in the number of lawsuits filed and the shear amount of money awarded plaintiff's poses a significant mechanism for the control of the police, particularly in the area of use of deadly force.

Department Administrative Regulations and Training

The mechanisms described thus far, including state criminal codes, Supreme Court decisions, and civil litigation have had varying degrees of effectiveness in controlling the misuse of deadly force by police. One commonality among these controls, however, is that they are all external to the police organization. In this respect, external controls can be characterized as the ultimate oversight—they help to insure that police are accountable to the public. But these external mechanisms also suffer from some serious limitations. For example, legal remedies pursued through state codes and civil litigation cannot provide *direct* control over the actions of police on the street. They are predominantly reactive in that they are used to redress instances where the misuse of deadly force already has occurred. Likewise, the specter of criminal and civil sanctions imposed on police from outside the organization may work to foster a lack of confidence and heightened uneasiness concerning the proper use of deadly force among officers (Langworthy & Travis, 1999).

In light of these concerns, most policing scholars have viewed the development of departmental regulations and training as the "first line" of defense in controlling the misuse of deadly force by police (Cheh, 1995; Klockars, 1995; Geller & Scott, 1992). Most large police agencies have articulated policies that include the following: (1) a clear definition of what constitutes deadly force, (2) parameters limiting its use, and (3) an explanation as to the manner in which deadly force is to be applied. In some departments, these guidelines provide restrictions in excess of what the law mandates, permitting the use of deadly force only in defense of life situations (Blumberg, 1982). These policies should be developed in conjunction with ongoing officer training that emphasizes the correct interpretation of restrictive policies, conflict management techniques designed to reduce the use of violence in general, and weapons training aimed at reducing the incidence of accidental shootings by police (Dunham & Alpert, 1995; Geller & Scott, 1992).

Existing research provides clear evidence regarding both the necessity and effectiveness of restrictive departmental policies and training in this area. For example, the creation of restrictive policies has been followed by reductions in police shootings in Los Angeles County, Kansas City, and New York City (Fyfe, 1979; Milton, Halleck, Lardner & Albrecht, 1977; Uelman, 1973). Sherman (1983) concluded that restrictive policies had these same effects in a study of officers in Kansas City and Atlanta. Likewise, Fyfe (1981) attributed differences in the rates of elective shootings by police officers in Memphis and New York City to the presence or absence of organizational guidelines controlling officer discretion in the use of deadly force.

Clearly, the creation of restrictive policies and adequate training has worked to reduce the number of discretionary police shootings, and the success of these measures highlights the advantage of internal controls in proactively preventing abuses before they occur. Despite three decades of progress however, critics have continued to press for further organizational reforms (Human Rights Watch 1995). These voices tend to become especially loud in the aftermath of egregious cases that garner significant media attention. Indeed, when these cases "fall through the cracks," citizens invariably lose confidence in the ability of the police to police themselves. Resulting calls for reform often highlight the need to strengthen existing external controls and legal remedies, and cite the need for more public oversight of police.

The Expansion of Less-than-Lethal Technologies

The debate regarding the most effective means of controlling the use of deadly force has been increasingly influenced by the development of a wide array of newer technologies designed to expand the range of options available to police in terms of subduing dangerous suspects. These "less-than-lethal" (LTL) technologies include electronic immobilization devices ("Taser" guns), chemically based weapons (tear gas, mace, and oleoresin capsicum pepper spray), and impact devices (projectile launchers) (Trostle, 1990). LTL technologies have been touted as providing a safe and effective non-lethal option for use in incapacitating suspects who may be armed and aggressive (Heal, 2000).

Two of the most widely adopted LTL technologies have been "Taser" guns and oleoresin capsicum (OC) pepper spray. Taser guns are a specific brand of electronic immobilization device. They are conducted energy weapons that fire a cartridge attached to two small probes. These probes emit an electronic charge that overwhelms the suspect's central nervous system on contact, thus "stunning" them into submission (Nielson, 2001). The second-generation ("advanced") Taser has been found to provide instant incapacitation in "virtually 100 percent "of the cases where it has been properly deployed (Nielson, 2001:57). OC pepper spray, the most widely used chemically based LTL technology, is discharged from pressurized canisters as a spray, stream, or fog (Nowicki, 2001). OC pepper spray produces temporary blindness and breathing difficulties after it has been sprayed into a suspect's face (NIJ, 2003).

The use of pepper spray in particular has elicited largely positive reviews within the law enforcement community. For example, Kansas City police report good to excellent results in a review of more than 800 cases where pepper spray had been used against suspects under the influence of drugs (NIJ, 1994). In addition, comparisons following the introduction of pepper spray in three North Carolina police departments concluded that the use of pepper spray decreased the number of injuries to both police and combative suspects, and coincided with a decrease in the number of excessive force complaints filed against police (NIJ, 1994).

In addition to these existing weapons, more futuristic technologies hold the promise of providing even greater nonlethal control capabilities to officers. Weapons that are largely in the developmental and testing phase of design include electrified water pistols, low-frequency radiation devices, dart guns, and "stench" gases (Trostle, 1990). While actual implementation of these types of devices may be years away, the continuing development of alternate nonlethal technologies appears certain.

These promising developments aside, the expanding adoption of LTL technologies also has introduced a number of significant issues, especially in terms of safety and the degree to which these technologies may work to expand the scope of police liability in use of force incidents. In terms of the safety of these weapons, there appear to be some instances where LTL technologies can produce unintended fatalities. Pepper spray, for instance, has been cited as a primary cause of death in cases when it is used against suspects who have pre-existing respiratory ailments such as asthma (NIJ, 2003). In these cases, the use of pepper spray induced asthmatic responses that fatally compromised the breathing ability of targeted suspects. So too, pepper sprays that are used in conjunction with alcohol-based carrier agents can be dangerously flammable. In one especially grisly incident, police used a stun gun after spraying an aggressive suspect with pepper spray. The electric charge ignited the spray and set the suspect aflame (NIJ, 2003). While cases such as these appear to be rare and isolated, they provide a vivid reminder that less-than-lethal weapons should not be considered *non-*

lethal in all possible scenarios. These concerns have forced police admin-istrators to recognize the importance of providing comprehensive training in the proper and effective use of LTL technologies in order to avoid costly litigation (NIJ, 1994).

Even the existence of adequate training in the use of LTL technologies does not preclude the possibility of expanded opportunities for litigation. An officer who chooses to use less-than-lethal weapons can still be sued, and the choice of using lethal weapons instead of available less-than-lethal tac-tics may invite charges of excessive force (Dorsch, 2001). For example, in *Deorle v. Rutherford* (2001) the United States Court of Appeals decided that the firing of "bean bag" impact weapons without prior verbal warnings con-stituted an excessive use of force because the weapon posed significant risk of injury to the suspect (Hopper, 2001). Courts may be unwilling to dis-tinguish between lethal and less-than-lethal weapons in deciding whether excessive force was applied in a particular case.

LTL technologies appear to have value in providing police an expanded number of avenues to deal with combative suspects. In this regard, LTL weapons offer an intermediary level of force that heretofore did not exist. However, the relatively recent advent of many of these weapons and the lack of empirical research regarding their use prevents firm conclusions regard-ing their utility in controlling the misuse of deadly force by police. For exam-ple, we do not know to what extent LTL technologies have been used as an alternative to shooting suspects. It may be that weapons such as pepper spray, Taser guns, and beanbag projectiles are primarily used in cases where officers rarely consider more lethal force. If this is the case, LTL weapons may simply work to increase the level of force used in a large num-ber of police-citizen encounters rather than mitigating the use of deadly force. Future research should provide data as to what situations tend to prompt the use of LTL technologies in order to clarify the most effective and appropriate role for these weapons.

Conclusion

The preceding analysis has highlighted both the strengths and limita-tions of existing controls on the police use of deadly force. The evidence shows that by expanding the strength of internal controls, police organi-zations have initiated an effective first line of defense by limiting the num-ber of elective shootings by officers. Is it reasonable to expect successful control through departmental restrictions and training in all cases? The prior discussion can be used to indicate ways in which external legal controls may be used to remedy internal control failures.

State criminal codes, while rarely used, are an essential mechanism in cases where police willfully abuse deadly force, as they serve to reinforce existing ideals concerning the ultimate accountability of police to the public. In cases where there is ambiguity among state codes concerning the appropriate application of deadly force, the Supreme Court has effectively stepped in to remedy legal inconsistencies and further limit officer discretion in this area. The expanding scope of police civil liability in the use of deadly force, whereby police administrators have been made to answer for the negligence of individual officers, has further restricted officer discretion and forced police agencies to act more proactively to prevent abuses through training and departmental restrictions. Still, police organizations must continue to provide avenues to remedy situations where departmental restrictions and training fail and innocent civilians are hurt or killed as a result of the misuse of deadly force, or they otherwise risk the imposition of "second-line" controls such as civil litigation or criminal prosecution.

The strengths and limitations of existing controls seem to suggest a balanced approach whereby internal and external controls can work in complimentary fashion. In this regard, Fyfe (1989) argues for clearly distinguishing between cases of willful and egregious misuse of deadly force and the more common cases resulting from officer negligence. As the research regarding the correlates of deadly force indicates, many cases of abuse stem from mistaken "split-second" judgments:

> Such violence occurs when police lack the eloquence to persuade temporarily disturbed persons to give up their weapons, but shoot them instead. It occurs when, instead of pausing to consider and apply less drastic alternatives, officers blindly confront armed criminals . . . it occurs when well-meaning police officers lack—or fail to apply—the expertise required to resolve as bloodlessly as possible the problems their work requires them to confront (Fyfe, 1989:467).

It appears that negligent mistakes resulting from split-second judgments—the majority of cases involving the misuse of deadly force by police—are most amenable to internal remedies designed to augment existing officer training. Fyfe (1989) advocates training that includes instruction of specific tactics designed to reduce the possibility of bloodshed and increase the chances of a nonviolent conclusion in these situations. This view clearly recognizes the situational exigencies that primarily influence officer decisionmaking in deadly force incidents, and suggests that legal punishments and other external controls are most appropriately applied only in cases where organizational controls have failed. In these cases, societal remedies provided through criminal and civil codes can act to punish rogue officers and poorly administered police organizations. At the same time, the increased use of LTL technologies has added to the options police officers have when attempting to subdue suspects. However, as our review of LTL force indicates, likely will be increasingly subjected to the same controls that have been applied more prominently to police use of deadly force.

Chapter Review Questions

1. How common—or uncommon—is police use of force? Why do you believe this is the case?

2. What is "situational risk?" Why is the concept of "situational risk" important to the study of police shootings?

3. Discuss the state of controls on the use of deadly force by the police prior to and during the 1960s. What led to changes by the late 1960s?

4. Why do the authors state, "While isolated prosecutions of rogue cops serve to garner headlines, the effectiveness of prosecutions in prevent the more typical cases involving officer negligence or recklessness appears to be severely limited?"

5. Discuss the contributions of the U.S. Supreme Court cases of *Tennessee v. Garner* (1985) and *Graham v. Conner* (1989) to the debate on police use of force.

6. What civil remedies exist to control police use of force? Do you believe that civil remedies can be effective controls? Why or why not?

7. What does the research evidence suggest regarding the effectiveness of internal controls of police use of force in the form of administrative regulations and training?

8. What are "less-than-lethal" technologies? How do they play into the debate on police use of force?

CHAPTER 7

Racial Profiling

Andra Katz-Bannister
David L. Carter

Introduction

Public concerns over "racial profiling" rapidly emerged in the 1990s and remains as a point of controversy between the police and minority communities today. A universally accepted definition of this phenomenon has yet to emerge, but the term generally refers to circumstances wherein police use "race [or more accurately, the perception of a driver's race] as a key factor in deciding whether to make a traffic stop" (Ekstrand, 2000:1). By extension, the term describes police-initiated behaviors that are the primary/sole product of a citizen's race/ethnicity, rather than behavioral/legal cues (Ramirez, McDevitt & Farrell, 2000). Racial profiling has been used to describe an officer's decision to initiate a traffic stop, as well as subsequent decisions (e.g., to conduct a search) made during the course of that encounter. The term has spawned catch phrases such as "driving while black" and has become a pivotal social and political issue across America.

As the profiling controversy began to gain momentum in the late 1990s, research projects were initiated by a range of state and federal political entities (Cox, Pease, Miller & Tyson, 2001; Ekstrand, 2000; Langan, Greenfeld, Smith, Durose & Levin, 2001; Nixon, 2001; Schmitt, Langan & Durose, 2002; Texas Department of Public Safety, 2001; Veniero & Zoubek, 1999; Zingraff et al., 2000), municipal police organizations (Cordner, Williams & Zuniga, 2000; Decker & Rojek, 2002; Lansdowne, 2000; Smith & Petrocelli, 2001; Spitzer, 1999; citation omitted for review), advocacy groups (Lamberth, 1996), academics (Barlow & Barlow, 2002; Engel, Calnon & Bernard, 2002; Harris, 1997, 1999, 2002; Hoover, 2001; Knowles, Persico & Todd, 2001; Meehan & Ponder, 2002a, 2002b; Norris, Fielding, Kemp & Fielding, 1991; Walker, 2001; Weitzer & Tuch, 2002) and private citizens (Davis, 2001). These projects used a wide range of methodologies, including legal analysis, anecdotal evidence, observational research, citizen surveys, self-reported data provided by officers, and the analysis of existing data. Many are of questionable generalizability, perhaps in part because of the haste with which they were initiated (Engel, Calnon & Bernard, 2002). In addition, no agreement has been reached on the true conceptual and operational definition of the concept of racial profiling, resulting in methodological inconsistencies that cloud insights into the phenomenon. Experience has highlighted the limitations of existent research endeavors and has illustrated the difficulty of conclusively establishing whether racial profiling exists in a given jurisdiction. The "denominator dilemma" discussed in the following section exemplifies this situation. Given these realities, truly understanding "racial profiling" may be elusive, although methodological implications do emerge for the broader study of police officer decision-making patterns during traffic enforcement encounters.

Problems with Data Collection
Which Must Be Considered

Police officers tend to oppose the idea of data gathering which is part of a racial profiling monitoring policy for two primary reasons. First, such a policy infers that all officers profile minorities. This presumption of guilt is not only offensive to officers it undermines the sense of fundamental fairness stressed in the justice system. Those who call for and support data collection argue that officers themselves are undermining this same sense of fairness by stopping people simply based on race or ethnicity. These views represent extreme ends of a continuum with the truth somewhere in the middle. A policy goal should be to fully educate officers that data collection is intended to be a check on officer behavior which can as easily exonerate a police department from racial profiling allegations as it can convict them.

It is naïve to say that if officers are doing their job properly, then they have no need to worry. Just as some officers will profile racial and ethnic minorities, there are also minority group members who will make this accusation against the police in the hope of being released from a traffic stop without a citation. The knife cuts both ways and all parties ought to recognize this.

In all likelihood, when a police department begins collecting driver demographic data during traffic stops, it will have a chilling effect on officer-initiated activity. Officers have repeatedly expressed concern that they will be targeted as a racist if "their numbers don't look right." The safest way to prevent this, in many officers' minds, is to significantly decrease proactive work and only respond to calls. This decreases service to the community, but officers have said, "that must be what the community wants."

Another reason to be concerned about data collection lies in a well-known axiom of statisticians: Statistics can lie. The critical element of data collection in traffic stops is not the data, per se, but the *interpretation* of the data. As an example, let us say that a white male police officer's traffic stop data show that 85 percent of all persons he stopped for traffic violations were black. What this means depends on the interpretation. Several interpretations can arise as examples:

- The officer is generally stopping blacks for equipment violations and whites for moving violations, thus he is using the traffic violations as a pretext stop, therefore he is profiling.

- The officer is generally stopping blacks for equipment violations and whites for moving violations, however, the area is poor and residents are predominantly black. Because of poverty, there is greater likelihood that vehicles remain in disrepair, thus more equipment violations among the residents and less likelihood the officer is profiling.

- The officer is assigned to an area where 95 percent of the residents are black. Because only 85 percent of the traffic stops were black, the officer was either not profiling or perhaps the officer was intentionally stopping more white drivers to make his statistics "look better."

- The area where the traffic stops are made is 65 percent black, however, there is a is a large commuting workforce of blacks and most stops are for moving violations during rush hour, thus the likelihood the officer is not profiling.

- An analysis of traffic accidents shows that most accidents occur between 4:00 P.M. and 6:00 P.M. on weekdays at a given intersection as a result of drivers making illegal left turns. Analysis of the officer's traffic citations shows that the citations issued are for left turn violations during the peak traffic problem hours thus no profiling.

A common concern expressed by police officers is "what percentage of people from different races will be acceptable." Herein lies the difficulty of interpreting the data. There is no standard that can be used to definitively conclude that there is racial profiling. Some members of minority communities state that there is no need to collect data because they know officers profile from their personal experience. Undoubtedly if they sincerely believe this, then policy and personnel actions cannot be taken without some form of objective evidence. Thus, both collection and interpretation of the data are critical ventures with long-ranging implications for the community, officers, and the department as a whole.

The issue of interpreting statistics from demographic data collection is critical. While the data should be public record, it must be recognized that this leaves open the opportunities for all people—e.g., police supporters, police critics, and the media—to draw their own conclusions. Even if the intent is to interpret the data accurately, it must be recognized that such interpretations are complex and cannot simply be a matter of comparing officer stops to general demographic characteristics of an area. Factors that should be considered include:

- Actual population demographics
- Accuracy of Census data
- Transient population in area (e.g., major streets)
- Demographic changes in area based on time (e.g., employers and businesses)
- Calls for service received by the police (e.g., suspicious persons; prowlers, etc.)
- Complaints received by the police (e.g., speeding traffic; open-air drug markets; prostitution; noise, etc.)
- Reported crime in the area (including types of crime, when crimes are occurring, known suspects' characteristics, etc.)
- Accuracy of information reported by officers

If officers are improperly stopping drivers by considering race or ethnicity as a criterion to stop, then police officials clearly want this practice stopped. If an officer's behavior is the product of insidious discriminatory practices, then the officer should be disciplined. If the officer's behavior is a product of unconscious consideration of race/ethnicity as one factor in an equation to stop motorists, then closer supervision and training may be the best remedies. One must be careful, however, to avoid generalization of all police practices based on spurious incidents.

There is a pragmatic issue that also must be addressed: the cost of the data collection process. Citizens and city officials alike must recognize that there are expenses associated with data monitoring. While each form only takes about 30 seconds to complete, when multiplied out times the number of times officers complete forms in a year's time, it can become a surprisingly high time commitment. Added to this is the time involved in processing the forms, the printing costs, and analysis—which is very labor intensive. Then, one can see that the costs rise quickly.

Discussing issues of race always is a sensitive process—it makes people uncomfortable and there always is a fear of offending someone or being unfairly labeled. Despite this sensitivity, if the issues are not openly discussed, then progress cannot be made. On this theme, one may find that statistically racial and ethnic minorities may indeed be stopped more frequently, but not necessarily due to police profiling. Police departments deploy officers proportional to demand. There always is a disproportionate amount of reported crime and calls for services in impoverished areas of all American cities. Unfortunately, minorities—notably blacks and Hispanics/Latinos—live disproportionately in lower-income neighborhoods. As a consequent, there are higher levels of contact between the police and minority communities. On a similar issue discussed by community members, poverty and racial/ethnic minorities have a strong correlation in America. Lower or limited income has an effect on certain types of police stops—notably, vehicle equipment violations—thus, there are disproportionately more stops of minorities for these violations.

The Dilemma of the Denominator

On the surface, studying the extent to which racial profiling occurs is a fairly simple process. A researcher should simply take the proportion of a particular category of citizens (Asian females between the ages of 18 and 24) represented in a group of drivers stopped by the police and divide this proportion by an appropriate denominator. If this basic equation yields a value greater than 1.0, it would suggest that police stopped that category of drivers at a disproportionately high rate; values less than 1.0 would indicate the converse was true. The stumbling block in this elementary mathematical process is defining and measuring an appropriate denominator for use in this equation. Scholars and practitioners have consistently had problems establishing a suitable denominator to analyze traffic stop data (Cox et al., 2001; Ekstrand, 2000; Ramirez, McDevitt & Farrell, 2000; Walker, 2001; Zingraff et al., 2000), complicating efforts to establish whether racial profiling occurs. This difficulty is partly a function of measurement difficulties and partly a matter of the vague definition of "racial profiling" as a behavioral concept.

In the context of our study, data were obtained detailing the demographics of citizens stopped by officers in Central City (a pseudonym). Given these demographic details, what could be used as a denominator to conclusively determine if bias or impropriety exists? Comparisons with census data from Central City would be inadequate because census data do not reflect the community's driving population. Department of Motor Vehicle records could be searched to find the demographics of licensed drivers residing in Central City, but such records often fail to capture race data, can be several years out of date, and do not account for unlicensed drivers. Even if accurate data reporting the demographic composition of licensed drivers within a given community were available, this could be an invalid denominator. Official data on licensed drivers within a community do not account for the many non-residents who may drive within that community in a given day.

These official data also would fail to account for the proportion of driving done by various demographic groups (e.g., 15% of a community could be age 60 or older, yet this age group might only account for 5% of all miles driven). Making estimates of roadway users is a methodologically

complex and costly endeavor, although recent research has made promising improvements (Meehan & Ponder, 2002a, 2002b). Even if the demographic distribution of the driving public or the proportion of road miles
driven by various demographic groups could be established, they might not
prove to be valid denominators as they do not account for driving violations.
Some research (Lange, Blackman & Johnson, 2001) has attempted to
develop the rate of violations committed by various demographic groups
to establish a partial picture of a more accurate denominator, but the conceptual and operational components of these efforts were widely criticized
by activists and the Justice Department.

> Even if establishing the rates of violations committed by different
> demographic groups was methodologically and pragmatically
> feasible, such a measure might still fail to serve as an appropriate
> denominator. Using a violation rate denominator assumes that both
> the occurrence of violations and police enforcement efforts are
> equal across time and space (Engel, Calnon & Bernard, 2002;
> Hoover, 2001). While rates describe violation patterns on an
> aggregate level, they ignore which groups of drivers are most likely
> to commit offenses in areas and times when police enforcement
> efforts are likely to detect infractions. Using these violations
> rates as a denominator would, of course, implicitly assume that
> all officers view the same offenses as equally serious across time,
> space, and situational characteristics (i.e., an officer is equally
> likely to stop a vehicle traveling 5 miles per hour over the speed
> limit in a congested school zone and a vehicle traveling 5 miles per
> hour over the speed limit on a deserted interstate highway).
> None of these conclusions should be made with certainty and all
> illustrate the complexity that surrounds efforts to answer the
> simple question of whether racial profiling exists.

A significant barrier to developing and measuring a suitable denominator for assessing racial profiling relates to this concept's vague conceptual
definition. Within the debate over racial profiling, it's unclear what this practice involves. For example, is racial profiling envisioned as: officers stopping
some drivers (e.g., Hispanic males) at a disproportional rate compared
with other drivers under equal circumstances (e.g., when speeding more than
10 miles per hour over the limit); officers using different standards for violations which invoke traffic stops (e.g., only stopping white drivers for
serious violations, while stopping minority drivers for even the most minor
infraction); or, officers stopping some drivers under pretext or false pretense?
Even if consensus could be reached about the proper conceptualization of
a denominator to use in assessing profiling, reaching agreement on the
most valid and reliable operational definition would be equally problematic.
These complicated situations have lead scholars to suggest that it would be
premature to make any conclusions about the existence and magnitude of
racial profiling (Engel, Calnon & Bernard, 2002; Verniero & Zoubek, 1999).

Within the context of this denominator dilemma, inquiry into racial profiling may need to be reframed to allow for meaningful research. At the present time, it may be infeasible to determine if race influences an officer's decision to initiate a traffic stop encounter. Even if the denominator dilemma could be resolved, it is unclear whether common data collection methodologies (i.e., officer-reported behavior) can validly capture a cognitive process. In addition, as the following data indicate, labeling this problem as *racial* profiling is a form of reductionism because other demographic and situational variables influence officer behavior. Despite these limitations on inquiry into racial profiling, meaningful research examining broader issues of officer behavior in traffic enforcement encounters is still feasible. While establishing whether profiling occurs may not be possible, developing insights into police behavior and discretionary conduct is feasible and meaningful.

Conclusion

The idea of "racial profiling" remains conceptually cloudy and operationally complex. As is often the case in scientific inquiry, a seemingly simple question reveals intricacies that elude direct answers. Most empirical research has not attempted to provide a full behavioral explanation of traffic stop encounters between the police and the public. Rather, they seek to illustrate how the interpretation of key variables in the racial profiling debate may be modified through more complex examinations of these interactions. Although a limited number of agencies have exhibited clear impropriety in the conduct of their officers, most research has failed to conclusively establish that racial profiling is a real and significant social issue (Buerger & Farrell, 2002). Existent research lack sufficiently rich data to make clear determinations that observed disparities are the product of the inappropriate use of discretion, as opposed to the product of some other lawful and legitimate explanation. Despite extensive and expensive inquiry, profiling remains a vague phenomenon about which little is conclusively understood. Yet, it remains a sensitive point of controversy between the police and minority communities, representing the reality that truly "colorblind communities" remains an elusive but admirable goal.

Chapter Review Questions

1. In your own words, briefly summarize the article.

2. The chapter discusses a fear that officers have about their "numbers not looking right." Explain what this means, and give your opinion as to whether their fears are justified?

3. Should officers decrease proactive policing in order to avoid being labeled racist?

4. In the example on data collection and interpretation of data, which of the interpretations do you feel would unjustifiably label a police officer as racist?

5. How much does the cost of data collection factor into investigating racial profiling?

6. Identify and explain one problem with finding a denominator for data collection on racial profiling.

7. Using the eight factors presented for interpreting statistics and the knowledge that minorities live disproportionately in lower-income neighborhoods, discuss whether or not racial profiling is an unavoidable consequence of the circumstances citizens and officers are in?

8. It has been established that the use of demographic data collected by the Department of Motor Vehicles does not provide an accurate source of information because "such records often fail to capture race data, can be several years out of date, and do not account for unlicensed drivers." In your opinion, what would be a more accurate source? Explain.

9. In your opinion, what are the significant reasons for not conclusively establishing racial profiling as a real and significant social issue?

10. Given all the information presented in the article, formulate your own theory on racial profiling. For example, is it circumstantial and unavoidable? If so, what options, if any at all, are left for preventing racial profiling?

CHAPTER 8

"As Time Goes By:" The Expansion of Women's Roles in Police Work

Donna C. Hale
Karen Finkenbinder

Introduction

At the beginning of the twenty-first century, citizens may not find it unusual to see women police officers driving patrol cars, carrying weapons, making arrests, and dealing with violent confrontations. After all, our society is inundated with crime stories on television and in movies that portray women as police detectives and profilers. However, few media depict the full story: women as patrol officers, or as chiefs of police.

Because we see women on television and in movies as police detectives/investigators, we might assume that a substantial number of women are sworn police officers. Unfortunately, the number of women police officers has not grown substantially in the ensuing 35 years after two policewomen first drove a patrol car in Indianapolis in 1968. According to the U.S. Census Bureau (2003:401), of the 586,000 public service police and detectives in 2002, 15.5 percent were women. Law enforcement agencies indicate "that the percentage of female officers in departments across the nation, which rose steadily for more than 20 years, has leveled off at about 13%" (Leinwand, 2004:13A).

The slow growth of women in policing is intriguing, especially when we realize that they first entered police work as sworn police officers in 1910. Beginning in the twentieth century, policewomen worked in Women's Bureaus—facilities that were structurally separated from police departments where policemen worked. Initially, policewomen were assigned crime prevention duties. It would not be until the late 1960s that they would assume the same patrol duties as their male counterparts.

The primary reason for the limited role of women in police work was the social attitudes regarding women's roles. In the late nineteenth and early twentieth centuries, a woman's place was in the home, taking care of the household and children. Social concepts of "separate spheres" and the "cult of domesticity," prescribed different roles for men and women. Although women were hired as police matrons near the end of the nineteenth century, their primary assignment was to work with female offenders. The early policewomen of the nineteenth century were responsible for protecting children and young women. Gender stereotyping of the period held that women were most suited for these duties because of their femininity.

In this chapter, we trace the role of women in policing by examining the decades of the twentieth century. By exploring the entry of women into police work, we explain the challenges women experienced in an occupation that was, and continues to be, primarily a man's domain. In our description of the role of women in policing during the twentieth century, we reference important historical events—economic, social, cultural, and legal—to explain how the changes of each decade affected women's roles in society. For each of the decades in our hourglass (see Figure 1, "As Time Goes By:" The Expansion of Women Roles in Police Work")[1] we selected a popular song of the period with a title that we believe corresponds to the changing role for women as police in that decade.

The hour glass metaphor is intended to briefly highlight some of the major events and challenges that women faced in the twentieth century. We note important milestones of each decade that provided opportunities for women to enter police work.

We conclude this chapter with some important recommendations made by both police leaders and researchers regarding how police work can be made more accessible for women. The first decade of the twenty-first century is the time for local governments and their police departments to utilize the research of the past 50 years to implement strategies and policies to recruit, retain, and promote women in policing.

"The Time and the Place and the Girl:" Policewomen and the Crime Prevention Model, 1910-1930

During the late nineteenth century when H.G. Wells wrote his book *The Time Machine* (1984 reprint), women worked in police departments as matrons responsible for the care of women and children. In *The Alienist* (1995), Caleb Cobb presents a fictional woman police officer, Sara Howard, who worked as the secretary for Police Commissioner Theodore Roosevelt. Cobb's role for Sara Howard is an accurate description of a career for women in the late nineteenth century workplace. After the Remington Arms Company manufactured the typewriter in 1873, it was not uncommon for a woman to be a secretary.

Figure 1

"As Time Goes By:" The Expansion of Women's Roles in Police Work

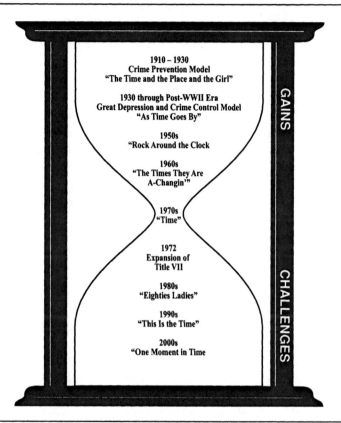

In 1905 the song, "The Time and the Place and The Girl," was first performed in the comic opera, *Mlle. Modiste*. Over the next two decades, the song was popular because the opera "had 202 performances and was frequently revived" (Gammond, 1991:392). This song's title is useful for our examination of women in policing. In the first decade of the twentieth century ("time"), in Oregon and California ("places"), two women ("girls") were the first to acquire the authority to make arrests.

The Travelers' Aid Society employed Lola Greene Baldwin as an agent to protect girls and women attending the Lewis and Clark Centennial Exposition in Portland (Myers, 1995). She was empowered by city officials in Portland, Oregon in 1905 to make arrests. Three years later, in 1908, Baldwin became the first director of the Women's Auxiliary to the Police Department for the Protection of Girls (Appier, 1998:29-30).

In 1910, Alice Stebbins Wells became the first sworn female police officer in Los Angeles, California. She possessed the authority to make arrests as well as to carry a gun. Wells is also recognized for the instrumental role she had in establishing Women's Bureaus across the United States. Policewomen were assigned to Women's Bureaus and were responsible for crime prevention and safeguarding women and children (Appier, 1998; 1992). In 1915 Wells established and served as the first president of the International Association of Policewomen (see Hale, 2002:1718).

During World War I, women began to leave home for employment in offices and factories. In 1920, after 72 years of campaigning for suffrage, women received the right to vote with the ratification of the Nineteenth Amendment. In 1922, the International Association of Chiefs of Police endorsed the employment of women in police work. Renowned police reformer, August Vollmer, Chief of Police in Berkeley, California established a crime prevention division and appointed Elizabeth Lossing, a psychiatric social worker, as the director (Liss & Schlossman, 1986). Policewomen conducted crime prevention duties during the first 30 years of the twentieth century (Appier, 1992; 1998). The Great Depression (Schulz, 1993) and the introduction of the crime control/military model of policing (Appier, 1998; 1992) were instrumental in limiting the role of women in police work.

"As Time Goes By:" 1930 through Post-WWII Era

Beginning with the Great Depression and continuing through World War II, women had a limited role in policing. They continued to work in clerical positions and provided support services for women and children. Certainly, the popular song "As Time Goes By" (1931) symbolized a period when women were not represented in large numbers in police departments. As time went by, though, women who entered police work "were able to maintain newly acquired positions and increase both their numbers and duties throughout the 1950s" (Schulz, 1993:6).

"Rock Around the Clock:" Women as Careerists

In 1952, "American Bandstand" premiered, a popular television dance show for teenagers. The following year, Bill Haley and His Comets defined a good time as "rocking around the clock." The 1950s was also a time for women to pursue a career in policing, as well as to seek opportunities for promotion (Schulz, 1993). But, the audience never saw a woman police officer in the popular "Dragnet" television show that first aired in 1951 and continued until the end of the 1950s. The main character, Sergeant Joe Friday, and his "just the facts, ma'am" style of investigation symbolized the crime control model of policing (Schulz, 1993).

However, the 1950s were neither a "quiet time" nor a slow growth period for women in policing (Schulz, 1993). Schulz (1993:5) reports that the 1950s witnessed an increase in the number of women in policing and an expansion of their responsibilities. The increase in women in policing in the 1950s was the first since after World War I. Schulz (1993) notes that policewomen of the 1950s:

> were interested in career opportunities and recognition within law enforcement, not within social work. Like their male colleagues who had become careerists in the 1930s, policewomen in the 1950s saw their future in civil service appointment and promotion and in diversified assignments with their department (Schulz, 1993:16).

Their activism was reflected in 1956 when the International Association of Policewomen (IAP) was re-established. The IAP was renamed the International Association of Women Police (IAWP) (Schulz, 1993:7).

One woman who had an important role in making promotions accessible to policewomen was Felicia Shpritzer. Shpritzer began her career in the New York City Police Department in 1942, in the Juvenile Aid Bureau. In 1961, she sued the department when she was denied an opportunity to take the promotional examination. She won her lawsuit in 1963. By challenging the department and winning her lawsuit in 1963, she opened the doors for other women to pursue promotional examinations (see Hale, 2002:1720).

"The Times They Are A-Changin:" Expansion of Women's Role in Police Work

Certainly the lyrics of Bob Dylan's "The Times They Are A-Changin" (1964) summarize the 1960s as a decade of social and political activism and reform. The 1960s were important as well for the changing role of women in society because of the feminist movement. In 1961, President Kennedy established the President's Commission on the Status of Women. In 1963 Congress passed the Equal Pay Act, and Betty Friedan's, *The Feminine Mystique* was published. And Title VII of the Civil Rights Act of 1964 was passed by Congress, prohibiting employment discrimination based on race, color, religion, sex, and national origin. In 1965, The Equal Employment Opportunity Commission was created to oversee the Civil Rights Act. In 1966, the American band, "The Outsiders" had a popular song entitled "Time Won't Let Me." This song's title is symbolic of policewomen of that period, who had struggled for advancements in police work and could not "wait forever" for both recognition and equity. The National Organization for Women was founded in 1966 and in 1967 was formally incorporated in Washington, D.C. In 1967, Simone De Beauvoir (Feminist Chronicles, Feminist Majority Foundation) first used the term "women's liberation," in her book, *The Second Sex*.

In 1967, just a year before women went on patrol, Paul McCartney of the Beatles immortalized the role of policewomen as giving parking tickets in "Lovely Rita Meter Maid," written with John Lennon. In their well-known song, McCartney described her uniform as a cap and a bag that made her "look a little like a military man." Peggy Lipton premiered in 1968 wearing bell-bottom pants as a member of the television undercover police story, "The Mod Squad"—a role she held until 1973. When "Dragnet" was revived (1967-1970), it included a role for a policewoman, as actress Merry Anders had a semi-recurring role as policewoman Dorothy Miller.

In 1968, The President's Commission on Law Enforcement and Administration of Justice and the U.S. National Advisory Commission on Civil Disorder recommended hiring more women in policing because they used empathy and sensitivity (Walker, 1985 cited in Zhao, et al., 2001:244). In 1968, Betty Blankenship and Elizabeth Coffal of the Indianapolis Police Department went on patrol in an automobile—previously a duty performed only by policemen. The Indianapolis Police Department was the first to assign women to full-time automobile patrol (Hale, 2002:1718).

The 1960s were an era of legislative changes that guaranteed women the opportunity to pursue careers in police patrol. The decade passed quickly and feminists and lobbyists would have agreed with Judy Collins as she sang "Who Knows Where the Time Goes" (1968).

"Time:" Women Enter Police Work

Pink Floyd's song "Time" (1973), with its chimes and hurried "tick-tock" music, echoes the theme of Andrew Marvel's seventeenth-century poem "To His Coy Mistress" that time is fleeting. The message of both is to not waste time, but "seize the day" (*carpe diem*) and make the most of opportunities presented, rather than waiting for a better time. The 1970s was a period of little wasted time. Publications, legislation, and the media all contributed to the changing image of women in nontraditional occupations such as policing.

The 1970s raced in with the publication of *Ms Magazine* (1972). Title VII of the Civil Right Act was extended to include public sector agencies, including, of course, police departments. Musician Helen Reddy won the Grammy in 1973 for "I am Woman" (written with Ray Burton, 1972). Her song about women's accomplishments relates to the success of the policewomen of the mid-1950s who succeeded in "dismantling their traditional sex based roles in policing" by using "the courts to challenge civil service regulations that severely limited their roles in police departments" (Schulz, 1993:6). Fuss and Snowden (2000:65) wrote that the extension of Title VII "helped pave the way for women to enter the male-dominated law enforcement field."

Beginning in the mid-1970s and continuing into the 1980s a number of television shows were produced depicting women as undercover police officers. Angie Dickinson was Sergeant Suzanne 'Pepper' Anderson in "Policewoman" (1974-1978). Actress Teresa Graves was the first African-American policewoman on television in "Get Christie Love!" (1974-75). And "Charlie's Angels" (1976-1981) starred Kate Jackson, Farrah Fawcett, and Jaclyn Smith as undercover detectives for the Townsend Detective Agency.

Undoubtedly, television audiences of the 1970s were not interested in comparing the performance of the fictional women police officers to actual police officers on the streets. However, performance evaluation studies were conducted beginning in the mid-1970s. These studies found no differences between men and women patrol duty performance (Bloch & Anderson, 1974; Sherman, 1975).

During the 1970s, police departments increased their efforts to hire more women due to either court orders or threats of discrimination lawsuits (Leinwand, 2004:13A). The National Advisory Commission on Criminal Justice Standards and Goals (1973:342) included Standard 13.6, specifying that all police agencies have policies that permit women to seek positions as either civilian or sworn officers. In the front of the National Advisory Commission on Criminal Justice Standards and Goals' (1973) *Police* monograph were two photographs depicting women as police officers. One was a recruitment photograph with a woman and male minority officer. The second photograph was a full-page depicting a policewoman—her arm fully stretched out—pointing a gun straight ahead. These photographs were effective illustrations that women and minorities were important to policing, and that women were capable of performing police work.

Near the end of the 1970s, police departments began to experiment with patrol strategies intended to bring the police officer into direct contact with neighborhood residents. Two early programs—the Newark, New Jersey and Flint, Michigan foot patrol programs—were pivotal in developing what is now commonly referred to as community policing. The purpose of community-oriented policing was to improve the residents' quality of life in neighborhoods and reduce their fear of crime.

In the 1980s, continuing legislation, police performance evaluations, and community policing research would strengthen the role of women in policing. Also, in the 1980s, the image of policewomen on television began to evolve from the physically attractive woman to professionally competent woman.

"Eighties Ladies:" Police Women and Domestic Violence

Pink Floyd's lyrics connect with K.T. Oslin's, "Eighties Ladies" (1987). Oslin tells the story of three women who grew up together in the 1950s, were the "stone rock and rollers in the 1960s," and found themselves as "Eighties Ladies" as the 1970s slipped away. Her song links the changing roles of women from crime prevention of the 1950s to patrol of the late 1960s through the 1970s. The 1980s found policewomen working effectively in community policing programs.

Social and legislative changes continued into the 1980s. Domestic violence gained national attention in 1980 with the first conference of the National Coalition against Domestic Violence. The Equal Employment Opportunity Commission issued new guidelines prohibiting sexual harassment in 1980. In 1981 Sandra Day O'Connor became the first woman Supreme Court justice. In 1985 Penny E. Harrington, who joined the Portland Police Bureau in 1964, became the "first woman chief of police of a major city in the United States" (see Hale, 2002:1722). In 1986 the United States Supreme Court upheld affirmative action as a remedy for past job discrimination.

Evaluation studies concluded that women were as effective as men in performing police work (Fry & Greenfield, 1980; Charles, 1981; 1982). Research by Grennan (1987) overall found no differences in the use of force by women and men police officers. Battered women reported policewomen as effective communicators in deescalating violent situations (Kenney & Homant, 1983).

In addition, the media image of the role of policewomen changed in the 1980s. The glamorous Pepper Anderson, Christie Love, and the "Charlie's Angels" trio were replaced by the extremely competent images of Christine Cagney and Mary Beth Lacey ("Cagney and Lacey," 1982-1988) and Officer/Sergeant Lucy Bates of "Hill Street Blues" (1981-1987). Perhaps K.T. Oslin's (1987) "Eighties Ladies" was correct: what complicated matters between men and women was when women became "educated and liberated."

"This Is the Time:" 1990s

Savatage's (1990) line that "we placed our years in the hourglass, they were never unearned" is relevant to summarize the advancement of policewomen for the past eight decades. If the number of television shows is any measure of success, policewomen were successful. Writers and producers continued to create successful police dramas throughout the 1990s beginning with "Law and Order" (1990 – present). In 1993, S. Epatha Merkerson joined the cast as Lieutenant Anita Van Buren. She is portrayed as an extremely competent leader of the homicide unit, but she encounters challenges by the rank and file.

In 1993, three more dramas joined the successful "Law and Order." Gillian Anderson starred as Agent Dana Scully in "The X-Files." Another successful police drama, "NYPD Blues," (1973) featured a number of women police officers over successive seasons (Officer Janice Licalsi, Detectives Adrianne Lesniak, Kelly Ronson, Rita Ortiz, and Abby Sullivan). In 1997, Actress Kim Delaney received an Emmy Award for Outstanding Supporting Actress in a Drama Series for her role as Detective Diane Russell. The third drama originating in 1993 was "Homicide: Life on the Street," starring actress Melissa Leo as Detective Sergeant Kay Howard. The decade of the 1990s ended with

Mariska Hargitay appearing as Detective Olivia Benson and Michelle Hurd as Detective Monique Jeffries in "Law and Order: Special Victims Unit."

However, television is not based on reality. The *Uniform Crime Reports* indicated in 1990 that women held 8.6 percent of the sworn police positions. Why such a low percentage of policewomen after so much legislation prohibiting discrimination and harassment against women (and others) since the 1960s? The public became more aware of the nature of sexual harassment, after Anita Hill's allegations against Clarence Thomas in 1991. Certainly, performance evaluations supported the notion that women were as effective as male police officers. Yet, the percentages of women in policing remained low.

By 1993 Ruth Bader-Ginsberg was appointed as the second woman to the United States Supreme Court. And, in the same year, President Clinton signed the Family and Medical Leave Act into law. President Clinton, in 1994, established the COPS Office when he signed legislation that would put 100,000 new police officers on the streets.

In 1995, two important organizations were founded to advance the entry of women in policing. The National Association of Women Law Enforcement Executives (NAWLEE) was established to both mentor and provide networks for women in law enforcement. The Feminist Majority Foundation established the National Center for Women in Policing (NCWP) to serve as a clearinghouse to promote the advancement of women in policing (Hale, 2002:1721).

A survey conducted in 1996 of more than 200 municipal police agencies from 47 states with city population more than 25,000 residents found that "female officers comprised an average of 9.58 percent of the officer workforce" (Zhao et al. 2001:248-249). Comparing this statistic with the percentage from an earlier survey administered in 1993, Zhao et al., (2001:249) reported that the "rate of increase in the percentage of female officers occurring between 1993 and 1996 as almost 11.5%." Zhao and his colleagues attribute the 6.05 percent increase in the overall number of officer positions between 1993-1996 to the Clinton Administration's endorsement of the implementation of community policing. Harrington and Lonsway (2004:507) recommend that police departments recruit individuals with communication skills and the ability to defuse volatile situations for community policing position. During a roundtable discussion at the sixth annual conference of the National Center for Women & Policing (NCWP), Kim Lonsway, Research Director for NCWP, concluded that to date:

> The research clearly indicates—although men and women are equally likely to use force in their routine duties as law enforcement officers—women are less likely to engage in excessive force. Rather, female officers tend to emphasize communication and de-escalation of potentially violent situations, a style that is more in line with community policing ideals (Lonsway, 2001:114).

A second reason Zhao et al. (2001:250) offered for the increase in officer positions was that "41% of the reporting agencies [indicated that they had] either a formal affirmative action program in place or [had] an affirmative action program that was the product of a court order or consent decree." Harrington and Lonsway (2004:507) agree that consent decrees "have a powerful effect on increasing the number of women within an agency."

"One Moment in Time:" Recommendations for the Future of Women in Policing

An important lyric from Whitney Houston's "One Moment in Time (2003) is "you're a winner for a lifetime if you seize that one moment in time." Her statement could be the motto of policewomen who had become chief executive officers of police departments. In 2003, women became police chiefs in Detroit, San Francisco, Milwaukee, Boston, and Fairfax County, Virginia (Leinwand, 2004:13A). In April 2004, Heather Fong became San Francisco's first female police chief. The *Uniform Crime Reports* indicates that in 2000, women held 11 percent of sworn positions. The increase for 2001 was very small—11.2 percent. The most recently published *Uniform Crime Reports* (2002) reports women holding 11.3 percent of sworn police positions.

As we noted above, there has been a plethora of research examining the performance of women police officers as well as the public and their peers' attitudes toward them since women began patrol duties in the 1970s. We also noted that during the past 50 years of television, the image of the policewomen has evolved from glamorous to more competent. The lineup of television police dramas for the first decade of the twenty-first century continues to portray competent women in the field of policing, including "C.S.I., Crime Scene Investigation" (2000) with actresses Marg Helgenberger as Catherine Willows and Jorja Fox as Sara Sidle. In 2001 "Law and Order: Criminal Intent" was introduced with Kathryn Erbe as Alexandra Alex Eames. Deanne Bray portrays *Sue Thomas: F.B. Eye* (2002) based on the actual life of Sue Thomas employed by the FBI to conduct deaf-work surveillance. Kathyn Morris is female homicide detective Lilly Rush assigned to old, unsolved *Cold Case* (2003) files.

The characters and the plots of the crime dramas shape the television audience's concept of police work. What the audience, perhaps, is not aware of is that police detectives enter police work as patrol officers, and become detectives through a highly competitive promotional process. The next sections of the chapter address aspects of recruitment, selection, retention, and promotion, and describe how women entering police work are affected by each of these.

Physical Agility/Fitness Testing: Disparate Impact?

Until the late 1970s, many police agencies used minimal height and weight standards as part of their selection process. This screened out most women applicants; thus, the courts rejected such standards under Title VII of the 1964 Civil Rights Act. Since that time, police departments have used physical agility testing or physical fitness standards as part of the selection criteria. This also has served to disproportionately affect women applicants. Gossert and Williams (1998) recognized that physical differences between men and women were commonly used to keep women out of patrol duties. Other researchers found that patrol work is fairly sedentary and requires a low level of aerobic conditioning (Gossert & Williams, 1998). In her recent study of police department physical agility tests, Kimberly Lonsway (2003:238) observed that the need for such tests are justified because policing is "widely assumed to require a great deal of physical prowess." She noted that in reality, incidents requiring large reserve of strength and fitness on the part of individual officers are "infrequent, critical incidents" (Lonsway, 2003:238). Further, her research supported the conclusion that "there is no consistency in the physical agility tests used by police agencies throughout the country and that evidence regarding their validity is almost completely lacking" (Lonsway, 2003:238). She attributes such problems to a number of theoretical and methodological problems that impede efforts to document what are truly the essential physical tasks for policing and to predict what can be characterized as "successful job performance."

The EEOC states that adverse impact of a selection test "is established when a plaintiff documents that passing rates for women fall below 80 percent of men's" (EEOC, 2001). If the passing rates of women are not sufficient, the agency must demonstrate the job relatedness and business necessity of the physical test. Recently, in the case of *Lanning v. Southeastern Pennsylvania Transportation Authority*, the court upheld the right of the agency to require all officers to run a mile and half in 12 minutes (*Lanning v. Southeastern Pennsylvania Transportation Authority*, 308 F. 3d 286 (3d Cir. 2002). In the *Lanning* case, the run was used to assess cardiorespiratory endurance and this type of testing is often used and increasingly upheld by the courts. It is an ordinarily part of a test battery that is age and gender neutral (there is one standard, for men and women). This battery of tests includes a test of absolute strength (bench press); muscular endurance (push-ups and sit-ups); explosive power (vertical jump); cardiorespiratory endurance ($1^1/_2$-mile run); and anaerobic conditioning (300-meter run). This type of testing must predict successful job performance and not just performance. This is a far different testing procedure than that used in physical agility testing.

In Lonsway's study of physical agility tests, she found that the most common test components were running events, a dummy drag, a solid wall climb, sit-ups, push-ups, and a sit-and-reach flexibility test . . . other events included a test of grip strength and a chain-link fence climb (Lonsway, 2003). Furthermore, other agility tests were used that included stairs, low barriers or low hurdles, ditch jumps and window climbs. This study also found a lack of consistency and validity in physical agility testing protocols.

Lonsway concludes in her research that there are four alternatives to physical agility testing—a major barrier for women entering police work. The first is to remove such testing from the selection procedure entirely and instead require a medical examination and do the physical training in the academy. A second alternative is to implement health-based screening that uses age and gender normed standards. The logic used for such screening is to prevent on-the-job injuries rather than predict successful job performance (Stanish et al., 1999). Lonsway noted that the courts have upheld the use of such normed standards for several reasons. Among these reasons are that the tests assess general fitness and not minimum standards for job performance; the standards are used to expand the competitive pool of qualified applicants and not to exclude anyone; and normed standards that appear different actually represent identical levels of underlying physical fitness. A third alternative is to offer job simulation tests that are truly representative of tasks that are essential to policing. The sticky point with such a strategy is where to set the cut off score for successful performance. One solution is to set cutoff scores at different levels for academy entrance and exit. Lastly, another option is to test recruits at the end of the academy after they have received fitness training. This option is probably a better alternative when done in conjunction with entry-level medical screening to ensure that a recruit is physically capable of participating in such fitness training.

Pregnancy

One of the few pieces of research regarding women in policing was published by the International Association of Chiefs of Police. The IACP (1998a) conducted a survey of 800 of its members (97% male) that looked at the future of women in policing. The most frequent reason used for women resigning from policing was *family/birth of a child*. It was reported that "women typically resign at the patrol level after five years of service primarily for family obligations or to seek better job opportunities" (IACP, 1998b:38).

Most departments do not have "maternity leave" or "light duty" for pregnant women. Polisar (1998:46) recommends training supervisors "on how to apply the light-duty policy to pregnancy." The U.S. Supreme Court has determined that pregnancy is akin to any other temporary disability. Whether or not a pregnant officer receives light duty is dependent upon the agency's "light duty policy." If the agency provides male officers light duty for off-duty injuries (such as an injury that occurred while playing softball off-duty), then the agency is required to find light duty for pregnant officers. But, if the agency does not allow light duty for off-duty injuries, it is not required to provide it for pregnant women. It also must be stated that only large departments may have the luxury of having any light duty at all. Pennsylvania is like many other states in that of more than 1,200 police departments, only 150 departments have more than 20 officers. In fact, many of these small departments have one or two officers. In such a setting, a department does not have the luxury of having an officer unavailable for any reason.

Under the Family Medical Leave Act, pregnant officers may take off from work (without pay), but this often puts a financial burden on them. Therefore, most women officers use their vacation, sick time and any other compensatory time. Many come back after delivery and recuperation for a period of time, but then leave because they do not have sick time or vacation time to deal with their children's illnesses. Also, many female officers are married to male officers and often they jointly decide that only one parent should be in a high-risk occupation; thus, they make a family decision that one must leave law enforcement and often the mother chooses to leave.

Recruitment, Promotion, and Retention Issues

In 1998 the International Association of Chiefs of Police sponsored a telephone interview of 800 police administrators who responded to 45 questions pertaining to the recruitment, promotion, and retention of women in policing (IACP, 1998b). The findings indicated that the recruitment strategies for women in policing were "more likely" in larger police departments (IACP, 1998b:36). "Larger departments are nearly three times more likely than smaller departments to actively recruit female applicants" (IACP, 1998b:36). Sixty-nine percent of the respondents reported that women officers actively seek promotions; almost two-thirds indicated that it was not difficult to move women into higher ranks in the department. The difficulty in promoting women was attributed to limited numbers of positions (IACP, 1998b:36). Overall, the respondents reported that women were effective in communication and interpersonal skills, domestic violence and abuse situations, and working with children and with the public. Forty-four percent reported no concerns with women handling physical confrontations (28% had concerns). Virtually all administrators reported that their department had a written policy addressing sexual harassment and "nearly all" of the departments reported that supervisors were trained to identify "sexual harassment in their workplace" (IACP, 1998b:38). Twenty percent of large police departments (compared to 4% of small police departments) had been sued for sexual harassment (IACP, 1998b:38). Ninety percent of respondents reported that they had written policies addressing gender discrimination, with 44 percent of the policies specific to "the issue of failure to promote women because of their gender" (IACP, 1998b:38).

Milgram (2002) recommends that police departments conduct a self-assessment of their present recruitment strategies. She recommends that they consider such recruitment strategies as using a Web page, an e-mail list, and sponsoring a women-in-policing career fair. Women attending the fair would benefit from the opportunities provided to attend panel sessions designed to assist them with the application and selection process. Personnel should be available to answer questions potential applicants may have about the physical ability test, police academy training, and police equipment. It is important to include a presentation by high-ranking women officers and to build-in time for audience questions and answers. Positions can be advertised in newspapers, on the department's Web page, and the World Wide Web. Recruitment materials can be distributed in malls, grocery store, sports facilities, military facilities, high schools, and colleges/universities (Milgram, 2002:25).

Promotional Issues

Leinwand (2004:13A) reports that only about 200 of the nation's 18,0000 police departments—or about 1 percent—have female chiefs. What are some of the reasons to explain the limited promotions for women in policing? Previous research found that the size of the jurisdiction made little difference in female representation in supervisory ranks in 1978 because women's representation was negligible (Martin, 1989). The proportion of women supervisors tripled from 1978 to 1986, but as Susan Martin notes, it was a change from the "minuscule to the minute." At the time, this low proportion was understandable—eligibility for promotion only occurred after several years of service at the entry-level. As women were fairly new to law enforcement, this could be explained. Further, bonus points were given for veterans and unlike today, very few women were military veterans.

The International Association of Chiefs of Police examined promotional issues in 1998 and observed that of 800 respondents, 75 percent believed that the number of women officers "will increase in the next five years and that there will be an increase in women supervisors" (IACP, 1998a:38,40). But a review of the latest Law Enforcement Directory (2002) did not bear this out, especially when examining the position of chief of police. There were more than 13,000 police departments totaling more than 437,000 officers. Only 171 women chiefs were found (.013%). In fact, those states commonly referred to as "progressive" have the fewest women chiefs (California and Oregon). Interestingly, the only state to have three women chiefs in some of its largest cities is North Carolina. The chiefs of Raleigh, Durham, and Winston-Salem are women.

Polisar (1998:50) recommends that in order for women to move up in ranks that "female officers" receive "opportunities for assignments and training that will lay the groundwork for their eventual promotion." He also recommends formal mentoring programs for women, and that supervisors encourage women to apply for promotions. Maglione (2002) suggests that mentoring begin early in recruit training to develop a women's network. She recommends that rank-and-file women meet informally with women recruits and provide them with support and advice regarding any concerns the recruits may be experiencing (Maglione, 2002:19). Women who are eligible for promotion need mentors to both advise and prepare them for each step of the promotional process.

The importance of mentoring cannot be overstated. Kranda (1998) reports that retaining highly qualified women is more of a problem than attracting applicants to police work. Therefore, she recommends that police departments implement a formal mentoring process as part of their recruitment, selection and training process. She says that a veteran officer should contact the new officer before her first day of employment. The mentor answers any questions the new officer may have about the job and continues to provide resources and support (Kranda, 1998).

Conclusion

Martha Graham (1894-1991), American dancer and choreographer, once said "I believe one thing: that today is yesterday and tomorrow is today and you can't stop" (Warner, 1992:298). Graham's long life parallels the time period of the changing role of women in policing. Just as women faced resistance in their attempts to pursue police work, Graham encountered opposition in her efforts to create a new dance style. Her quote reminds us that the future is shaped by what was accomplished in the past as well as today. Therefore, it is important to implement changes, even if incrementally, to improve and further strengthen the entry of women in policing.

This chapter concludes with Lonsway et al.'s (2003) six reasons why police departments can benefit from hiring and retaining women as police officers. These six principles are the results of the determined individuals who recognized that "today is yesterday and tomorrow is today and you can't stop."

1. Women are as competent as men are.

2. Women are less likely to use excessive force; they rely on communication not physical force.

3. Women utilize "community-oriented policing."

4. Women will improve law enforcement's response to violence against women.

5. Women in greater numbers in policing will reduce problems of discrimination and harassment within a law enforcement agency.

6. Women hired and retained in policing will benefit both women and men in the areas of training, selection, performance, and supervision.

Endnote

1   The authors thank Dr. Signe Kelker, Mr. Berkley Laite, and Ms. Karla Schmit, reference librarians at Shippensburg University, as well as Chris Leighty of Fye's music store at the Chambersburg, PA mall, and Pauline Clinkenbeard, friend of Donna Hale, for their research assistance with the song titles. Sarah Henrie, graduate assistant at Shippensburg University, is acknowledged for her assistance with the hourglass graphic.

Chapter Review Questions

1. Discuss the role of women in the field of policing in the nineteenth and twentieth centuries. According to the authors, why did women serve in these capacities? Do you agree with the author? Why or why not?

2. The authors of this chapter make a point to provide the reader with the context under which women and policing are examined. Why is this "context" important to our understanding of women in policing?

3. In what ways did the role of women in policing change in the 1950s?

4. How did the depiction of women police officers on television in the 1970s differ from the experiences of women in policing in the 1970s?

5. What is the authors' opinion on the issue of women and community policing? Do you agree or disagree? Why?

6. In your opinion, what contributed to the increased number of women police officers in the 1990s?

7. How are age and gender normed standards different than more traditional physical agility tests? Why have the courts upheld such standards?

8. View an episode of a police television show that depicts a female police officer. Describe and discuss how the character was portrayed in the show.

9. Discuss why the authors suggest that a formal mentoring process is an important part of the recruitment, selection and training process for women police officers.

10. Do you believe that police departments should actively recruit females into the policing profession? Why or why not?

SECTION IV

Ethical Issues and Police Deviance

CHAPTER 9

Ethical Issues in Policing

Joycelyn M. Pollock

An officer confesses to planting drugs on suspects and, at least in one case, shooting an unarmed citizen, paralyzing him for life, and providing false testimony to justify the shooting (Ramparts scandal).

A man is arrested and at the police station is anally assaulted with a broomstick by an officer. Several officers observe the assault and cover up for the offending officer (Abner Louima scandal).

A ring of officers engage in robbery, drug sales, and murder. Despite their obvious involvement in drug crimes, no one in the department comes forward to turn them in (River Rats scandal in Miami).

Introduction

This chapter is about ethics in law enforcement. Do the actions above represent a breakdown in ethical decisionmaking, or are they criminal acts of people who happen to wear police uniforms? This chapter examines this question, as well as others. In every profession, there are a few individuals who have criminal inclinations and eventually use the profession, whether law, medicine, teaching, or law enforcement, to facilitate their criminal inclinations. We often see these actions analyzed as ethical violations, but should they simply be considered criminal acts? Why is it that when a gang member brutally assaults another, it is a crime, but when a police officer brutally assaults a citizen, it is an ethical transgression? Should not the same theories (and punishment) apply to both? As one police officer vehemently explained in an ethics training class, "when an officer steals, he is a thief; don't refer to him as a police officer, he's a thief who happens to wear a uniform." It does a disservice to all law enforcement officers to discuss the obviously criminal acts of a very few officers as if they were similar to other officers' ethical dilemmas. Whether or not criminal acts and other forms of serious corruption should enter a discussion on ethics, there is definitely a dilemma presented by such deeds, and that is: what should an officer do when he or she becomes aware of the wrongdoing of a colleague?

In this chapter we will provide a brief introduction to the field of ethics and then focus specifically on how the field applies to law enforcement. The types of dilemmas that officers face will be reviewed, along with strategies officers and others might use to solve such dilemmas. Also considered will be management efforts to minimize and reduce corruption.

The Field of Ethics

Ethics is the study of behavior, but more specifically, how behavior is defined as right or wrong. In the most common use of the term, ethics is the study of how one defines behavior as right and wrong in one's public life, for instance, in one's profession; while morality refers to the study of right or wrong behavior in one's private life (Pollock, 1998:6-7). Ethics is different from law. While our laws spell out prohibited behaviors and punishments; ethics are more encompassing. The sanctions one might experience for committing unethical acts may be only informal, or, perhaps, one would experience no punishment at all. In fact, at times, one might be informally sanctioned for rejecting an unethical behavior, and behaving, instead, in an ethical manner (i.e., whistleblowing). Further, it is entirely possible to have a behavior be "wrong," but not necessarily against the law, such as most forms of lying. Too much may be made of this, however, and one of the first and most powerful "checks" on behavior for police officers, as well as all others, should be the simple question: "Is it against the law?"

In every profession there is some emphasis on the "ethics" of that profession. Law schools teach a "professional responsibility" class, medical schools offer a medical ethics class, and business schools teach a business ethics class. The educated professional is presumed to know, understand, and accept the ethics of his or her chosen profession. Often, scandals precipitate a newfound interest in the ethics of certain professions. The Watergate scandal of the Nixon administration led people to ask how could it be that all the major players in the illegal breaking and entering of the Democratic party headquarters were lawyers who should know better. The scandal spawned a flurry of activity in law schools and new and improved ethics classes emerged. The business scandals of 2002, including the bankruptcy of WorldCom and Enron, and the trading scandals on Wall Street, will no doubt lead to a flurry of new ethics classes in business schools. It may also be true that the scandals in law enforcement in recent years, including the Ramparts scandal in Los Angeles will focus greater attention on ethics training in law enforcement academies and criminal justice programs in universities and colleges.

The ethical choices of individuals in these professions are at least partially influenced by the norms, values, and desires of the larger community. If unethical business practices are accepted or "winked at," it should come as no surprise when such practices eventually harm a large number of people. Unethical practices in politics continue because they are effective and the public, despite loud rhetoric, tolerates them. Some would say that widespread instances of police brutality may be a natural byproduct of the public's willingness to allow police *carte blanche* discretion in the so-called "war on drugs" or more general "war on crime." In other words, we (meaning the majority) get the policing we ask for, just as we get the politicians we deserve.

Ethics, Crime, and Law Enforcement

Discussions of ethics in law enforcement typically focus on police corruption and/or police brutality. The fact is that cities across this nation are rocked by corruption scandals in depressing regularity. Table 1 shows a partial list of some incidents just in the past 10 years.

Table 1
Scandals Between 1988 and 1998

City	Year	Number Involved	Acts
Atlanta	1995	6	federal corruption charges
Chicago	1996	10	extortion, robbery, sale of drugs
Cleveland	1998	44	protection
Detroit	1991	9	conspiracy to sell, money laundering
Los Angeles	1994	27	theft of drug money
Miami	1980s	100	drug related charges
New Orleans	1994	11	protection, murder
New York	1992	36	drug crimes
Philadelphia	1995	10	planting drugs, shakedowns, burglary
Savannah	1994	10	protection, sale of illegal guns
D.C.	1994	12	protection

Gaines, L. and V. Kappeler (2003). *Policing in America*, Fourth Edition. Cincinnati, OH: Anderson Publishing Co., pp. 388-389.

There are a number of different typologies of the range of corrupt behaviors committed by police officers (for instance, see Caldero & Crank, 2004; Perez & Moore, 2002). They can be loosely grouped into two categories—corruption that is in furtherance of individual gain or benefit, and corruption that is in furtherance of organizational goals. Some activities, such as cover-ups, might be placed in either category.

Examples of individual corruption include: gratuities, shakedowns, protection, bribes, extortion, "shopping" on a burglary call, theft, selling/buying drugs, using drugs or alcohol on duty, sexual coercion, harassment or assault of female officers or civilians, misreporting overtime or court duty, not performing work related tasks during a shift, shirking duties by ignoring calls, and lying in a cover-up.

Examples of means-end corruption include: use of drugs by undercover officers, physical coercion/threat in interrogation, deception in interrogation, lying on affidavits, "testilying," allowing continued criminality by informants, supplying informants with drugs, planting evidence, brutality, lying for fellow officers or covering up/not reporting, misinformation through crime statistics.

More thorough discussions of some of these issues can be found. Kania (1988), for instance, provides an expansive analysis of gratuities, as does Pollock (1998). Carter (1999) discusses drug use and other forms of corruption related to drugs. Barker and Carter (1991, 1999) discuss various forms of police lying. Kraska and Kappeler (1995) explore police sexual misconduct, including harassment and assault. Police use of force is covered by a number of authors (for instance, Skolnick & Fyfe, 1994; and Nelson, 2000). Cohen and Feldberg (1991) explore misuse of police authority.

One of the most intriguing distinctions made is between personal forms of corruption and "noble cause" corruption (referred to as means-end corruption in the list above) (Caldero & Crank, 2004; Klockars, 1983). While the first is merely for personal profit or gain, the other has noble aims (crime fighting). There is nothing noble, so goes this argument, about stealing from a burglary location, accepting a bribe, or shaking down a prostitution ring; however other acts such as coercing a confession, conducting an illegal search, or lying to obtain a search warrant, are utilized by officers who seek nothing for themselves, but are doing such things in order to catch criminals. Crank (2004), Caldero and Crank (2004), and others argue that in order to guard against such acts, training must take cognizance of the noble motives of these officers.

Noble cause corruption stems from good officers who employ bad means to get to a good end. But can these bad means be justified? Often, the acts lead to very negative consequences. An officer who lies on an affidavit for a search warrant, must also then lie to the prosecutor, his superiors, and on the witness stand in order to stay out of trouble. It may be, in fact, that lying or otherwise subverting due process is not the only way to catch criminals, just the easiest way. And what would we make of those officers who brutalize suspects already in custody? According to one retired New York City officer, it was an unwritten rule that anyone who assaulted a police officer should not be able to walk, unassisted, into the stationhouse (Doyle, 2000). Do we consider this "noble cause corruption" (deterring would-be assaulters of police) or simply brutal vengeance?

Let's look at some acts that might be called "noble cause" corruption: In Tulia, Texas, the work of a hired undercover agent led to the arrests of 43 persons—a sizeable proportion of Tulia's small minority community. The trouble is that the so-called police officer hired by this small town police department had outstanding warrants in Houston, was fired from several law enforcement jobs, and would have received extremely negative recommendations if Tulia officials had bothered to do a background check. His "investigations" centered only on African-Americans and whites who were either married to, or dating, African-Americans. Convictions were obtained almost solely on his testimony, with virtually no corroborating evidence, and it has been proven in several cases that he must have lied. For instance, one gentleman was accused of selling drugs on a day that he was in Oklahoma. His employer testified to that fact, yet he was still convicted by the white jury. The NAACP, the Justice Department, and the Texas Attorney General's office have all indicated they are investigating the matter, but only the NAACP and its lawyers have managed to obtain any results in getting any of the 43 arrested out of jail and/or prison (Herbert, 2002).

In the early 1990s, Richard Danziger and Christopher Ochoa confessed to robbing and killing a female employee of Pizza Hut in Austin, Texas. Recently, they have been released from prison after another confessed to the murder and DNA evidence confirmed that he committed the crime, not Danziger and Ochoa. They served 12 years in prison for a crime they did not commit because the officers involved allegedly coerced them to confess by threatening them with the death penalty and threatening one of them that his family in Mexico would be harmed by the Mexican police if he did not cooperate (Hafetz, 2002).

Coincidentally, about the same time that these two men were being released in Texas, the juveniles accused and convicted of the Central Park jogger rape case were also exonerated by the confession of another and DNA evidence. They also explained that they confessed because of police coercion, a fact that seems easy to understand considering one of them was only 14 years old when he underwent intensive police interrogation (Getlin, 2002). The Innocence Project reports that more than 27 guilty verdicts have been overturned in the past decade because of false confessions that were coerced by police tactics (Tanner, 2002). Thus, the means these officers used to obtain a confession resulted, not in justice but a gross injustice to those involved, and the real criminal was free to continue to victimize. Regardless of their motives, these officers violated the rights of individuals and engaged in acts that were illegal or, at best, unethical, leading to unjust outcomes.

A Tale of Two Cities

Any discussion of law enforcement ethics almost inevitably must discuss New York City and Los Angeles—highly professional police departments that have both experienced their share of corruption scandals. The two city police departments are very different—Los Angeles covers 463 square miles and has 9,000 officers to serve four million people, while New York spans 309 square miles and serves 8 million people with 39,000 officers (LeDuff, 2002).

Former Police Commissioner William Bratton and former Mayor Rudy Giuliani have both made headlines with their boast that the zero-tolerance policy instituted in New York City toward minor "lifestyle" crimes was primarily responsible for the crime decline enjoyed by New Yorkers. From 1993 to 1997 felony complaints dropped by 44 percent, murder and nonnegligent homicide dropped by 62 percent, forcible rape by 12 percent, robbery by 48 percent, and burglary by 45 percent. They attribute the decline to Compstat (a state-of-the-art computer data system) and the zero-tolerance management strategy. Police officers were encouraged to pick up and arrest loiterers, the homeless, "squeegee men," vandals, subway jumpers, and public intoxicants. The idea in this "Broken Windows" approach to crime was that these minor criminal offenders somehow led to more serious crimes. And the numbers seemed to speak for themselves, except that New York City was also not alone in experiencing a decline in crime. San Diego, for instance, also saw almost the same drop but did not employ zero tolerance policing (Greene, 1999).

However, what is not often discussed is that, during the same period, citizen complaints against the police rose by 75 percent, and the number of complaints where there was no arrest (just perceived harassment) jumped substantially (Greene, 1999). In 1999, lawsuits and settlements of civil rights claims against N.Y.P.D. reached $40 million (Nelson, 2000). In a poll taken during the 1990s, 93 percent of New Yorkers believed that police were corrupt (Kraus, 1994).

The most gruesome and outrageous incident, of course, was the Abner Louima case in which a Haitian man, arrested for a dispute at a bar, was anally assaulted by Officer Justin Volpe. The incident was witnessed by at least one other officer and others were implicated in a cover-up. The Amadou Diallo case also very nearly sparked race riots. In this case, an unarmed Diallo attempted to enter his apartment house after being told to stop by police who were looking for an armed robber, and was shot 41 times by officers. The subsequent trial (moved away from the Bronx to Albany) resulted in acquittals for the four officers involved. Observers believe that zero tolerance has led to increased police harassment of minorities, as well as the greater use of deadly force (Nelson, 2000). Despite some critics, Bratton now plans to employ the same approach in Los Angeles.

William Bratton is now the Chief of Los Angeles, a city that has had its own well-publicized problems. The Rodney King scandal reinforced the widespread perception of L.A.P.D. as a police department where police were highly trained, but brutality was tolerated, if not encouraged, especially against minorities. Just eight years after the Christopher Commission issued its scathing commentary regarding L.A.P.D.'s management policies and how they led to racism and brutality, L.A.P.D. was in the news again. The Ramparts scandal in 1994 exposed the department to scrutiny and disgust when a number of officers in an anti-gang unit (CRASH) were exposed by one officer who was being prosecuted for stealing cocaine worth millions from the police evidence room. The officers in this unit evidently had acted as a force unto themselves, harassing youth, planting evidence, lying to obtain affidavits, and destroying property. The worst charges included shooting an unarmed suspect, planting a gun, and then lying to support their version of what happened. More bizarre allegations included stories of "killing" parties to celebrate shootings, spreading ketchup to imitate blood at crime scenes, spraying graffiti such as "L.A.P.D. rules" on searched premises, and handing out plaques for killing gang members (Jablon, 2000). The District Attorney's office has been burdened with the cost of reexamining hundreds of old cases and filing appeals against their own convictions because of doubts regarding the officers' testimonies (Glover & Lait, 2000). So far, 40 convictions have been overturned and 11 officers have been relieved of duty (Jablon, 2000).

William Bratton has taken on a department that is under a federal consent decree as a result of the Ramparts scandal, with a demoralized police force, and rising crime rates. More than 1,000 officers have left the department and all gang officers were reassigned leaving a vacuum of intelligence. Subsequently, there has been a 240 percent increase in crime in the gang-ridden areas of Los Angeles since 1998 (LeDuff, 2002). Whether the zero-tolerance policy used in New York will reduce crime or merely exacerbate relations with the minority community and open the door to further misconduct remains to be seen.

Understanding Police Corruption

In explanations that have been proposed to explain corruption in police departments, some argue that certain types of individuals are attracted to policing, some argue the subculture encourages it, and some argue other theories better explain the existence of corrupt and/or brutal officers. One thing that most analysts don't do, however, is present comparative evidence. Do more police officers engage in unethical/corrupt behavior than other professionals? Obviously, the profession of policing gives its members certain opportunities that others don't have, but, in every profession, there are opportunities. For instance, how many doctors misuse controlled substances? How many lawyers cheat their clients? How many inspectors take bribes? How many soldiers mistreat foreign nationals? How many politicians are influenced by campaign contributions or gifts? Of course, this is not to excuse such deviance; it is, however, important to gain some perspective in our study of police corruption. Corruption by police may be *qualitatively* different because of the power inherent in the role of law enforcers, but there is no evidence that it is *quantitatively* different from other professional or occupational groups.

Given those caveats, it does seem that law enforcement has some unique aspects that open the door for temptation. Specifically, these elements are *exposure*, *discretion*, and *socialized "deviance."* First, officers, perhaps more than any other group in society, are *exposed* to a steady diet of the worst elements of society. Their perspective on human nature may become warped because they routinely deal with people at their worst and the worst people, leading to cynicism and, for some, an attitude of "everyone is crooked, so why not me?" They are also exposed to opportunities that many of us will never be exposed to, such as access to large amounts of money as evidence, bribes, and other temptations. So, while all jobs may have opportunities for ethical lapses, law enforcement may be unique in the type and pervasiveness of the exposure to both negative behavior and the opportunity to engage in it themselves.

Further, their job is such that they operate without a great deal of oversight or supervision and are called upon daily to make a myriad of decisions, most of them affecting citizens in some way or another. In other words, they have *discretion* or power. And, as the saying goes, power corrupts. What may be the case is that those who are corrupt will use power if they have it. Late at night, working alone, officers make decisions on the spur of the moment. Some of these officers will make decisions that would have been made differently if there had been supervisors around or their behavior was more public.

Finally, officers are *socialized* in both formal and informal ways to ignore laws that apply to everyone else. This may occur in very minor ways like driving faster than the speed limit or parking in a no-parking zone. But the socialization to flaunt laws extends into serious actions as well. Officers pick up the distinct message that they are in a different category and they may feel that their privileges are small reward for the responsibilities they undertake as police officers. So some officers expect to get out of speeding tickets, and some expect gratuities from business owners, and some expect that "professional courtesy" may extend to other forms of behavior as well, such as when neighbors call on a noise disturbance or a family violence call. Many officers are socialized into an us-versus-them attitude toward the citizens they are sworn to protect, as well as their own supervisors. This socialization sets up the condition whereby some officers take advantage of their role and others feel unable to do anything about it.

These elements of policing—exposure, discretion, and socialized deviance create a situation that is ripe for unethical decisions by officers. Why some choose unethical behaviors and others do not is our next question.

Individual, Organizational, and Societal Explanations

The problem of corruption in law enforcement can be discussed at the level of the *individual*, the *organization*, and *society* (looking at the role of policing in society). At the *individual level*, the "rotten apple" theory explains that corruption starts with an individual deviant who either acts alone or contaminates a small number of fellow officers to commit deviant and corrupt acts. This explanation is usually used for the most egregious cases of corruption (i.e., those acts uncovered by the Mollen Commission in New York or the Ramparts scandal in Los Angeles).

Sometimes along with the "rotten apple" explanation is the "slippery slope" explanation. In this explanation of police corruption, unethical acts of police are viewed as a progression from the least serious to the most serious. Once an officer starts down the path of corrupt behaviors, for instance, by taking gratuities, then it is a slow but inevitable slide into more serious forms of corruption (Sherman, 1982, Malloy, 1982). Officers themselves tend to reject this definition and argue that it is a long jump from gratuities to stealing from a burglary location. However, another relevant observation is that when officers engage in minor transgressions, they are less able to stand up to and report major transgressions by others (Skolnick & Fyfe, 1994).

It is not coincidental that solutions focus on hiring, training, and supervision, for these would all address individual deviance. For instance, it is often explained (by older officers) that corruption occurs because of "bad hires." They point to time periods when departments hired quickly without extensive background investigations, or with reduced qualifications for hire. "What do you expect," say some officers, "when you hire guys who admit to having used drugs?" Of course this position does not explain the consistent, if periodic, exposes of police corruption that have occurred with depressing regularity over decades.

The second level of analysis is at the *organizational level*. In this discussion, explanations revolve around the structure of the organization, formal and informal subcultures, and training. It is probably no coincidence that the worst scandals seem to occur in the largest cities. In a department of 37,000 officers, such as the case with N.Y.P.D., it is extremely difficult for top administrators to affect the organizational culture. Larger departments have sub-units that operate semi-autonomously; thus, in many instances of corruption scandals, the misdeeds take place in an isolated division or tactical unit that receives little supervision or oversight from the larger organization.

Formal and informal subcultures in an organization also affect the potential for corruption. When brutal officers are not punished, that is a message from leadership. When whistleblowers are sanctioned and transferred or fired, that sends a message. In two recent cases, Internal Affairs officers or others were told to suppress or limit their investigation and to "keep the lid on" rather than expose corrupt officers. John Tromboli in New York City attempted to expose Michael Dowd long before the Mollen Commission exposed the widespread drug dealing and criminal activity of him and his group of fellow officers. Similarly, a Sergeant Poole in Los Angeles had early indications of the extent of the Ramparts scandal when investigating a homicide involving one of the officers, but was told by his superiors to limit and curtail his investigations (Golab, 2000). In both these cases management could have ordered an extensive and comprehensive investigation, but instead evidently wanted to avoid "airing dirty laundry." This tendency of management to not want to hear about corruption among its officers is perhaps one of the most serious barriers to reducing corruption.

Even if the formal culture supports ethical decisionmaking, it may be subverted by the informal subculture. We discussed above the socialization of police to flaunt the law. In some ways, their very job depends on their ability to break the law (i.e,. to buy drugs, to solicit sex, to lie). Undercover work and interrogation place police officers in a situation where they must become very comfortable lying.

Barker and Carter (1999) discuss the pervasive deception that characterizes law enforcement. Police are trained and expected to be deceptive in a number of different tasks (i.e., undercover work, interrogation, even in controlling the flow of information to the media). They identify "accepted lying," "tolerated lying," and "deviant lying." The important point, however, is that for some officers, the lines become blurred. What becomes second nature in investigation, is harder to turn off in other situations when truthfulness is expected.

The last level of analysis is at the *societal level*. Here we would look to the role of policing in society and examine when such corruption is likely to occur. Historically, law enforcement was used by the majority to oppress the disenfranchised. Police agencies were responsible, for instance, for harassing and brutalizing labor union organizers in the early part of the twentieth century (Fogelson, 1977; Crank, 2003; Skolnick & Fyfe, 1994). Police officers in the south protected and even participated in the lynchings and race-based assaults and firebombings (Nelson, 2000).

Some would argue that police are still involved in oppressing the disenfranchised and the "drug war" is only one example of how the formal machinery of social control is subverted to be used against the poor and minority groups. All this to say, that while in the United States, the rhetoric is equal justice for all, but the reality is that law enforcement's basic function is to control groups the majority and/or power-holders fear—the poor and minority. When public (majority) fear goes up, the "gloves come off" and police are given a green light to use extralegal means to control if necessary. When public fear goes down and/or when there are too many exposed cases of abuse, then law enforcement is reined in by laws, policies or civil rights lawsuits. This analysis implies that while individual officers commit the abuses, they would be less likely to do so without the implicit acquiescence of the public and the tacit consent of management.

Confronting Dilemmas in Law Enforcement

A dilemma, large or small, occurs when an individual has trouble making the right decision. It could be that the officer knows what is right, but to "do the right thing" will mean that he or she will be ostracized or suffer in some other way from what happens. In some cases, there are a number of possible alternatives in a situation and the officer is truly confused about what is right. That is also a dilemma. But when an officer finds a large amount of money executing a search warrant for drugs, is it an ethical dilemma whether to steal the money or not? Is the officer who does steal, simply a criminal? Honest officers may feel that to consider this an ethical issue demeans the profession and insults all officers. When an act clearly has no support other than crass egoism, it may not be appropriate to discuss it as a dilemma.

The realm of ethics does cover issues such as: Should officers take free coffee or meals? Should officers ticket their fellow officers for speeding? Should officers "testi-lie" (i.e., perjure themselves in order to obtain a warrant, or make sure evidence is admitted in a trial)? What should an officer do when he observes another officer use unlawful force on a suspect?

Officers face these very real dilemmas. How do they make their decisions? Ordinarily decisionmaking is quick and without much thought. One might consider these decisions the consequence of character (Delattre, 1989). When a motorist offers an officer a bribe, do most police officers weigh the decision and debate with themselves whether or not to take it, each time it happens? Of course not. It is wrong and most police officers, in fact, most of us, do not have to think about it. If we have never been inclined to take bribes or violate the law, then it is highly unlikely that we would begin to do so in our profession.

However, what would happen if your field training officer was the one taking the bribe, and further, several other officers in your division indicated that it was the "normal" thing to do? "Everyone does it," they explain and kid you about your scruples. Further, there are veiled threats that indicate to you that if you "tip the applecart," your life will be made miserable and your career sabotaged. Then what would you do? In this case, the individual is presented with conflicting pressures—the pressure to do what's right versus the pressure to support fellow officers, and/or the pressure to protect oneself. This is why ethics in policing must be addressed at the organizational level as well as the individual level. One can hire good officers, but if they are placed in a system of entrenched corruption with subcultural pressures to deviate, then some will or they will quit.

These are serious dilemmas for individual officer and deserve a careful response. It is all too easy for armchair theorists to say "do the right thing" or some other platitude that implies that to be ethical is easy. The costs should not be underestimated; therefore, in this section, we will discuss how an officer might approach such dilemmas.

It should also be noted that "doing" is different from "believing." We may believe something is wrong and do it anyway. In fact, that's when our conscience kicks in, even if it didn't prevent us from doing the act to begin with. There is a big difference between believing something is okay, doing it, and justifying your actions with a rationalization afterward; and a true belief that the action was perfectly acceptable. For instance, officers may take a bribe, and then justify it to themselves with the explanation that they aren't paid enough or they needed the money or no one was injured. But these are rationalizations. This officer knows the bribe is wrong.

On the other hand, an officer who lies to cover up for a fellow officer may believe that he is doing the right thing. He may, in fact, rather be punished for perjury than turn on his fellow officer, at the same time he may be tormented because to do the right thing he must also lie, which he knows to be wrong. This is a true ethical dilemma. There are sometimes no easy answers and sometimes the answer will come at a great cost, but there are time-worn, proven ways to address ethical dilemmas.

Ethical Systems and Decisionmaking

Pollock (1998) discusses the major ethical systems, as well as some pragmatic steps one might take to resolve an ethical dilemma. An ethical system is a type of moral theory or set of principles that define right and wrong. For some, ethics is a matter of individual perception. Ethical relativists believe that ethics are more like opinions (i.e., the prettiest color is blue) than absolutes (it is wrong to steal). This would mean that everyone's opinion is just as good as anyone's. Of course the obvious argument against moral relativism is that we would have to agree that a child rapist who believes there is nothing wrong with using children for sexual pleasure has just as much legitimacy as the those who view such behavior as evil. Most people reject moral relativism when it comes to such forms of behavior, although they may be tolerant of other, less serious forms of behavior.

Ethical systems are either consequence-based or non-consequence-based. This means that the system looks to the end (or consequence) of the act to determine its goodness, while a non-consequentialist system looks to the inherent nature of the act itself to determine its goodness. For instance, if killing is wrong, it is wrong in all circumstances according to non-consequentialist systems, but can be a good if it results in a good end according to consequentialist systems.

Egoism is a consequentialist system. The egoist weighs every action in a way that considers the consequence—for herself. The act that results in the most utility for oneself is good, according to an egoist way of thinking. An "enlightened egoist" may consider the needs of others, but only for the long-term good for the egoist. Egoism has some supporters, but most philosophers reject the tenets of egoism as an unworkable way to define good, and an unworkable way to live. The weakness of this system is its inconsistency—how can all of us strive to maximize our own interests? We would be constantly in conflict if we all pursued only our own ends. Having said that, it is true that much of human behavior is probably motivated by egoistic thinking. Officers who testify against others may be doing so because they want the department to be a better place, or they believe it is their duty, but they may be testifying because they will avoid a prison sentence themselves by doing so. This isn't an ethical act, it is merely an egoistic one.

The most well-known consequentialist system is utilitarianism. Jeremy Bentham and John Stuart Mill developed the major precepts of this ethical system. What is good is that which benefits the greatest number. Each act and its alternative(s) have a certain utility. To determine the right thing to do, one simply weighs the total utility of every possible act for all involved. To illustrate: an officer is faced with an opportunity where a lie would mean that a search was legal. If she tells the truth, the evidence obtained will be thrown out. The utility of the lie is a criminal conviction—it would be good for the officer, good for the prosecutor, good for the victim, good for society, and bad for the criminal. This appears to weigh in favor of lying; however, "rule based utilitarianism" specifies that before weighing the utilities, one must figure out what would happen if that act was made a rule for all similar situations. In this case, every time an officer had to lie to save evidence, she should do so. Now weighing the utility of lying versus not lying, something else happens. In all likelihood, the officer's lies will eventually be exposed and, before long, the prosecutor will not trust the officer at all. If all officers lied, then no one would believe anything police officers said. That would lead to more acquittals than convictions for a net negative utility for all concerned (except the criminals). Many argue that this very situation is occurring in Los Angeles. The jury who acquitted O.J. Simpson of killing his wife simply did not believe the L.A.P.D. officers, and after the Ramparts scandal described above, juries may be even less likely to believe L.A.P.D. officers testimonies. It is important, when using a utilitarian ethical system, to weigh all possible future consequences of each act.

Two weaknesses of utilitarianism are that it assumes one can predict the future, and the other is that it ignores individual rights. In order to weigh utility accurately, one must know what the outcome will be of the act. Of course this is impossible. In the coerced confessions cases described earlier, the officers presumed they knew they were dealing with the real criminals and so coerced a confession to get a conviction. It may be that you would agree that the coercion to obtain a confession (physical, emotional, or mental) is justified because it results in greater utility for the victim and society than harm to the individual; however, in these cases, society and the victim gained nothing because they had the wrong person. Therefore it was a net disutility. The officers did not know that another person would ultimately confess because one can never know the future, which is a serious weakness of the "end justifies the means" reasoning.

The other weakness, of course, is that many would argue even if the confession was accurate, there are still rights against being mistreated, and the officer oversteps when using either physical or extreme mental coercion. Due process protects all individuals against the power of the state (not just criminals). There are constant pressures to curtail rights in the interest of safety. This is even more true after 9/11. Civil liberties may be sacrificed because of public fear, but some argue that liberties and individual rights are more important than safety. Utilitarianism, of course, as a consequence based system, would support acts that violate individual rights, if they led to increased public safety. Other ethical systems would never support such a trade.

The major non-consequentialist system is ethical formalism or duty-based ethics. Immanuel Kant, the architect of this system, believed that good was defined as doing one's duty, and that in order for an act to be a good act, it must conform to one's duty, not treat people as a means to an end, and satisfy the concept of universalism (that the actor would be happy with such an act being a universal law). This system would not support coerced confessions, nor any violation of the law because the police officer's duty is to enforce the law, not break it. Ethical formalism would support an officer who testified against other officers if his or her motivation was duty rather than self interest, and it would support an officer who gave tickets to other officers—because this is the duty of a police officer.

The weakness of this system is that its absolutist nature makes it extremely rigid and unbending when other factors may be important to consider. For instance, such an ethical system would support enforcing the law whenever there was a crime committed. It evaluates each act under the criteria above with no regard to the consequences of such acts, so if an officer did her duty and did so with good motives, it would still be a good act, even if it resulted in a negative outcome.

For instance, a strict interpretation of ethical formalism would dictate that an officer working undercover could never engage in any illegal acts, no matter how minor. While this is admirable, it may not be feasible. An undercover officer may have to watch drug sales, perhaps even engage in drug use, in order to keep his cover. The non-consequentialist would argue that there is no difference between illegal use of drugs when committed by an officer as when committed by a drug criminal, both are breaking the law. Under this view, if undercover work cannot be done without breaking the law, then one should not engage in it. Consequentialists, on the other hand, would argue, that minor crimes committed by or ignored by officers are acceptable if the end is to catch a more serious criminal. Of course, once one opens the door to these trade-offs, how does one determine which acts are more important than others. Should an undercover officer involved in a major drug operation allow an assault to occur? A burglary? A rape? A murder?

Of course, most individuals do not consciously apply these ethical systems in full measure every time they are faced with a dilemma or decision.

A number of different authors have provided more simple methods for evaluating ethical actions. When faced with a number of choices Close and Meier (1995) suggest the individual ask themselves the following:

1. Does the action violate another person's constitutional rights, including the right of due process?

2. Does the action involve treating another person only as a means to an end?

3. Is the action under consideration illegal?

4. Do you predict that your action will produce more bad than good for all persons affected?

5. Does the action violate department procedure or professional duty?

These questions seem to encompass aspects of both ethical formalism and utilitarianism.

As stated earlier, one of the best checks on anyone's behavior is whether or not the action is legal. If it is not, one must have a clear and persuasive argument for why violating the law conforms to some higher ethical principle. Almost all of the actions listed above as corruption violate some law or another. A second question one could ask is whether or not it would be embarrassing to have the act reported in the newspaper. If one has performed an unethical act, it is unlikely that this exposure would be pleasant or comfortable. Likewise, those who perform unethical actions seek always to hide or cover up their actions. The desire to cover up or hide one's act is a red flag and should be heeded. Finally, with any action, one should ask whether or not it is fair to everyone involved. Even police officers who arrest someone can do so fairly to all involved. It is fair to arrest when there is probable cause. It is fair to subdue in order to effect an arrest. But it is not fair to continue hitting a suspect handcuffed and cowed. The simple questions in Table 2 work when one does not have the time or inclination to apply ethical systems to a dilemma. Of course, it is first necessary to want to do the right thing.

Table 2

Is it legal?
Would you mind if it was on the front page of the newspaper?
Is it fair to all concerned?

Management's Role in Law Enforcement Ethics

Some departments have never had much of a problem with corruption and others have a long history of periodic scandals. What differentiates these departments? Is leadership important? Several authors have speculated that, in large measure, the relative "ethics" of an agency has everything to do with leadership. If the top managers in an organization are honest and ethical, it does not necessarily mean that they will be successful in rooting out corruption, but if an organization's leader is unethical and corrupt, then it seems that it would be inevitable that there will be corruption among the rank and file as well.

Prenzler and Ransley (2002) discuss corruption in police organizations across the world and provide an exhaustive list of organizational improvements that can minimize and/or reduce the extent of corruption among officers. They are listed in Table 3.

Table 3
Reducing Police Corruption

Internal affairs units
Independent civilian oversight agencies
Overt recording devices (video cameras in cars)
Covert high-technology surveillance
Targeted integrity testing
Randomized integrity testing
Drug and alcohol testing
Quality assurance test (customer service monitors)
Internal informants
Complaints profiling
Supervisor accountability
Integrity reviews
Mandatory reporting
Whistleblower protection
Compulsory rotation in corruption prone sections
Asset and financial reviews
Surveys of police
Surveys on public
Personnel diversification
Comprehensive ethics training
Inquisitorial methods (fact finding rather than due process emphasis)
Complaint resolution
Monitoring and regulation of police procedures (of informants)
Decriminalizing vice
Risk analysis (to see what areas are vulnerable to corruption)

Others have also presented their own lists. Carter (1999), for instance, mentions the following as being important in combatting corruption: leadership from the chief's office, management and supervision, supervisory training, organizational control and information management internal auditing of the use of informants, internal affairs, drug enforcement units having audit controls and turnover of staff, better evidence handling, early warning systems, training and discipline as methods of controlling corruption. Hunter (1999) discusses decertifying officers who have committed serious misconduct, community policing, college education, enhanced discipline, civilian review boards, and training.

These suggestions all relate to the individual and organizational explanations for corruption. In order to address corruption completely, however, each organization and the individuals within it must come to terms with the role law enforcement plays in society and address societal supports for unethical actions.

If law enforcement is to undertake purely a crime fighter role, and criminals are viewed as the enemy to be vanquished, then there will always be "noble cause" corruption because there will always be some officers who feel that the "end" of crime fighting will justify any "means." However, if law enforcement is given a more expansive role and embraces public service rather than purely crime fighting, then there will be less support for subverting the law to serve the end of crime control (Pollock, 1998).

Law Enforcement Ethics after 9/11

What does the future of law enforcement hold? One might argue that the challenge to law enforcement after the terror of 9/11 is to be not just "crime fighters," but "super crime-fighters." We know now that a public service role can have a large impact on crime reduction (Zhao, Scheider & Thurman, 2002); however, will such evidence be considered given public fear about terroristic acts? "Community policing" seems almost anachronistic when one considers the new image of "Homeland Security" and the reaches of the "Patriot Act."

The most recent discussions concerning the sacrifice of civil liberties in the interest of public safety make it clear that we are in a new age of utilitarian reasoning. All the basic arguments concerning utilitarianism and policing must be rewritten after the tragedy and terror of 9/11. The "end" of catching criminals may justify different "means" when the criminal is a terrorist. For instance, racial profiling, almost universally condemned when used for drug dealers, has become accepted again when used against Middle Eastern men who have some remote chance of being terrorists. Restrictions on wiretapping have been relaxed, we are using indefinite detentions without charges, and other civil rights are in danger because the "end" of safety is more important than ever before.

Are these sacrifices warranted? Does the end of safety justify the means of invasion of privacy, indefinite detentions, suspension of civil liberties, or coerced confessions? Let us examine these crime fighting methods in the same manner that we analyzed "testilying" before. Can supporters guarantee that these sacrifices will protect us against future terroristic acts? Remember, the weakness of utilitarianism was that one cannot predict the future. Is it possible, for instance, that holding an Iranian immigrant for six months and then deporting him for what appears to be no reason, might create a terrorist out of his son who was born in Topeka, Kansas? Methods/means that are justified by the "end" of safety, may, in the end, lead to more terrorism. The message that the end justifies any means may encourage those officers who are inclined to "noble cause" corruption and, as in the drug war, we will see the misuse of power for good "ends." Do we want this or is the most ironic consequence of terrorism that we become more like those who are our enemies?

Alderson (1998) writes of the dangers of using oppressive police tactics to suppress public dissidents and political unrest. Countries such as Great Britain have had a longer history of balancing police power and civil rights in such places as India and Ireland: "to stress security to unnecessary extremes at the price of fundamental freedoms plays into the hands of would be high police despots. Such despots are quick to exploit fear in order to secure unlimited power" (Alderson, 1998:23). It seems imperative at this juncture in history that all concerned be cognizant of the dangers of societal messages that the end is more important than the means. As many have said throughout history, one cannot trade liberty for security, for, in the end, we will lose both. An ethical use of law enforcement power is to recognize its potential to subvert the very essence of the source of its power—the public's right to be protected and served.

Chapter Review Questions

1. Define the term "ethics," and how it differs from morality and the law.

2. Discuss how "noble cause" corruption is seen as justifiable in some cases, but not in others.

3. In New York City, while the crime rate dropped complaints against police rose by 75 percent. In your opinion, how would a "broken windows" approach to crime lead to higher citizen complaints? Take into consideration the communities that are most prone to "broken window" offenses. Also consider the impact that a higher police presence may have on the citizens of that community.

4. How do exposure, discretion, and socialized deviance lead to police corruption?

5. In your own words, explain the theories presented for the "individual level" of police corruption.

6. How may formal and informal organizational subcultures encourage or deter police corruption?

7. In policing, do you feel that utilitarianism is a justifiable means to a positive end? Why or why not?

8. What do you think could be done in order to minimize/eliminate pressure on officers to deviate from the path of being a "good, law-abiding officer"?

9. ". . . A strict interpretation of ethical formalism would dictate that an officer working undercover could never engage in any illegal acts, no matter how minor . . . An undercover officer may have to watch drug sales, perhaps even engage in drug use, in order to keep his cover." How would instances like these not be considered an ethical transgression for the undercover officer?

10. Compare and contrast legal ethics before and after 9/11.

CHAPTER 10

Police Officers, Excessive Force, and Civil Liability

John L. Worrall

Introduction

Police officers increasingly are being sued for the use of excessive force, something which is supported by a large body of research. For example, Americans for Effective Law Enforcement (AELE), in an early civil liability study, found that from 1967 to 1971 the number of civil suits filed against the police increased by 124 percent (AELE, 1974). Expanding their survey to include later years, the AELE concluded that between 1967 and 1976 lawsuits increased by more than 500 percent (AELE, 1982). A similar study carried out by the International Association of Chiefs of Police (1976) at around the same time revealed that one in 34 police officers were sued. The AELE predicted that these figures would yield more than 26,000 lawsuits against the police annually (AELE, 1980).

A more contemporary study by Kappeler, Kappeler, and del Carmen (1993) focused on cases decided by the U.S. Federal District Courts between 1978 and 1990. Their research uncovered a significant increase from approximately 40 decisions in 1978 to well over 140 in 1990, results which are consistent with earlier assumptions about trends in civil lawsuits filed against law enforcement officials (e.g., Silver, 1996; Littlejohn, 1981; Meadows & Trostle, 1988; Stafford, 1986). The authors suggested that, "by inference, this research adds further support to the notion that there has been a substantial and sustained increase in the volume of civil liability cases brought against the police" (Kappeler et al., 1993).

Chiabi's (1996) study of Section 1983, and *Bivens* claims, is one of several recent inquiries into trends in civil lawsuits filed against the police. He examined Fourth Amendment (alleging unlawful searches and seizures) cases filed against the New York City Police Department from 1983-1987, and concluded that "the failure of other available remedies to protect the public from police violations . . . [and] the additional incentive of monetary damages in Section 1983 actions will continue to make [lawsuits] appealing to victims of police abuses in the future" (1996:101). More recently, a survey of municipal attorneys conducted by Worrall and Gutierrez (1999) revealed that lawsuits are not necessarily being filed more frequently, but that certain *types* of lawsuits are being filed with increased frequency.

In short, it appears that civil liability lawsuits against the police "go with the territory" in the law enforcement profession. They are often viewed in a negative light as they can take a serious financial toll on police organizations. However, civil liability trends over the years have resulted in some positive changes in both training and law enforcement practice. Regardless of which perspective the reader may subscribe to, civil liability is an important problem that cannot be ignored. This chapter begins by examining the benefits and costs of civil litigation, then continues by defining important terms, drawing distinctions between deadly force, nondeadly force, "indirect" force, and excessive force. Next, it provides an overview of the means by which law enforcement officials can be held civilly liable for excessive force. Finally, it critically examines the leading court decisions surrounding police civil liability for excessive force.

The Benefits of Civil Litigation

Administrators can view civil liability lawsuits as "a barometer of police performance" (Wagner & Decker, 1997:310). Insofar as most police officers act without constant supervision, lawsuits can serve as an indicator to management regarding how well police officers are behaving on the street. In support of this contention, the United States Commission on Civil Rights has stated that lawsuits can act as "important indicators of public perception of the agency" (1981:50). Police departments can draw on the information generated from lawsuits—especially when the police are in the wrong—to improve their performance, enhance their public image, and strengthen police-community relations.

Civil lawsuits can also serve as something of a quality-of-service yardstick against which to measure police officers' performance. Many important court cases, resulting from a lawsuit being filed against a police officer, supervisor, or agency, have fostered improvements in police training and more responsible law enforcement in general, especially in the area of use of force (Kappeler, 2001). To this end, an important Supreme Court decision was *Tennessee v. Garner* (1985), which placed serious restrictions on the ability of the police to use deadly force.

Changes in public organizations are often akin to "bending granite" (Guyot, 1979); few civil servants enjoy parting with the comforts of tradition. However, lawsuits can give police agencies a strong incentive to change. Alpert and Dunham (1996:244) have stated that "suits against the police that prove inadequate administrative controls, deficient policies, or customs and practices that are improper or illegal, can force the department to correct its specific deficiencies and review all policies, practices, and customs." While civil lawsuits may be undesirable, they serve an important function, which allows police agencies to grow and evolve to meet the demands placed on them by a changing public.

The Costs of Civil Litigation

Civil liability also can have many negative consequences. A study of 101 police cadets, for example, found that nine percent of the officers interviewed felt their fears of civil litigation had reached the point of being irrational or excessive (Scogin & Brodsky, 1991). Later discussions with these cadets led the researchers to conclude that "the percentage of litigaphobic candidates is considerably higher than the nine percent self-identified figure" (Scogin & Brodsky, 1991:44). A fairly recent replication confirmed the same results. Police cadets in another state academy worried excessively about the threat of suit (Kappeler, 1996), though fears of suit do not necessarily pervade the ranks of new officer trainees.

According to Reynolds (1988:7), the ". . . *fear* of potential liability permeates nearly all police department policy and procedure and, in both obvious and subtle ways, unnecessarily restricts and impedes the effectiveness of legitimate law enforcement procedures." The threat of citizens' negative reactions to police encounters can cause officers to withdraw and otherwise take measures to protect themselves from grievances filed by the public. According to another police commander, "any perfectly law-abiding police officer can be sued, perhaps maliciously by just about anybody at just about any time. [It's] an unfortunate and unjust side effect of pinning on the badge" (Garner, 1991:34). Civil litigation, in other words, can strike at police officers' confidence and willingness to act in pressing situations. "Even worse, law enforcement officers who have an unrealistic or exaggerated fear of personal liability may become overly timid or indecisive and fail to arrest or search to the detriment of the public's interest in effective and aggressive law enforcement" (Schofield, 1990:26-27).

Notwithstanding its effects on officers themselves, civil liability can take a financial toll on cities and counties. Researchers have reported an increase in both the size and number of awards given to plaintiffs who sue the police (e.g., Fabrizio, 1990; Rudovsky, 1992). For example, del Carmen (1987) estimated that the cost of the average jury award of liability against the typical municipality is about $2 million. In 1982, for example, there were more than 250 cases where juries awarded at least $1 million to plaintiffs (National League of Cities, 1985). Bates, Cutler, and Clink (1981) took this figure and speculated that if current estimates of jury award figures were applied to the existing 39,000 local governments, there could be as much as $780 billion in pending litigation against police agencies. More recent studies, however, have revealed that the average reported award is $118,698 (Kappeler et al., 1993).

Litigation is costly not just because of settlements or jury awards, but also because of potential jumps in liability insurance premiums. In 1975, for example, before the decision in *Monell v. Department of Social Services* (1978) insurance premiums for Dade County, Florida increased from $60,000 to $150,000 in the space of one year (these figures would obviously be higher in today's dollars). *Monell* exposed municipalities—not just police officers and supervisors—to litigation, and, consequently, many municipal governments are facing an "insurance crisis" (Hagerty, 1976). Some commentators have noted:

> Quite clearly, absent insurance, a substantial judgment or series of judgments could monetarily cripple a municipality and force it to forgo or reduce services in vital areas. Yet insurance is unavailable to some municipalities and for many others it has become prohibitively expensive. Due to the expanding liability of local governments and concomitant disappearing [legal] defenses, insurers are facing greater underwriting costs and will not significantly lower municipal premiums (Vitullo & Peters, 1981:335).

All told, police civil liability for the use of excessive force (not to mention other varieties of misconduct) is a pressing issue that cannot be ignored. It appears, in fact, that the costs may outweigh the benefits. Lawsuits are a fearsome prospect to many police officers and potentially devastating to local government finances. And there is no research suggesting that civil litigation against the police is on the decline or likely to turn in that direction any time soon.

Important Definitions

The focus of this chapter is on civil liability for excessive force. Excessive force can be defined as physical force (e.g., beating, shoving, touching, or neglect) beyond what is necessary and reasonable to achieve a law enforcement objective. Excessive force need not result in death or serious injury. It can assume a more subtle form, such as by way of a non-injurious push or shove. Only when force is excessive can a police officer be held civilly liable for it. Force that is not excessive is a common and necessary component of the law enforcement profession. As Bittner (1970:40) has observed:

> Whatever the substance of the task at hand, whether it involves protection against an undesired imposition, caring for those who cannot care for themselves, attempting to solve a crime, helping

to save a life, abating a nuisance, or settling an explosive dispute, police intervention means above all making use of the capacity and authority to overpower resistance to an attempted solution in the native habitat of the problem. There can be no doubt that this feature of police work is uppermost in the minds of people who solicit police aid or direct the attention of the police to problems, that persons against whom the police proceed have this feature in mind and conduct themselves accordingly, and that every conceivable police intervention projects the message that force may be, and may have to be, used to achieve a desired objective.

Three varieties of force that go with the law enforcement profession can be identified. The first, and most uncommon, is deadly force. Black (1990:398) has defined deadly force as "force likely or intended to cause death or great bodily harm." A number of weapons and devices besides firearms can be used to apply deadly force. For example, repeated beatings with a police baton could turn deadly.

Nondeadly force is the second type of force. It is the opposite of deadly force, that which is unlikely and not intended to cause death or serious bodily injury. Nondeadly force is almost always preferable and, as a result, is used more frequently by the police. Stun guns, pepper mace, and numerous other devices can be used to apprehend suspects when deadly force would otherwise be considered unreasonable.

Deadly and nondeadly force are similar insofar as both require some degree of physical force to be applied to a suspect. That is, the police actually do something to the suspect which is intended to secure his or her compliance. A third variety of force identified by Kappeler (2001:78) is called "indirect" force. In his words:

> Most excessive force cases involve the direct application of force by a police officer against a citizen or suspect. In these cases a police officer intentionally uses force to control, detain, or seize a suspect. The classic case of excessive force is one in which a police officer uses direct application of force, most often by way of a firearm, to seize a citizen. There are, however, circumstances where police officers may indirectly use force to bring about a seizure. Brandishing weapons . . . or keeping a suspect in a frisk position for an extended period of time are behaviors that can place officers at a risk of liability for excessive use of force.

Indirect force can occur even when a suspect is never physically handled by the police or injured, say, from a gunshot. For example, if a person is hog-tied and placed in the back of a patrol car and later dies (frequently called positional asphyxiation by the courts), the death can be said to have resulted from indirect force. We will return to civil liability for deadly, nondeadly, and indirect force later. Let us now briefly review the avenues for bringing civil lawsuits against the police.

Avenues for Suit

There are two common avenues for civil litigation against law enforcement officials. The first of these avenues is known as a Section 1983 claim. It stems from 42 U.S.C. Section 1983. Section 1983 lawsuits are most often filed in the federal courts. The second avenue for suit is a state tort claim. Tort law covers personal injury, and can be used by plaintiffs to sue the police. Each avenue for suit is examined more fully in the following subsections.

Section 1983

42 U.S.C. Section 1983 reads:

> Every person who, under color of any statute, ordinance, regulation, custom, or usage, or any State or Territory or the District of Columbia, subjects, or causes to be subjected, any citizen of the United States or any other person within the jurisdiction thereof to the deprivation of any rights, privileges, or immunities secured by the Constitution and laws, shall be liable to the party injured in an action at law, suit in equity, or other proper proceeding for redress . . .

This statute can be interpreted to mean that the police will be held liable if (1) they violate a federal right, most often a constitutional right, and (2) they act under color of state law while doing so. A number of constitutional claims can be made, but most Section 1983 suits stem from the Fourth (e.g., *Graham v. Connor*, 1989; *Jenkins v. Averett*, 1970; *Pierson v. Ray*, 1967), Eighth (e.g., *Hudson v. McMillian*, 1992), and Fourteenth Amendments (e.g., *Fargo v. San Juan Bautista*, 1988; *Nishiyama v. Dickson County*, 1987) to the Constitution (del Carmen & Smith, 1997:228).

There is also some confusion surrounding the definition of "color of law." Two researchers have attempted to clarify the issue by suggesting that officers act under color of law when they "identify themselves as law enforcement agents, perform duties of a criminal investigation, file official police documents, attempt or make an arrest, invoke their police powers outside their lawful jurisdiction, settle a personal vendetta with police power, display or use police weapons or equipment, act pursuant to a state statute or city ordinance," and so on (Vaughn & Coomes, 1995:409).

Liability under Section 1983 can be far-reaching. At the individual-level, police officers can be held liable for a variety instances of constitutional misconduct. To the benefit of defendant officers, however, the courts have begun to require that constitutional violations alleged under Section 1983 be committed with a certain level of culpability. That is, plaintiffs generally have to prove that the defendant officer(s) intended for the violation to occur. The level of culpability required for a constitutional violation varies depending on the type of unconstitutional conduct alleged by the plaintiff (see Worrall, 2001). The standards are "objective reasonableness" for Fourth Amendment search and seizure claims (*Tennessee v. Garner*, 1985), "deliberate indifference" for Eighth Amendment conditions of confinement claims (e.g., *Estelle v. Gamble*, 1976), "malicious and sadistic" conduct for Eighth Amendment excessive force claims (*Hudson v. McMillian*, 1992), behavior that "shocks the conscience" for Fourteenth Amendment substantive due process claims (*Rochin v. California*, 1952), and "deliberate indifference" for Fourteenth Amendment procedural due process claims (*Wood v. Ostrander*, 1989). Other culpability standards have been identified, but, again, their nature depends on the type of constitutional violation alleged.

Defendant police officers also benefit from qualified immunity, which shields them from liability if they acted in an objectively reasonable fashion (*Pierson v. Ray*, 1967; *Anderson v. Creighton*, 1987). A defendant police officer is said to have acted in an objectively reasonable fashion if he or she does not violate clearly established rights of which a reasonable person would have known (*Harlow v. Fitzgerald*, 1982). In some Section 1983 cases, defendants have benefited from qualified immunity even for violating clearly established constitutional rights, provided that the defendant's mistaken belief is objectively reasonable (see *Anderson v. Creighton*, 1987; *Malley v. Briggs*, 1988).

Municipalities, counties, and police supervisors can also be sued under Section 1983. In the past, the common practice was to name only police officers in a lawsuit. Nowadays, however, the tendency has been for plaintiffs to name all parties that could have anything to do with the alleged misconduct. This legal strategy is based on the "deep pockets" theory; the agency—as opposed to an individual officer—is most likely to have more money to pay in a settlement or court disposition (del Carmen & Smith, 1997).

For a municipality or county to be held liable, it must not only be shown that a violation of the plaintiff's rights occurred while officers were acting under color of law, but also that a policy or custom (of the agency or municipality) caused the injuries to the plaintiff. In *Monell v. Department of Social Services* (1978) the court held that agencies may be held liable if they "implement or execute a policy statement, ordinance, regulation, or a decision officially adopted and promulgated by municipal officers . . . or a custom." The courts have spent considerable energies deciding what constitutes policy or custom and who can be considered a policymaker (e.g., *Jett v. Dallas Independent School District*, 1989; *Pembauer v. City of Cincinnati*, 1986).

Municipalities and counties also can be held liable under Section 1983 for failure to train. In *City of Canton v. Harris* (1989) the Supreme Court held that failure to train can be the basis of liability if the failure amounts to deliberate indifference. "Deliberate indifference" was later clarified to include training standards that are "arbitrary, "conscience shocking," or "grossly negligent" (*Baker v. Putnal*, 1996). Agency or municipal liability can be imposed more readily than individual liability because cities and their law enforcement agencies cannot assert the "good-faith" defense and thus have no qualified immunity (*Owen v. City of Independence*, 1980).

Section 1983 supervisory liability can be imposed in circumstances similar to municipal and county liability. As with subordinates, supervisors can also be sued in their individual or official capacities (and they can also assert qualified immunity). Typically, supervisors in public agencies (with the possible exception of sheriffs) cannot be held liable for what their subordinates do. Courts have held that the common law doctrine of *respondeat superior* (i.e., let the "master" answer) does not apply because supervisors in public agencies are not so much "masters" of their subordinates as they are employees who serve another master, the government (e.g., *James v. Smith*, 1986). Nevertheless, supervisors can be held liable if they: (1) authorized the act in question; (2) participated in the act; (3) directed the act; (4) ratified the act; (5) were present at the time the act occurred; and/or (6) created the policy or custom which led to the act. According to del Carmen and Smith (1997:233), "supervisors may be liable in Section 1983 cases only if there is an 'affirmative link' between the plaintiff's injury and the action or inaction of the supervisor."

The only *Supreme Court* case concerning supervisory liability in the Section 1983 context was *Rizzo v. Goode* (1976). In *Rizzo*, plaintiffs sued the Mayor of Philadelphia, the city's Managing Director, the Police Commissioner, and two other police department supervisors, and alleged a "pervasive pattern of illegal and unconstitutional mistreatment by police officers . . . directed against minority citizens in particular and against all Philadelphia residents in general" (*Rizzo v. Goode*, 1976:366-367). The plaintiffs further charged supervisors with "conduct ranging from express authorization or encouragement of this mistreatment to failure to act in a manner so as to assure that it would not recur in the future" (*Rizzo v. Goode*, 1976: 367). The lower federal courts found in favor of the plaintiffs, but the Supreme Court stated, disapprovingly, that "there was no *affirmative link* between the occurrence of the various incidents of police misconduct and the adoption of any plan or policy by [the supervisors]—express or otherwise—showing their authorization or approval of such misconduct" (*Rizzo v. Goode*, 1976: 371, emphasis added).

State Tort Law

Not all allegations of police misconduct involve deprivations of constitutional rights. Lawsuits based on state tort law are reserved for those plaintiffs not wishing to seek recovery under the provisions of Section 1983. State tort claims are an important avenue of redress because negligent acts by the police and/or misconduct that result in minor injuries are usually not serious enough to invoke a Section 1983 claim (*Cathey v. Guenther*, 1995). Indeed, the Supreme Court has stated that "not every push or shove" is a constitutional violation (*Graham v. Connor*, 1989), so state tort actions are often reserved for matters not reaching the level of constitutional significance.

There are at least three levels of state tort claims. First, *strict liability* torts include offenses that are particularly harmful to the public will. Strict liability is usually defined in terms of *crimes*, where the elements of *mens rea* and foreseeability are irrelevant. Strict liability rarely applies to police officers; published cases imposing strict liability on law enforcement officials are all but nonexistent.

Intentional torts are a second and more readily observable conduct in policing under state law. According to Kappeler (2001:20), "intentional torts are usually those behaviors that are substantially certain to cause injury or damage where the officer knowingly engaged in the behavior." To be liable for an intentional tort, an officer need not *intend* to harm; it need only be shown that the officer intended to engage in the behavior that *led* to the harm. Common forms of intentional torts applicable to policing include wrongful death, assault and battery, false arrest, and false imprisonment.

A third—and more far reaching—variety of tort claim is a tort based on *negligence*. In a negligence tort the mental state of the defendant officer is not at issue. Plaintiffs need only demonstrate the presence of four elements to succeed with a negligence claim: (1) a legal duty between the officer and the plaintiff; (2) a breach of that duty; (3) proximate causation between the officer's actions and the alleged harm; and, (4) actual damage or injury (*Estate v. Willis* 1995). Of course, there is some controversy surrounding precisely what these criteria mean. Many case decisions have revolved around the ambiguous notion of "legal duty," for example.

The issue of state tort negligence is complex and has a rich history which cannot be reviewed in depth here (see Kappeler & Vaughn, 1989). Space limitations merely allow for an overview of state tort negligence. At the individual-level there are several common forms of police negligence. The most common forms of negligence addressed in the literature include, but are not limited to, negligent operation of emergency vehicles (see Kappeler & del Carmen, 1990b), negligent failure to protect (see Vaughn 1994; Carrington 1989), negligent failure to arrest (see Kappeler & del Carmen, 1990a), and negligent failure to render assistance (Kappeler, 2001).

A Critical Examination of Existing Case Law

Because plaintiffs can file excessive force lawsuits in both federal and state courts, case law surrounding excessive force is logically divided into two categories: (1) Section 1983 case law and (2) state tort case law. . Federal and state courts rely on different standards for determining whether excessive force was used. Indeed, at the state level, standards can vary from one jurisdiction to the next. In the interest of consistency then, it is worth focusing carefully on federal standards, as most civil liability lawsuits alleging excessive force are filed pursuant to 42 U.S.C. Section 1983 (see Kappeler, 2002:68).

One of the requirements for making a claim under Section 1983 is that a constitutional rights violation take place. Unfortunately, it is not always clear what constitutes a federal constitutional rights violation. Throughout the years the federal courts—and the Supreme Court—have relied on differing standards. For example, many courts once relied on the Due Process clause of the Fourteenth Amendment for deciding when a constitutional rights violation takes place (e.g., *Gumz v. Morrissett*, 1985; *Johnson v. Glick*, 1973). Other courts relied on the Fourth Amendment's proscription against unreasonable searches and seizures, and still other courts held that the Eighth Amendment's cruel and unusual punishment standard was the appropriate constitutional provision. This confusion led to a large body of case law that failed to provide the law enforcement community with a clear message about the definition of excessive force. Prior to the Supreme Court's landmark decision in *Tennessee v. Garner* (1985), one researcher commented on the confusion in the courts:

> Perhaps because of the seeming analogy between deaths caused by police shootings of fleeing felons and deaths effected by the system by executions after trial, plaintiff's attorneys and scholars have frequently argued that fleeing felon police shootings are punishment and should be subject to Eighth Amendment protections. There are faults in this analogy, however, because execution is a court-ordered final disposition of an offender who has been given all the benefits of due process, and who has been found guilty beyond a reasonable doubt of a capital offense. Shootings to apprehend felony suspects, by contrast, occur earlier in the process, and are a last resort means of seizing suspected offenders. Thus, they are clearly subject to Fourth Amendment restrictions (Fyfe, 1983:528).

In addition to confusion over what constitutional amendment was necessary to judge police officers' use of force, the courts were also divided over what actual *amount* of force was necessary for a police officer's actions to rise to the level of a constitutional rights violations. For example, several courts have held that plaintiffs must suffer some form of meaningful physical injury to succeed with an excessive force lawsuit (e.g., *Hinton v. City of Elwood, Kansas* 1993; *Palmer v. Williamson*, 1989). Still other courts have decided that the acts of shoving, pushing, and restraining suspects do not rise to a constitutional level (e.g., *Brown v. Noe*, 1989; *Eberle v. City of Anaheim*, 1990). In the words of one such court, "not every push or shove, even if it later seems unnecessary in the peace of a judge's chambers, subjects defendants to Section 1983 liability for excessive force" (*Trout v. Frega*, 1996:121).

Still, however, some courts have held that relatively minor methods of using force, such as twisting a suspect's arm, can lead to civil liability (e.g., *Brown v. Glossip*, 1989; *Browning v. Snead*, 1995). As the Fourth Circuit once observed, "The suggestion that . . . constitutional rights are transgressed only if he suffers [serious] physical injury demonstrates a fundamental misconception . . . Police can violate a suspect's constitutional rights . . . without leaving [a visible sign of any beating] (*Riley v. Dorton*, 1996:117). Either way, if a police officer's decision to use force is inappropriate, and the resulting actions can be considered excessive, plaintiffs can always proceed with a state tort claim if the conduct in question does not violate any federally protected rights.

What, then, are the appropriate standards governing the use of excessive force by the police? At least two important Supreme Court decisions have finally answered this question as well as minimized some of the confusion of the past. In particular, the Supreme Court's decisions in *Tennessee v. Garner* (1985) and *Graham v. Connor* (1989) set the standards for deadly and nondeadly force, respectively. Indirect excessive force has also been considered by the Supreme Court, more than once in fact. The following subsections consider the relevant federal standards in each of these categories.

Deadly Force

It can scarcely be disputed that *Tennessee v. Garner* (1985) is the most important excessive force case ever decided by the U.S. Supreme Court. Given its importance, the facts are worth considering briefly. In that case, a Memphis police officer shot and killed an unarmed fifteen-year-old boy who was fleeing the scene of a residential burglary. The officer called to Garner to stop, but he did not. When Garner was about to climb a fence, the officer shot him in the back of the head, fatally wounding him. Garner's surviving family members filed a Section 1983 lawsuit, claiming the force used was excessive. The Supreme Court agreed.

The Court ruled that deadly force may be used when two criteria are present: (1) it is necessary to prevent the suspect's escape and (2) the officer has probable cause to believe the suspect poses a serious threat of death or serious physical injury to other people or police officers. One would think that the Supreme Court would be unanimous in a decision such as this, but three justices dissented, noting that the statute struck down by the majority "assist[s] the police in apprehending suspected perpetrators of serious crimes and provide[s] notice that a lawful police order to stop and submit to arrest may not be ignored with impunity" (*Tennessee v. Garner* (1985:28).

Most court decisions following *Garner* have focused on the second criterion more so than the first. In other words, more attention has been given to deciding what, if any, threat is posed by a fleeing felon, rather than whether force is necessary in order to prevent the suspect's escape. According to Kappeler (2001:72), the case law surrounding the "threat of death or serious physical injury" standard has taken two considerations into account: (1) the degree to which the suspect's escape would pose an "immediate and serious danger" and (2) the suspect's past dangerousness.

Immediate and Serious Danger. The level of dangerousness posed by the suspect as well as the immediacy of the threat must both be considered in determining whether deadly force is appropriate. According to Kappeler (2001:72), "[a] dangerous suspect is, generally, an armed suspect who can inflict serious physical harm." Suspects who are armed with a deadly weapon, be it a gun, knife, or other device, can safely be considered dangerous (e.g., *Butler v. City of Detroit*, 1985; *Nelson v. County of Wright*, 1998). For the suspect to be considered dangerous, the weapon he or she brandishes must be capable of inflicting death or serious bodily harm. Fingernail clippers, for example, cannot be considered a deadly weapon (*Zuchel v. Spinarney*, 1989).

Just because a suspect is armed with a deadly weapon does not permit the use of deadly force by police. The danger posed by the suspect must be immediate. For example, if the suspect is armed with a gun, the gun must be pointed at a police officer or some other individual for deadly force to be appropriate. As one court noted with regard to this point, the threat posed by the suspect could not be considered immediate because "there appear[ed] to be some doubt as to whether the decedent's hand was raised in a shooting position" (*Hicks v. Woodruff*, 1999). In another case, a district court concluded that the police used deadly force in an unconstitutional fashion. It stated that:

> . . . Hegarty repeatedly asked the officers to leave, but she neither threatened them nor did she fire any shots while the officers were present. In fact, the officers decided to enter Hegarty's home forcibly only after it appeared that she had put down her rifle. Hegarty did not threaten injury to herself at any time, nor were there other individuals in danger (*Hegarty v. Somerset County*, 1994:257).

Past Dangerousness. A threat of injury or serious physical injury can also be posed by a suspect's past dangerousness, that is, based on the nature of the crime he or she committed. Suspects who have committed murder, armed robbery, and similar offenses can be stopped via deadly force on occasion (e.g., *Ford v. Childress*, 1986; *Ryder v. City of Topeka*, 1987). Less serious offenses such as burglary or motor vehicle theft, however, do not grant the police authority to use deadly force (*Kibbe v. Springfield*, 1985; *Tennessee v. Garner*, 1985).

It needs to be emphasized that only a handful of courts have permitted deadly force based solely on past dangerousness. Further, the Supreme Court has yet to sanction such action. And at least one circuit court of appeals has held that the use of deadly force to apprehend a suspect charged with a serious crime is unconstitutional (*Hemphill v. Schott*, 1998). For example, if a suspect committed robbery but was then accosted by the police and, pursuant to their orders, raised his hands, he could not then be shot. Deadly force in such an instance would be unreasonable.

Another important point with regard to past dangerousness is that the serious crime committed by the suspect should be in close temporal proximity to the use of deadly force. If, for instance, the police use deadly force based solely on the fact that a suspect committed homicide several days, weeks, or months ago, his/her actions may be considered unconstitutional. This is especially true if other methods besides the use of deadly force could be used to apprehend the suspect (e.g., *Wright v. Whiddon*, 1990).

Nondeadly Force

Four years after *Garner*, the Supreme Court decided the landmark case of *Graham v. Connor* (490 U.S. 386 [1989]), which set the standard for *nondeadly* force. The Court emphatically declared that all claims involving allegations of excessive force against police officers must be analyzed under the Fourth Amendment's reasonableness requirement:

> . . . all claims that law enforcement officers have used excessive force—deadly or not—in the course of an arrest, investigatory stop, or other "seizure" of a free citizen should be analyzed under the Fourth Amendment and its "reasonableness" standard.

Further, the Court adopted an "objective reasonableness" test to decide when excessive force is used. This requires focusing on what a *reasonable* police officer would do "without regard to [the officer's] underlying intent or motivation."

In helping to decide what a reasonable police officer would do, the Court looked to three factors: (1) the severity of the crime; (2) whether the suspect poses a threat; and (3) whether the suspect is resisting and/or attempting to flee the scene. Courts must, in focusing on these three factors, allow ". . . for the fact that police officers are often forced to make split-second judgments—about the amount of force that is necessary in a particular situation" (1989:386). Generally, then, if the crime in question is a serious one, the suspect is dangerous and resists arrest, the suspect will have difficulty succeeding with an excessive force claim.

Indirect Force

At least two Supreme Court cases appear to address the issue of liability for indirect excessive force. In *Brower v. County of Inyo* (1989), Brower stole a car and eluded the police in a high-speed chase which took place over a 20-mile stretch. The police parked an 18-wheeler truck and trailer across the both lanes of the highway on which Brower was traveling, blocking his path. They also pointed the headlights of their police cars in Brower's direction, which was intended to blind him. Brower crashed into the roadblock and was killed. Brower's family and estate brought a Section 1983 civil lawsuit against the police, alleging that the roadblock violated Brower's Fourth Amendment right to be free from unreasonable seizures. The Court did not decide directly on the constitutionality of the indirect force used in this case, but it did make the following observation:

> Brower's independent decision to continue the chase can no more eliminate respondents' responsibility for the termination of his movement effected by the roadblock than Garner's independent decision to flee eliminated the Memphis police officer's responsibility for the termination of his movement effected by the bullet.

In another case, *County of Sacramento v. Lewis* (1998), a police officer observed a motorcycle approaching at high speed. The officer turned on his lights, yelled for the motorcycle to stop, and unsuccessfully attempted to block the motorcycle by moving his cruiser close to that of a county sheriff's deputy. The deputy switched on his lights and siren and began chasing the motorcycle. During the chase, the motorcycle tipped over. The deputy was unable to bring his cruiser to a halt before hitting and killing the motorcycle's passenger. Representatives of the passenger's estate brought a Section 1983 action, alleging a substantive due process violation under the Fourteenth Amendment to the U.S. Constitution. The Supreme Court did not view the indirect force applied in this case as excessive. It held that for the police to be liable in such instances, their conduct must "shock the conscience." In the Court's words:

> Respondents' allegations are insufficient to state a substantive due process violation. Protection against governmental arbitrariness is the core of due process . . ., including substantive due process . . ., but only the most egregious executive action can be said to be 'arbitrary' in the constitutional sense . . .; the cognizable level of executive abuse of power is that which shocks the conscience . . . In the circumstances of a high-speed chase aimed at apprehending a suspected offender, where unforeseen circumstances demand an instant judgment on the part of an officer who feels the pulls of competing obligations, only a purpose to cause harm

unrelated to the legitimate object of arrest will satisfy the shocks-the conscience test. Such chases with no intent to harm suspects physically or to worsen their legal plight do not give rise to substantive due process liability.

Conclusion

Has case law promoted clarity? This question cannot be answered easily. On the one hand, it appears that most police departments around the country adopted deadly and nondeadly force policies well before the Supreme Court decided *Garner* and *Graham* (e.g., Blumberg, 2001; Fyfe, 1988). This suggests that police departments adopted their own views on what is considered excessive force. In addition, many agency policies are far more restrictive with regard to the use of, say, deadly force than the *Garner* decision is.

On the other hand, even though police departments may have adopted force policies independently of the Supreme Court's leading decisions on the subject, it cannot be said that the case law is totally clear. In fact, when Fourth Amendment claims of excessive force are raised, the courts can quickly become confused. This is because while Fourth Amendment reasonableness is judged from an objective standard, so is qualified immunity. That is, to determine whether the Fourth Amendment has been violated by an officer's decision to use force, the court must consider what a reasonable police officer would have done under the circumstances. A similar test, however, is used for determining whether the officer should be granted qualified immunity.

If the case law in a particular area is not entirely clear, an officer may be immune from suit even though he or she acted in a constitutionally unreasonable fashion. This can lead to the paradoxical result of "reasonably unreasonable" conduct. According to Worrall (2001):

> A finding of reasonably unreasonable conduct can be reached because the test for determining whether a Fourth Amendment violation occurs is, like the test for determining qualified immunity, one of objective reasonableness. In other words, when focusing on Fourth Amendment conduct, a court can rule that an officer's actions were in violation of the Fourth Amendment (that they were not objectively reasonable), but that qualified immunity should attach nevertheless because the law in the area was not clearly established (that the actions *were* objectively reasonable).

The only case where the Supreme Court has directly addressed the paradox of reasonably unreasonable conduct was *Anderson v. Creighton* (1987). In that case an FBI agent conducted a forcible, warrantless search of a home on the mistaken belief that a bank robbery suspect might be found inside. The homeowners filed suit against the agent under Section 1983, claiming that the search was unreasonable. The *Anderson* Court rejected the plaintiff's argument that "it is not possible . . . to say that one 'reasonably' acted unreasonably," and that "it is inappropriate to give officials alleged to have violated the Fourth Amendment—and thus necessarily to have unreasonably searched or seized—the protection of qualified immunity intended only to protect reasonable official action" (*Anderson v. Creighton* (1987:643).

No other Supreme Court cases, however, have directly addressed the paradox of reasonably unreasonable conduct. Recently, in *Wilson v. Layne* (1999), the court considered "whether a reasonable officer could have believed bringing members of the media into a home during the execution of an arrest warrant was lawful, in light of clearly established law and the information the officers possessed" (*Wilson v. Layne*, 1999:8). It concluded that while this activity constituted a Fourth Amendment violation, "it was not unreasonable for a police officer to have believed that bringing the media observers along during the execution of an arrest warrant (even in a home) was lawful" (*Wilson v. Layne*, 1999:8). In effect, the Court decided that the defendants in *Wilson* acted in a reasonably unreasonable fashion, but without commenting on its seemingly paradoxical ruling.

To some observers the paradox of reasonably unreasonable conduct is not a source of confusion, but a review of federal opinions concerning the nexus between qualified immunity and Fourth Amendment excessive force suggests otherwise. It would seem, therefore, that as far as Section 1983 is concerned, there is not a great deal of clarity in existing case law. The *Garner* and *Graham* decisions set forth fairly clear standards as to when deadly and nondeadly force is appropriate, but as soon as qualified immunity enters the fray, a decision can be returned in favor of the police even if excessive force was used. The law enforcement community would probably benefit from some clearer standards in the future.

Chapter Review Questions

1. The author of this chapter delineates a number of benefits to civil litigation directed toward a police officer, supervisor, or an agency itself. What other benefits might come from civil litigation?

2. The author of this chapter suggests that the threat of civil lawsuits against police officers may, in fact, alter their behavior on the streets. Provide two examples of how police officer behavior can change as a result of the threat of a civil lawsuit.

3. Define and discuss the differences among deadly, nondeadly, and indirect force.

4. What is Section 1983? Define its scope with regard to individuals and municipalities/counties. How have the courts decided levels of culpability for alleged constitutional violations under Section 1983?

5. The United States Supreme Court case of *Anderson v. Creighton* (483 U.S. 635, 1987) discusses the issue of "objective reasonableness" for defendant police officers. After reading this case, what does "objective reasonableness" mean in the context of qualified immunity under Section 1983?

6. Discuss the similarities and difference among strict liability torts, intentional torts, and torts based on negligence.

7. Discuss the U.S. Supreme Court decisions of *Tennessee v. Garner* (1985) and *Graham v. Connor* (1989). What was the decision in each case?

8. What does "reasonably unreasonable" conduct refer to? How did the Court in *Anderson v. Creighton* address this issue?

Conclusion

Andrew Giacomazzi

Half Police, Half Human

As you now undoubtedly have experienced, this volume has provided the reader with quite a bit to think about when it comes to policing in the United States and beyond. Our goal was to provide a mix of very contemporary controversies in policing—including post-September 11, 2001 concerns, with others that have surfaced over the course of American policing's various reforms throughout the past 100 years. If we have provided you with many questions—many more than answers—I believe we, and especially our esteemed contributors, can be credited for a job well done!

Considerable progress has been made in American policing since the great institution-building phase in the mid-1800s. Improved standards for the recruitment and selection of police officers, as well as their corresponding training have resulted in largely professional police officers who are asked to do what amounts to an impossible job. And while improvements in technology and transportation have facilitated both reactive and proactive police practices, we still expect a considerable amount from line-level police officers, whose human qualities are sometimes masked once their uniform, badge and gun are worn. For example, these days we ask police officers to efficiently and effectively respond to our calls of reported crimes; we ask them to settle disputes with our neighbors who are playing loud music at night; we ask them to care for our kids at school; we ask them to be partners in the problem-solving process and attend requisite neighborhood association meetings; and we ask them to be efficient crime fighters, so long as it is not we who are doing wrong—and to do all of this and more for a little bit of money!

As Carl Klockars once noted, the police are institutions and individuals, and they carry out a varied police mandate on a daily basis—most often very well. It is at both levels—but especially the individual level—that allow us to scrutinize police decisionmaking. Policing, therefore, is a human enterprise. Sure there are rules and procedures about proper policing, books and training on the nuts and bolts of law enforcement, but when it comes right down to it, we often expect officers in a highly stressful profession to be perfect—in a way, to be super human.

Several months ago, I was struck by a question my 7-year-old daughter Sydney made to me at the dinner table. Out of the blue, she asked, "Dad, you're half police, half human, right?" While I chuckled at her question at the time, and told her, "I've never been 'police,' but I've always been 'human,'" her question was a case in point: is our perception that the men and women in blue are *either* police officers *or* human beings? The answer, of course, is that those who make up the hundreds of thousands of police officers at the city, county, state and federal levels are both.

But we tend to constantly second-guess police officer decisionmaking—especially when it comes to the police use of deadly force. And many citizens become outraged at the police when such incidents are reported in the media. We expect perfection of the police, especially when it comes to life and death decisions that they make. Sometimes, even when deadly force is deemed reasonable, we continue to question the motivations and actions of officers.

A few months back, a Boise City police officer was exonerated for the shooting of a citizen in front of a grocery store. The suspect, not more than 20 feet from the officer, pointed a gun toward the officer's head. The officer shot first, and the suspect's injuries were fatal. While discussing this critical incident in class one day, several students questioned whether it would have been more appropriate for the officer to use less-than-lethal force. And citizen callers to a local radio talk show asked for the chief's resignation. "We need a new chief who can reign in the gun slingers." Indeed, the police have a difficult job.

As the contributions to this volume are reviewed below, you might ask yourself which ones are controversies—at least in part—because of a condition called "humanness." Sometimes being human manifests itself in the pursuit of self-interest, in particular agendas, in unethical behavior, such as sexual misconduct or corruption, and in a variety of other discretionary decisions that are the crux of American policing. Of course, the good news is that this distinct human quality allows us to learn from mistakes and engage in reforms that can improve policing, and the ultimately of neighborhood quality of life. Many of the conclusions, solutions, and recommendations made by our colleagues in their respective chapters are encouraging indeed.

Controversies in Policing

In Chapter 1, Anthony Bouza asserted that there are too few controversies in policing. Ironically, his contribution to this volume is undoubtedly highly controversial! Bouza offered numerous examples of "anti-intellectualism" of police executives, who often respond to social problems with overly knee-jerk solutions. These solutions, in their variety of forms, including reactive responses as well as more proactive programs, were touted by police executives as the reasons for the crime declines by the mid 1990s. But Bouza offered some compelling, alternate explanations for these declines that are wholly independent of the police, further strengthening his argument. According to Bouza, if this anti-intellectualism of police executives continues, we are likely to have more of the same—in times of crime declines, police executives will take credit on account of their programs, and in times of crime increases, they will shrug off responsibility. Implied in Bouza's chapter is a push toward police departments becoming learning organizations, where police ask the tough questions, and use objective information to answer them. In this way, police decisionmaking at the highest levels—would be better informed. As Bouza so eloquently put it years ago, we should beware of simple solutions to complex problems.

David Perkins, in Chapter 2, addressed the longstanding controversy surrounding the order versus freedom debate, but in the more contemporary context of a post-9/11 world. Here, Perkins examined the reallocation of scare police resources in an age of terrorism, including allocations of funds for increases in personnel, intelligence sharing, upgraded technology, and training for terrorist interdiction. This discussion led to his observation that police reforms in the area of community policing and problem solving may be threatened if a balance between terrorist related initiatives and community policing initiatives is not struck. Perkins raised thought-provoking questions concerning the nature of these terrorist attacks. Can these acts be equated with warfare, or are they some kind of grand criminal activity? This particular unanswered question has ramifications for rules of engagement, and the specific actions that may be taken by agents of government against terrorists. Perkins' examples of what already has been done in this arena clearly demonstrates that the rules of engagement already have become relaxed in favor of more order, but that the debate goes on, as is evidenced by the growing support for preserving liberties with the Safe Act.

In Chapter 3, Victor Kappeler and Karen S. Miller-Potter continued the discussion of policing in the age of terrorism by offering a commentary on the expansion of capitalism through globalization and the policing of terrorism. Globalization, they argued, requires open borders, free trade and accommodating importation laws, practices that are antithetical to the policing of terrorism. Kappeler and Miller-Potter discussed how the police have historically defined—then redefined those who are dangerous as well as the geographic orientation of the police, all of which revolves around threats to the expansion of capital. The authors argued that in the twenty-first century, the new economic revolution dictates that the police focus on those places where capital circulates and on those deemed to be a threat to the emerging global economy. Terrorists, then, have become the newer targets of agents of social control. But Kappeler and Miller-Potter pointed out, and in support of their argument, that definitions of terrorism have expanded, and law enforcement has begun to identify those who are dangerous as "globalization protesters." As such, the authors contend that the policing of terrorism is leading to the federalization of local police agencies and an internationalization of federal police agencies. The authors concluded that the policing of terrorism requires something different than the policing of globalization protesters. In this developing era of terrorism and globalization, only time will tell if history truly repeats itself.

In Chapter 4, Jihong Zhao, Matthew Scheider, and Quint Thurman argued that community policing, touted by some to be soft on crime, really equates to "smarter" policing. What we learned from Zhao and his colleagues is that rigorous, quantitative, studies can be undertaken to determine the effectiveness of community policing, not just in terms of its effects on the more common outcome variables of satisfaction with the police and fear of crime, but also in terms of crime rates. Here, the authors determined that the amount of federal COPS Office funding significantly impacted the drop in crime in U.S. cities with populations greater than 10,000. And while we are still left wondering what specifically about the COPS funding may have led to the aforementioned decreases, Zhao and colleagues advocated for a broad definition of community policing, which might include, but is not limited to collaborative partnerships and problem-solving. These activities, combined with more traditional reactive responses by the police, encompass a philosophy of policing that holds the greatest chances of improving neighborhood quality of life.

Noted policing scholar John P. Crank provided us with his standpoint on police culture in Chapter 5. Crank argued that culture exists in the eyes of the beholder, essentially offering a rather post-modern view of culture, which is reflective of an observer's interpretation of a group's behavior. What we learned from Crank's work is that just when we thought we could identify, in an objective manner, a common police culture, there really is no such thing as a police culture itself—at least not one that truly, objectively can be observed and understood. Crank's provocative piece has significant implications for social science research generally, and the study of police culture specifically. It is a reminder to us all that human understanding is continually influenced and shaped by the world around us.

John Liederbach and Robert W. Taylor, in Chapter 6, reminded us that while instances of police use of deadly force are rare, their effects can be significant. The authors discussed the notion of situational risk as it relates to the decision to use deadly force, and offered a number of ways that deadly force can be controlled, including use of state criminal codes for the prosecution of officers—which in reality rarely occurs, U.S. Supreme Court decisions that serve as guidelines for the use of force, civil liability, and department administrative regulations and training. Liederbach and Taylor advocated the use of restrictive departmental policies and training on police use of deadly force, especially in light of the research suggesting their effectiveness. But they argued that external controls are necessary, especially when internal controls fail. The authors' reviewed developing less-than-lethal technologies that may provide other options for police officers who are confronted with making difficult, split-second judgments about use of force.

In Chapter 7, Andra Katz-Bannister and David L. Carter discussed yet another human quality of the police: does a police officer's discretionary decisionmaking sometimes lead to racial profiling? While Katz-Bannister and Carter pointed out that a number of researchers in this area have attempted to answer this question, the lack of sound research methodologies preclude us from truly knowing the extent of racial profiling. The authors insightfully discussed the barriers that must be overcome in this important research, including problems with racial profiling data interpretation, appropriate "denominators" that would assist us in determining whether a particular racial group is being disproportionately stopped, and appropriate conceptual and operational definitions of the term. What we learned from Katz-Barrister and Carter is that what appear to be rather simple questions (i.e., "Are officers improperly stopping drivers by considering race or ethnicity as a criterion to stop?" or "Is an officer engaging in discriminatory practices?"), ultimately are difficult to answer. This chapter undoubtedly will help us all to assess research that makes the claim that police officers are engaging in racial profiling.

In Chapter 8, Donna C. Hale and Karen Finkenbinder explored the history of women in policing. Beginning in the late nineteenth and early twentieth centuries, women had limited roles in policing by holding clerical positions and in assisting females and children. As they moved throughout the decades of the twentieth century, Hale and Finkenbinder provided us with a number of important contextual references—economic, social, cultural, and legal—which help us to understand the place of women in policing throughout our history. The authors argued that while women have made great strides in the policing profession over the years, there is more that can be done. They concluded their chapter by discussing issues of recruitment, selection, retention, and promotion, pointing out ways which might facilitate not only attracting prospective women police officers, but also retaining and advancing them through the ranks.

Joycelyn Pollock's chapter on police ethics epitomized the human qualities of police officers—their decisions to engage in either ethical or unethical behavior and the moral reasoning systems they might use to come to such decisions. Pollock's chapter reminds us that the field of ethics in policing is vast and complex. For example, while some officers might engage in corruption for personal gain, others engage in corruption for the "noble cause," which is exacerbated when the police mandate focuses on crime fighting. Extreme acts of known police misconduct often are reported in the media, but Pollock suggested that there is no evidence that police corruption is *quantitatively* different from other professions. Conversely, Pollock maintained that police corruption is *qualitatively* different from other professions due to police exposure, discretion, and formal and informal socialization. Pollock's discussion of individual, organizational, and societal factors, along with her review of ethical systems, not only help us to understand police decisionmaking, but also open the door for a variety of strategies to prevent and control corruption in law enforcement.

In Chapter 10, John L. Worrall provided us with an in-depth discussion of police officer excessive force and civil liability. Worrall discussed the costs and benefits of civil litigation, three varieties of force—nondeadly, deadly, and indirect force, and delineated the avenues for suit, including Section 1983 and state tort law. Many readers may have been surprised to learn about how far reaching Section 1983 actually is with regard to liability. For example, not only can individual police officers be held liable for excessive use of force, but, under certain circumstances, so too can municipalities, counties, and supervisors. Police officers, as Worrall pointed out, also can benefit from qualified immunity if they acted in an objectively reasonable fashion. Worrall's chapter also included an examination of existing case law, including a review of the landmark U.S. Supreme Court cases of *Tennessee v. Garner* and *Graham v. Connor*. Most importantly, Worrall called for clearer standards as to when deadly and nondeadly force is appropriate, especially in the rather complex milieu of "reasonably unreasonable" conduct, a scenario in which an officer's actions are in violation of the Fourth Amendment, but where qualified immunity exists.

In closing, I believe that the contributions of this book not only lend themselves readily to scholarly debate on these subjects, but they also serve to invite police practitioners into discourse about how public safety might be re-defined in the future. In so doing, we recognize that our contributors do not have the final say in these matters, but certainly they have helped to light the way for leadership in American Policing.

References

Adams, K. (1999). "What We Know About Police Use of Force." In J. Travis & J.M. Chaiken (eds.) *Use of Force by Police: Overview of National and Local Data*, pp. 1-15. Washington, DC: U.S. Dept. of Justice, Office of Justice Programs, National Institute of Justice.

Albritton, J. (1999). "Is There a Distinct Subculture in America Policing? No." In J. Seewell (ed.) *Controversial Issues in Policing*, pp. 162-172. Boston, MA: Allyn & Bacon.

Alderson, J. (1998). *Principled Policing: Protecting the Public with Integrity*. Winchester, MA: Waterside Press.

Alpert, G.P. & R.G Dunham (1996). *Policing Urban America*, Third Edition. Prospect Heights, IL: Waveland Press.

Alpert, G.P. & M. Moore (1997). "Measuring Police Performance in the New Paradigm of Policing. In R. Dunham & G. Alpert (eds.) *Critical Issues in Policing*, pp. 265-282. Prospect Heights, IL: Waveland Press, Inc.

Americans for Effective Law Enforcement (1982). *Impact*. San Francisco, CA: AELE. Anderson Publishing Co.

Americans for Effective Law Enforcement (1980). *Lawsuits against Police Skyrocket*. San Francisco, CA: AELE.

Americans for Effective Law Enforcement (1974). *Survey of Police Misconduct Litigation: 1967-1971*. San Francisco, CA: AELE.

Anonymous. (1998). "Young Black Males under Criminal Justice Control." The Sentencing Project. Report Summary. Washington, D.C.

Anzaldua, G. (1987). *Borderlands/La Frontera*. San Francisco, CA: Aunt Lute.

Appadurai, A. (1990). "Disjuncture and Difference in the Global Cultural Economy." *Public Culture*, 2(2):1-24.

Appier, J. (1998). *Policing Women: The Sexual Politics of Law Enforcement and the LAPD*. Philadelphia, PA: Temple University Press.

Appier, J. (1992). "Preventive Justice: The Campaign for Women Police, 1910-1940." *Women & Criminal Justice*, 4(1):3-36.

Baker, M. (1985). *Cops: Their Lives in Their Own Words*. New York, NY: Pocket Books.

Barker, J. (1999). *Danger, Duty, and Disillusion: The Worldview of the Los Angeles Police Officers*. Prospect Heights, IL: Waveland.

Barker, T. & D. Carter (1999). "Fluffing Up the Evidence and Covering Your Ass: Some Conceptual Notes on Police Lying." In L. Gaines & G. Cordner (eds.) *Policing Perspectives*, pp. 342-351. Los Angeles, CA: Roxbury.

Barker, T. & D. Carter (1991). "Police Lies and Perjury: A Motivation Based Taxonomy." In *Police Deviance*, Second Edition. Cincinnati, OH: Anderson Publishing Co.

Barker, T. (1978). "An Empirical Study of Police Deviance Other than Corruption." *Journal of Police Science and Administration*, 6:264-272.

Barrineau III, H.E. (1987). *Civil Liability in Criminal Justice*. Cincinnati, OH: Pilgrimage.

Bates, R.D., R.F. Cutler & M.J. Clink (1981). "Prepared Statement on Behalf of the National Institute of Municipal Law Officers." Presented before the subcommittee on the Constitution. Senate Committee on the Judiciary, May 6, 1981.

Baum, F. (1900). *The Wonderful Wizard of Oz*. Chicago, IL & New York, NY: George M. Hill Co.

Becker, H.S. (1963). *Outsiders: Studies in the Sociology of Deviance*. New York, NY: The Free Press.

Binder, A., P. Scharf & R. Galvin (1982). *Use of Deadly Force by Police Officers*. Washington, DC: National Institute of Justice.

Bitnner, E. (1972). *The Functions of the Police in Modern Society*, Second Edition. Washington, DC: National Institute of Mental Health.

Bittner, E. (1970). *The Functions of Police in Modern Society*. Washington, DC: National Institute of Mental Health.

Bittner, E. (1967). "The Police on Skid Row: A Study of Peace Keeping." *American Sociological Review*, 32:699-715.

Black, D. (1980). *The Manners and Customs of the Police*. New York, NY: Academic Press.

Black, H.C. (1990). *Black's Law Dictionary*, Sixth Edition. St. Paul, MN: West Publishing Co.

Bloch, P. & D. Anderson (1974). *Policewomen on Patrol.* Washington, DC: The Police Foundation.

Blumberg, M. (2001). "Controlling Police Use of Deadly Force: Assessing Two Decades of Progress." In R.G. Dunham & G.P. Alpert (eds.) *Critical Issues in Policing*, Fourth Edition, pp. 559-582. Prospect Heights, IL: Waveland Press.

Blumberg, M. (1989). "Controlling Police Use of Force: Assessing Two Decades of Progress." In R.G. Dunham & G.P. Alpert (eds.) *Critical Issues in Policing: Contemporary Readings*, pp. 442-464. Prospect Heights, IL: Waveland Press.

Blumberg, M. (1981). "Race and Police Shootings: An Analysis in Two Cities." In J.J. Fyfe, *Contemporary Issues in Law Enforcement.* Beverly Hills, CA: Sage.

Bouza, A.V. (1976). *Police Intelligence.* New York, NY: AMS Press.

Brewer, D. (1893). "An Independent Judiciary as the Salvation of the Nation," Proceedings of the N.Y. Bar Association, 37-47.

Brown, M.K. (1988). *Working the Street: Police Discretion and the Dilemmas of Reform.* New York, NY: Russell Sage Foundation.

Bryant, T. & N. Parish (2000). "3 Policemen Are Fired over Allegations of Sex Acts with Teens." *St. Louis Post-Dispatch*, (November 1):A1.

Buerger, M.E. (2002). "Supervisory Challenges Arising from Racial Profiling Legislation." *Police Quarterly*, 5:380-408.

Buerger, M.E. & A. Farrell (2002). "The Evidence of Racial Profiling: Interpreting Documented and Unofficial Sources." *Police Quarterly*, 5:272-305.

Bursik, R. (1988). "Social Disorganization and Theory of Crime and Delinquency: Problems and Prospects." *Criminology*, 26(4):519-551.

Caldero, M. & J. Crank (2004). *Police Ethics: The Corruption of Noble Cause*, Second Edition. New York, NY: Matthew Bender.

Carabillo, T., J. Meuli & J.B. Csida (1995). *Feminist Chronicles.* The Feminist Majority Foundation and New Media Publishing, Inc.

Carlisle, J. (1995). "A Police Corps will Reduce Crime Rates and Improve Police-Community Relations." In P. Winters, *Policing the Police*, pp. 60-68. San Diego, CA: Greenhaven Press.

Carlson, D. (2002). *When Cultures Clash: The Divisive Nature of Police-Community Relations and Suggestions for Improvement.* Upper Saddle River, NJ: Prentice-Hall.

Carrington, F. (1989). "Avoiding Liability for Police Failure to Protect." *Police Chief,* 56:22-24.

Carter, D. (1999). "Drug Use and Drug-Related Corruption of Police Officers." In L. Gaines & G. Cordner (eds.) *Policing Perspectives,* pp. 311-324. Los Angeles, CA: Roxbury.

CBS's "60 Minutes," "Protecting New York," March 23, 2003.

Chan, J. (1996). "Changing Police Culture." *British Journal of Criminology,* 36(1):109-134.

Charles, M. (1982). "Women in Policing: The Physical Aspect." *Journal of Police Science and Administration,* 10:194-204.

Charles, M. (1981). "The Performance and Socialization of Female Recruits in the Michigan State Police Training Academy." *Journal of Police Science and Administration,* 9:209-223.

Cheh, M.M. (1995). "Are Lawsuits an Answer to Police Brutality?" In W.A. Geller & H. Toch (eds.) *And Justice For All: Understanding and Controlling Police Abuse of Force,* pp. 233-260. New Haven, CT: Yale University Press.

Chevigny, P. (1995). *Edge of the Knife: Police Violence in the Americas.* New York, NY: The New Press.

Chiabi, D.K. (1996). "Police Civil Liability: An Analysis of Section 1983 Actions in the Eastern and Southern Districts of New York." *American Journal of Criminal Justice,* 21:83-104.

Cincinnati Enquirer (2001). "Cincinnati's Call to Change." (April 19).

CNN.COM (2000). "Report Faults LAPD Culture for Corruption." (September 11). http://www.cnn.com/2000/US/09/11/lapd.report/

Cobb, C. (1995). The *Alienist.* New York, NY: Bantam Books.

Cohen, H. & M. Feldberg (1991). *Power and Restraint: The Moral Dimension of Police Work.* New York, NY: Praeger.

Colb, S.F. (1998). "The Qualitative Dimension of Fourth Amendment 'Reasonableness'." *Columbia Law Review,* 98(7):1642-1725.

Cole, D. (1999). *No Equal Justice: Race and Class in the American Criminal Justice System.* New York, NY: The New Press.

Cordner, G. (1997). Community Policing: Elements and Effects. In D. Dunham & G. Alpert (eds.) *Critical Issues in Policing*, Third Edition, pp.451-468. Prospect Heights, IL: Waveland,

Cordner, G., B. Williams & M. Zuniga (2000). *Vehicle Stops for the Year 2000.* San Diego, CA: San Diego Police Department.

Cox, S.M., S.E. Pease, D.S. Miller & C.B. Tyson (2001). *2000-2001 Report of Traffic Stops Statistics: July 2000 to June 2001.* Rocky Hill, CT: Division of Criminal Justice.

Crank, J. (2003). *Imagining Justice.* Cincinnati, OH: Anderson Publishing Co.

Crank, J. (2004). *Understanding Police Culture*, Second Edition. New York, NY: Matthew Bender.

Crank, J. & R. Langworthy (1992). "An Institutional Perspective of Policing." *The Journal of Criminal Law and Criminology*, 83:338-363.

Davis, K.C. (1975). *Police Discretion.* St. Paul, MN: West Publishing Co.

Davis, K.R. (2001). *Coverup: Driving While Black.* Cincinnati, OH: Interstate International Publishing of Cincinnati.

Decker, S.H. & J. Rojek (2002). *Saint Louis Metropolitan Police Department Traffic Stop Patterns.* St. Louis, MO: University of Missouri–St. Louis.

del Carmen, R.V. & M.R. Smith (1997). "Police, Civil Liability, and the Law." In R.G. Dunham & G.P Alpert (eds.) *Critical Issues in Policing: Contemporary Readings*, Third Edition, pp. 225-242. Prospect Heights, IL: Waveland.

del Carmen, R.V. (1987). *Criminal Procedure for Law Enforcement Personnel.* Monterey, CA: Brooks/Cole.

Delattre, E. (1996). *Character and Cops: Ethics in Policing*, Third Edition. Washington, DC: The AEI Press.

Denzin, N. (1997). *Interpretive Ethnography: Ethnographic Practices for the 21st Century.* Thousand Oaks, CA: Sage Publications.

DiCristina, B. (1995). *Method in Criminology: A Philosophical Primer.* New York, NY: Harrow and Heston.

Dinh, V.D. (2002). "Freedom and Security after September 11." *Harvard Journal of Law and Public Policy*, 25(2):399-406.

Donohue III, J.J. & S.D. Levitt. (2001). "The Impact of Legalized Abortion on Crime." *Quarterly Journal of Economics*, 116(2):379-420.

Dorsch, D. (2001). "Opened Door for Lawyers, Burden for Officers." *Law and Order*, 49(9):102.

Doyle, A. (2000). "From the Inside Looking Out: Twenty-Nine Years in the New York Police Department." In J. Nelson (ed), *Police Brutality*, pp. 171-189. New York, NY: W.W. Norton & Co.

Durkheim, E. (1938/1963). *Rules of Sociological Method*. New York, NY: The Free Press.

Eck, J. & M. Edward (2000). "Have Changes in Policing Reducing Violent Crime? An Assessment of the Evidence." In A. Blumstein & J. Wallman (eds.) *The Crime Drop in America*. pp. 207-265. New York, NY: Cambridge University Press.

Ekstrand, L.E. (2000). *Limited Data Available On Motorist Stops*. Washington, DC: U.S. General Accounting Office.

Engel, R.S., J.M. Calnon & T.J. Bernard (2002). "Theory and Racial Profiling: Shortcomings and Future Directions in Research." *Justice Quarterly*, 19(2):249-273.

Fabrizio, L.E. (1990). *FBI National Academy: A Study of the Change in Attitude of Those Who Attend*. Chicago, IL: Officer of International Criminal Justice, University of Illinois at Chicago.

Feldman, N. (2002). "Choices of Law, Choices of War," *Harvard Journal of Law and Public Policy*, 25(2):457-485.

Feuer, A. (2000). "Ex Officer Details Surge of Rage as He Began Attack on Louima." *New York Times*. Retrieved on 2/18/00 from http://www.nytimes.com/yr/mo/day/news/national/regional/ny-louima.html.

Fick, R. (1997). "California's Police Pursuit Immunity Statute: Does It Work?" *Police Chief*, 64:36-43.

Flowers, R. B. (1994). *The Victimization and Exploitation of Women and Children: A Study of Physical, Mental, and Sexual Maltreatment in the United States*. Jefferson, NC: McFarland & Company, Inc.

Fogelson, R. (1977). *Big City Police*. Cambridge, MA: Harvard University Press.

Freeh, L. (2001). Statement for the Record on the Threat of Terrorism to the United States before the United States Senate Committees on Appropriations, Armed Services, and Select Committee on Intelligence, May 10, 2001.

Fry, L. & S. Greenfield (1980). "Examination of Attitudinal Differences between Policeman and Policewoman." *Journal of Applied Psychology*, 65(1):123-126.

Fuss, T. & L. Snowden (2000). "Surveying Sexual Harassment in the Law Enforcement Workplace." *Police Chief*, 67(6):65-68, 70-72.

Fyfe, J. (1989). "The Split-Second Syndrome and Other Determinants of Police Violence." In R.G. Dunham & G.P. Alpert (eds.) *Critical Issues in Policing: Contemporary Readings*, pp. 465-479. Prospect Heights, IL: Waveland Press.

Fyfe, J. (1988). "Police Use of Deadly Force: Research and Reform." *Justice Quarterly*, 5(2):165-205.

Fyfe, J. (1981). "Race and Extreme Police-Citizen Violence." In R. McNeeley & C.E. Pope (eds.) *Race, Crime, and Criminal Justice*, pp. 89-108. Beverly Hills, CA: Sage.

Fyfe, J. (1979). "Administrative Interventions on Police Shooting Discretion." *Journal of Criminal Justice*, 7:313-335.

Gammond, P. (1991). *The Oxford Companion to Popular Music*. New York: Oxford University Press.

Garner, G. (1991). "Off-Duty: Off the Hook?" *Police*, 15:32-34; 71-73.

Garner, J.H. & R.G. Dunham (1999). "Measuring the Amount of Force Used by and Against the Police in Six Jurisdictions." In J. Travis & J.M. Chaiken (eds.) *Use of Force by Police: Overview of National and Local Data*, pp. 25-44. (NCJ 176330)

Geertz, C. (1983). *Local Knowledge: Further Essays in Interpretive Anthropology*. New York, NY: Basic Books.

Geller, W.A. & M.S. Scott (1992). "Deadly Force: What We Know." In C.B. Klockers & S.D. Mastrofski (eds.) *Thinking about Police: Contemporary Readings*, pp. 446-476. Washington, DC: Police Executive Research Forum.

Gerhardt, M. J. (2002). "Crisis and Constitutionalism." *Montana Law Review*, 63:277-292.

Getlin, J. (2002). "DA Suggests Overturning Convictions in Jogger Case." *Austin American Statesman*, (December 6):A16.

Giacomazzi, A.L., Q. Thurman & J. Zhao (2001). *Community Policing in a Community Era*. Los Angeles, CA: Roxbury Publishing Co.

Glover, S. & M. Lait (2000). "71 More Cases May be Voided Due to Rampart." *LA Times*, retrieved on 4/20/00 from www.latimes.com/news/state/reports/rampart/lat.rampart000418.html.

Golab, J. (2000). "LA Confidential." Salon.com. Retrieved January 17, 2003 from http://www.dir.salon.com/news/feature/2000/09/27/Rampart/index.html.

Goldstein, H. (1975). *Police Corruption: A Perspective on its Nature and Control.* Washington, DC: Police Foundation.

Goldstein, S.L. (1987). *The Sexual Exploitation of Children: A Practical Guide to Assessment, Investigation, and Intervention.* New York, NY: Elsevier.

Gossert, J. & J. Williams (1998). "Perceived Discrimination among Women in Law Enforcement." *Women & Criminal Justice*, 10(1):53-73.

Greene, J.A. (1999). "Zero Tolerance: A Case Study of Police Policies and Practices in New York City." *Crime & Delinquency*, 45(2):171-187.

Greene, J.R. (2000). "Community Policing in America: Changing the Nature, Structure, and Function of the Police." In Julie Horney (ed.) *Criminal Justice 2000, Vol. 3: Policies, Processes, and Decisions of the Criminal Justice System*, pp.299-370. Washington, DC: National Institute of Justice.

Grennan. S. (1987). "Findings on the Role of Officer Gender in Violent Encounters with Citizens." *Journal of Police Science and Administration*, 15(1):78-85.

Guyot, D. (1979). "Bending Granite: Attempts to Change the Rank Structure of American Police Departments." *Journal of Police Science and Administration*, 7(3):253-284.

Hafetz, D. (2002). "Their Innocence Proved, Men Sue." *Austin American Statesman*, (November 8):B1.

Hagerty, T.J. (1976). "Insurance Coverage and Civil Rights Litigation." *Federation of Insurance Counsel Quarterly*, 27:3-17.

Hale, D. (2002). "Women and Policing." In D. Levinson (ed.) *Encyclopedia of Crime and Punishment*, Volume 4, pp. 1718-1722. Thousand Oaks, CA: Sage Publications.

Hale, D. & S. Wyland (1999). "Dragons and Dinosaurs: The Plight of Patrol Women." In L. Gaines & G. Cordner (eds.) *Policing Perspectives: An Anthology*, pp. 450-458. Los Angeles, CA: Roxbury Publishing Co.

Harrington, P. & K. Lonsway (2004). "Current Barriers and Future Promise for Women in Policing." In B.R. Price & N.J. Sokoloff (eds.) *The Criminal Justice System and Women: Offenders, Prisoners, Victims, and Workers*, Third Edition, pp. 495-510. New York, NY: McGraw-Hill.

Harris, D.A. (2002). *Profiles in Injustice.* New York, NY: New Press.

Harris, D.A. (1999). "The Stories, the Statistics, and the Law: Why 'Driving While Black' Matters." *Minnesota Law Review*, 84:265-326.

Harris, D.A. (1997). "'Driving While Black' and All Other Traffic Offenses: The Supreme Court and Pretextual Traffic Stops." *Journal of Criminal Law & Criminology*, 87(2):544-582.

Harvey, D. (1989). *The Conditions of Postmodernity: An Inquiry into the Origins of Cultural Change*. Oxford: Blackwell.Hawkins Press.

Hatty, S.E. & M.D. Schwartz (2003). *Controversies in Critical Criminology*. Cincinnati, OH: Anderson Publishing Co.

Heal, S. (2000). "Push for Less Lethal." *Law Enforcement Technology*, 27(11):72-79.

Herbert, B. (2002). "In Tulia, Justice Has Gone Into Hiding," *Austin American Statesman*, (August 13):A9.

Hickman, M. & B. Reaves (2001). "Community Policing in Local Police Departments 1997 and 1999." *Bureau of Justice Statistics Special Report*. Washington DC: Office of Justice Programs, U.S. Department of Justice.

Homant, R.J. & D.B. Kennedy (1994). "Citizen Preferences and Perceptions Concerning Police Pursuits." *Journal of Criminal Justice*, 22(5):425-435.

Hoover, L. (2001). "Interpreting Racial Profiling Data." *TELEMASP Bulletin*, 8(5):1-7.

Hopper, J.A. (2001). "Less-Than-Lethal Litigation: Departments and the Courts React to Less-Than-Lethal Standards." *Law and Order*, 49(11):87-91.

Hubler, S. (1991). "Grand Jury To Investigate Shootings." *Los Angeles Times* (September 20).

Human Rights Watch (1998). *Shielded From Justice: Police Brutality and Accountability in the United States*. New York, NY: Human Rights Watch.

Hunter, R. (1999). "Officer Opinions on Police Misconduct," *Journal of Contemporary Criminal Justice*, 15(2):155-170.

International Association of Chiefs of Police (1998a). *The Future of Women in Policing: Mandates for Action*. Washington, DC: International Association of Chiefs of Police.

International Association of Chiefs of Police (1998b). "Women in Policing: IACP Gallup Assess Recruitment, Promotion, and Retention Issues." *Police Chief*, 65(10):36, 38, and 40.

International Association of Chiefs of Police (1976). Survey of Police Misconduct Litigation 1967-1976.

Jablon, R. (2000). "L.A. Confronts Police Scandal That May Cost Tens of Millions," *Austin American Statesman*, (February 19):A18.

Janco, M.A. (2002). "Delco Jury Convicts Officer of Rape Charges," *Philadelphia Inquirer*.

Johnson, D. (1996). "Chicago Officials Complain of Too Many Sting Operations." *New York Times*. (January 18).

Johnson, P. (2000). *On Gadamer*. New York, NY: Wadsworth.

Kania, R. (1988). "Police Acceptance of Gratuities." *Criminal Justice Ethics*, 7(2):37-49.

Kappeler, V.E., R.D. Sluder & G.P. Alpert (1998). Forces *of Deviance: Understanding the Dark Side of Policing*. Prospect Heights IL:W aveland Press, Inc.

Kappeler, V.E., M. Blumberg & G. Potter (1998). *Understanding the Dark Side of Policing*, Second Edition. Prospect Heights, IL: Waveland Press.

Kappeler, V.E., M. Blumberg & G. Potter (1993). *The Mythology of Crime and Criminal Justice*. Second Edition. Prospect Heights, IL: Waveland Press.

Kappeler, V.E. & J.B.Vaughn (1989). "The Historical Development of Negligence Theory." *American Journal of Police*, 8(1):1-36.

Kappeler, V.E. & P.B. Kraska (1998). "A Textual Critique of Community Policing: Police Adaptation to High Modernity." *Policing: An International Journal of Police Strategies and Management*, 21(2):293-313.

Kappeler, V.E. & R.V. del Carmen (1990). "Police Civil Liability for Failure to Arrest Intoxicated Drivers." *Journal of Criminal Justice*, 18(2):117-131.

Kappeler, V.E. & R.V. del Carmen (1990). "Legal Issues in Police Negligent Operation of Emergency Vehicles." *Journal of Police Science and Administration*, 17:163-175.

Kappeler, V.E. (2001). *Critical Issues in Police Civil Liability*, Third Edition. Prospect Heights, IL: Waveland.

Kappeler, V.E. (1996). "The Fear of Civil Liability Among Kentucky Police Cadets." Unpublished paper, Eastern Kentucky University, Richmond, KY.

Kappeler, V.E., S.F. Kappeler & R.V. del Carmen (1993). "A Content Analysis of Police Civil Liability Cases: Decisions of the Federal District Courts, 1978-1990." *Journal of Criminal Justice*, 21(4):325-337.

Kappler, V. E. & M.S. Vaughn (1997). "Law Enforcement: When the Pursuit Becomes Criminal- Municipal Liability for Police Sexual Violence." *Criminal Law Bulletin*, 33:352-376.

Kelly, T. (1999). "Officer Accused of Sexually Assaulting a Woman While On-Duty." *New York Times*, (January 12).

Kenney, D. & R. Homant (1983). "Attitudes of Abused Women toward Male and Female Police Officers." *Criminal Justice and Behavior* 10:391-405.

Kerner, O. (1968). *Report of the National Advisory Commission on Civil Disorder.* New York, NY: New York Times Co.

Kleinig, J. (1996). *The Ethics of Policing.* Cambridge, MA: Cambridge University Press.

Klinger, D.A. & D. Grossman (2002). "Who Should Deal with Foreign Terrorists on U.S. Soil? Sociolegal Consequences of September 11 and the Ongoing Threat of Terrorist Attacks in America." *Harvard Journal of Law and Public Policy*, 25:815-834.

Klockars, C.B. (1995). "A Theory of Excessive Force and its Control." In W.A. Geller & H. Toch (eds.) *And Justice For All: Understanding and Controlling Police Abuse of Force*, pp.11-29. New Haven, CT: Yale University Press.

Klockars, C.B. (1983). "The Dirty Harry Problem," In C. Klockars, *Thinking about Police: Contemporary Readings*, pp. 428-438. New York, NY: McGraw-Hill.

Klockars, C.B. (1983). *Thinking about Police: Contemporary Readings.* New York, NY: McGraw-Hill.

Knowles, J., N. Persico & P. Todd (2001). "Racial Bias in Motor Vehicle Searches: Theory and Evidence." *Journal of Political Economy*, 109(1):203-229.

Kobler, A. (1975). "Police Homicides in a Democracy." *Journal of Social Issues*, 31:163-181.

Kranda, A. (1998). "Women in Policing: The Importance of Mentoring." *Police Chief*, 65(10):54, 56.

Kraska, P. (1996). "Enjoying Militarism: Political/Personal Dilemmas in Studying U.S. Paramilitary Units." *Justice Quarterly*, 13(3):405-429.

Kraska, P.B. & V.E. Kappeler (1997). "Militarizing American Police: The Rise and Normalization of Paramilitary Units." *Social Problems*, 44(1):1-16.

Kraska, P. & V.E. Kappeler (1995). "To Serve and Pursue: Exploring Police Sexual Vioence Against Women." *Justice Quarterly*, 12(1):85-111.

Kraska, P. B. & V.E. Kappeler (1995). "Top Serve and Pursue: Police Sexual Violence against Women." *Justice Quarterly*, 12(1):85.

Kushner, H.W. (1998). *The Future of Terrorism Violence in the New Millennium.* Thousand Oaks, CA: Sage Publications, Inc.

Lakoff, G. & M. Johnson (1992). *Metaphors We Live By.* Chicago, IL: University of Chicago Press.

Lamberth, J. (1996). *A Report to the ACLU.* New York, NY: American Civil Liberties Union.

Langan, P.A., L.A. Greenfeld, S.K. Smith, M.R. Durose & B.J. Levin (2001). *Contacts between Police and the Public: Findings from the 1999 National Survey.* Washington, DC: U.S. Department of Justice, Bureau of Justice Statistics.

Lange, J., K.O. Blackman & M.B. Johnson. (2001). *Speed Violation Survey of the New Jersey Turnpike: Final Report.* Calverton, MD: Public Services Research Institute.

Langworthy, R. & L. Travis (1999). *Policing in America: A Balance of Forces.* Upper Saddle River, NJ: Prentice Hall.

Langworthy, R. (1986). 'Police Shootings and Criminal Homicide: The Temporal Relationship." *Journal of Quantitative Criminology*, 2(4):377-388.

Lansdowne, W.M. (2000). *Vehicle Stop Demographic Study.* San Jose, CA: San Jose Police Department.

Lash, S. & J. Urry (1994). *Economies of Signs and Space.* Newbury Park, CA: Sage.

Lash, S. & J. Urry (1987). *The End of Organized Capitalism.* Madison, WI: University of Wisconsin Press.

LeDuff, C. (2002). "Los Angeles Police Chief Faces a Huge Challenge." *New York Times*, retrieved 10/25/02 from http://www.nytimes.com/2002/10/24/national/24GANG.html.

Leinwand, D. (2004). "Lawsuits of '70s Shape Police Leadership Now." *USA TODAY*, Monday, April 26, 2004, 13A and 14A.

Littlejohn, E.J. (1981). "Civil Liability and the Police Officer: The Need for New Deterrents to Police Misconduct." *University of Detroit Journal of Urban Law*, 58:365-370.

Liss, J & S. Schlossman (1984). "The Contours of Crime Prevention in August Vollmer's Berkeley." *Research in Law, Deviance and Social Control* 6:79-107.

Lonsway, K., M. Moore, P. Harrington, E. Smeal & K. Spillar (2003). "Hiring and Retaining More Women: The Advantages to Law Enforcement Agencies." National Center for Women and Policing. A Division of the Feminist Majority Foundation.

Lonsway, K. (2003). "Tearing Down the Wall: Problems with Consistency, Validity, and Adverse Impact of Physical Agility in Police Selection." *Police Quarterly*, 6(3):237-277.

Lonsway, K. (2001). "Law and Order Roundtable Discussions: First Topic: Police Women and the Use-of-force." *Law and Order*, 49(7):109-114.

Lorber, J. (1998). *Gender Inequality: Feminist Theories and Politics*. Los Angeles, CA: Roxbury.

Lyons, W. (2002). *The Politics of Community Policing: Rearranging the Power to Punish*. Ann Arbor, MI: University of Michigan Press.

MacIntyre, A. (1988). *Whose Justice? Which Rationality?* Notre Dame, IN: University of Notre Dame Press.

Maglione, R. (2002). "Recruiting, Retaining, and Promoting: The Success of the Charlotte-Mecklenburg Police Department's Women's Network." *Police Chief*, 69(3):19-24.

Malloy, E. (1982). *The Ethics of Law Enforcement and Criminal Punishment*. Lanham, NY: University Press.

Manning, P. (1999). "The Police: Mandate, Strategies and Appearances." In V.E. Kappeler (ed.) *Police and Society: Touchstone Readings*, Second Edition, pp. 94-122. Prospect Heights, IL: Waveland Press.

Manning, P. (1999). "Violence and Symbolic Violence." In V.E. Kappeler (ed.) *Police and Society: Touchstone Readings*, Second Edition, pp. 395-401. Prospect Heights, IL: Waveland Press.

Manning, P.K. (1989). "The Police Occupational Culture in Anglo-American Societies." In L. Hoover & J. Dowling (eds.) *Encyclopedia of Police Science*. New York, NY: Garland.

Martin, S. (1980). *Breaking and Entering: Policewomen on Patrol*. Berkeley, CA: University of California Press.

Martin, S. (1997). "Women Officers on the Move: An Update on Women in Policing." In R. Dunham & G. Alpert (eds.) *Critical Issues in Policing*, Third Edition, pp. 363-381. Prospect Heights, IL: Waveland Press.

Martin, S. (1989). "Women on the Move? A Report on the Status of Women in Policing." *Women & Criminal Justice*, 1(1):21-40.

Marx, K. (2000). "Capital." In D. McLellan (ed). *Karl Marx: Selected Writings*, Second Edition, pp. 452-546. New York, NY: Oxford.

Matza, D. (1969). *Becoming Deviant*. Englewood Cliffs, NJ: Prentice Hall.

Mastrofski, S.D., J.B. Snipes, R.B. Parks & C.D. Maxwell (2000). "The Helping Hand of the Law: Police Control of Citizens on Request." *Criminology*, 38:307-342.

Mastrofski, S.D., R.E. Worden & J.B. Snipes (1995). "Law Enforcement in a Time of Community Policing." *Criminology*, 33(4):539-563.

Mastrofski, S. & R.B. Parks (1990). "Improving Observational Studies of Police." *Criminology*, 28(3):475-496.

McClendon, K.J. (1994). *Multiple Regression and Causal Analysis*. Itasca, IL: F.E. Peacock.

McGurrin, D. & V.E. Kappeler (2002). "Media Accounts of Police Sexual Violence: Rotten Apples or State-Supported Violence?" In K.M. Lersch (ed.) *Policing and Misconduct*. Upper Saddle River, NJ: Pearson Education.

McLaren, J. & D. Perkins (1998). "The Posse Comitatus Act and Its Amendments," a paper from the Annual Meeting of the Academy of Criminal Justice Sciences. Albuquerque, NM:

Meadows, R.J. & L.C. Trostle (1988). "A Study of Police Misconduct and Litigation: Findings and Implications." *Journal of Contemporary Criminal Justice*, 4:77-92.

Meehan, A.J. & M.C. Ponder (2002a). "How Roadway Composition Matters in Analyzing Police Data on Racial Profiling." *Police Quarterly*, 5(3):306-333.

Meehan, A.J. & M.C. Ponder (2002b). "Race and Place: The Ecology of Racial Profiling African American Motorists." *Justice Quarterly*, 19(3):399-430.

Mencken, H.L. (1983). "Recollections of Notable Cops," In C. Klockars, *Thinking about Police: Contemporary Readings*. New York, NY: McGraw-Hill.

Mijares, T.C., R.M. McCarthy & D.B. Perkins (2000). *The Management of Police Specialized Tactical Units*, pp. 63-66. Springfield, IL: Charles C Thomas, LTD.

Mijares, T.C. (1993). "Tower of Lessons." *Command*, Summer:8-10.

Milgram, D. (2002). "Recruiting Women to Policing: Practical Strategies That Work." *Police Chief*, 69(4):23-25, 26, & 29.

Miller, L.S. & K. M. Hess (2002). *The Police in the Community: Strategies for the 21st Century*. Belmont, CA. Wadsworth/Thomson. National Bulletin on Police Misconduct Sexual Misconduct by Officer - Department's Policy of Silence. December.

Milton, C., J. Halleck, J. Lardner & G. Albrecht (1977). *Police Use of Deadly Force*. Washington, DC: Police Foundation.

Moore, M. (2002). "How Effectively Does Your Police Agency Recruit and Retain Women?" *Police Chief*, 69(3):29.

Morash, M. & R.N. Haarr (1995). "Gender, Workplace Problems, and Stress in Policing." *Justice Quarterly*, 12(1):113-140.

Moriarty, L.J. (2003). *Controversies in Victimology*. Cincinnati, OH: Anderson Publishing Co.

Morn, F. (1995). *Academic Politics and the History of Criminal Justice Education*. Westport, CT: Greenwood Press.

Mustaine, E.E. & R. Tewksbury (2003). *Controversies in Criminal Justice Research*. Cincinnati, OH: Anderson Publishing Co.

Myers, G. (1995). A *Municipal Mother: Portland's Lola Greene Baldwin, America's First Policewomen*. Corvallis, OR: Oregon State University.

National Center for Women and Policing, Feminist Majority Foundation (1999). Equality *Denied. The Status of Women in Policing: 1998*. Los Angeles, CA: National Center for Women and Policing.

National Institute of Justice (NIJ) Technology Assessment Program (1994, March). "Oleoresin Capsicum: Pepper Spray as a Force Alternative."

National Institute of Justice (NIJ) Research for Practice Series (2003, April). *The Effectiveness and Safety of Pepper Spray*. (Publication No. NCJ 195739).

National Institute of Justice (1997). *Criminal Justice Research under the Crime Act—1995 to 1996*. Washington, DC: U.S. Department of Justice.

National League of Cities (1985). "Seeking Solutions on Liability Insurance." *Nations Cities Weekly* (Nov. 25). Washington, DC: N.C.W.

NBC Nightly News, January 29, 2004.

NBC Nightly News, March 19, 2003.

Nelson, J. (ed.) (2000). *Police Brutality*. New York, NY: W.W. Norton & Co.

Neuman, W.L. (2000). Social *Research Methods: Qualitative and Quantitative Approaches*. Boston, MA: Allyn & Bacon.

Niederhoffer, A. (1969). *Behind the Shield: The Police in Urban Society*. Garden City, NY: Doubleday.

Nielson, E. (2001). "The Advanced Taser." *Law and Order*, 49(5):57-62.

Nixon, J. (2001). Annual Report on Missouri Traffic Stops [Online]. Available: http://www.ago.state.mo.us/rpexecsummary.htm [2002, January 24].

Norris, C., N. Fielding, C. Kemp & J. Fielding (1992). "Black and Blue: An Analysis of the Influence of Race on Being Stopped by the Police." *British Journal of Sociology*, 43(2):207-224.

Nowicki, E. (2001). "OC Spray Update." *Law and Order*, 49(6):28-29.

O'Harrow, R. Jr. (2003). "Police in Florida Compiling Counter-Terrorism Database." *The Washington Post*, (August 6).

O'Neill, P. & J. Oliva (1995). This Is the Time (1990) [Recorded by Savatage]. On *Dead Winter Dead* [CD]. New York, NY: Atlantic Records.

Osborne, J. (2003). "Will Austin Join Patriot Act Revolt?" *Austin American Statesman*, (August 7). (citing at least 140 local governments): NBC Nightly News, January 29, 2004 (now asserting over 200 local jurisdictions).

Osgood, D. & J. Chambers (2000). "Social Disorganization outside the Metropolis: An Analysis of Rural Youth Violence." *Criminology*, 38(1):81-115.

Parish, N. (2000a). "Cover-up in Webster Groves." *St. Louis Post-Dispatch*.

Parish, N. (2000b). "Ferguson Officer Sentenced to Nine Months Jail." *St. Louis Post-Dispatch*.

Parish, N. (2000c). "Three Florissant Officers Accused of Sex with Police Explorer." *St. Louis Post- Dispatch*.

Parsons, D. & P. Jesilow (2001). *In the Same Voice: Women and Men in Law Enforcement*. Santa Ana, CA: Seven Locks Press.

Pate, A.M. & L.A. Friddell (1993). *Police Use of Force: Official Reports, Citizen Complaints, and Legal Consequences*. Washington, DC: Police Foundation.

Peak, K. J. & R.W. Glensor (1996). *Community Policing and Problem Solving*. Upper Saddle River, NJ: Prentice Hall

Peck, M.S. (1998). *The Road Less Traveled*. New York, NY: Touchstone Books.

Perez, D. & J. Moore (2002). *Police Ethics: A Matter of Character*. Cincinnati, OH: Copperhouse/Atomic Dog Publishing.

Petrillo, L. (1990). "When a Cop Shoots, Who Takes a Close Look . . .?" *San Diego Union*, (December 21).

Pochurek, L.M. (1994). "From the Battlefield to the Homefront: Infrared Surveillance and the War on Drugs Place Privacy under Siege." *St. Thomas Law Review*, 7:137-167 (citing Stewart, David, "The Drug Exception," A.B.A.J., May, 1990.)

Polisar, J. (1998). "Recruiting, Integrating and Retaining Women Police Officers: Strategies that Work." *Police Chief*, 65(10):42-52.

Potter, G.W. (2002). *Controversies in White-Collar Crime*. Cincinnati, OH: Anderson Publishing Co.

Potter, G.W. & V.E. Kappeler (1998). *Constructing Crime: Perspectives on Making News & Social Problems*. Prospect Heights, IL: Waveland Press.

Prenzler, T. & J. Ransley (2002). *Police Reform: Building Integrity*. Sydney, Australia: Gaunt, Incorporated.

President's Commission on Crime and the Administration of Justice (1967). *The Challenges of Crime in a Free Society*. Washington, DC: U.S. Government Printing Office.

President's Commission on Law Enforcement and Administration of Justice (1967). *"The Challenge of Crime in a Free Society: A Report by the Presidential Commission on Law Enforcement of the Administration of Justice."* Washington DC: U.S. Government Printing Office.

Ragonese, P. (1991). *The Soul of a Cop*. New York, NY: St. Martin's Paperbacks.

Ramirez, D., J. McDevitt & A. Farrell (2000). *A Resource Guide on Racial Profiling Data Collection Systems*. Washington, DC: U.S. Department of Justice.

Reiner, R. (1992). *Politics of the Police*, Second Edition. London: Wheatsheaf.

Reiss, A.J. (1971). *The Police and the Public*. New Haven, CT: Yale University Press.

Reiss, A.J. (1968). *Police Brutality: Answers to Key Questions*. New Brunswick, NJ: Transaction.

Reynolds, C.D. (1988). "Unjust Civil Litigation: A Constant Threat." *The Police Chief*, 55(12):7.

Ritti, R.R. & S. Mastrofski (2002). *The Institutionalization of Community Policing, Final Report*. National Institute of Justice Grant 2000-IJ-CX-0021.

Ritti, R.R. & J.H. Silver (1986). "Early Processes of Institutionalization: The Dramaturgy of Exchange in Interorganizational Relations." *Administrative Science Quarterly*, 31(1):25-42.

Rudovsky, D. (1992). "Police Abuse: Can the Violence Be Contained?" *Harvard Civil Rights - Civil Liberties Law Review*, 27(2):465-501.

Salant, P. & D.A. Dillman (1994). *How to Conduct Your Own Survey*. New York, NY: John Wiley & Sons.

Samaha, J. (2002). *Criminal Procedure*. Bellmont, CA: Wadsworth.

Sampson, R. & W. Groves (1989). "Community Structure and Crime: Testing Social Disorganization Theory." *American Journal of Sociology*, 94(4):774-802.

Sampson, R. (1985). "Neighborhood and Crime: The Structural Determinants of Personal Victimization." *Journal of Research in Crime and Delinquency*, 22(1):7-40.

Sapp, A.D. (1997). "The Seductions of Sex." In John P. Crank (ed.) *Understanding Police Culture*. Cincinnati, OH: Anderson Publishing Co.

Sapp, A.D. (1986). "Sexual Misconduct by Police Officers." In T. Barker & D.L. Carter (eds.) *Police Deviance*. Cincinnati, OH: Anderson Publishing Co.

Savage, D.G. (2002). "Lawyers Debate Response to Sept. 11." *Los Angeles Times*, (August 11).

Scheingold, S. (1984). *The Politics of Law and Order*. New York, NY: Longman.

Schmitt, E.L. (2002). "Wider Military Role in U.S. Is Urged," *New York Times*, (July 21).

Schmitt, E.L., P.A. Langan & M.R. Durose (2002). *Characteristics of Drivers Stopped By Police, 1999*. Washington, DC: U.S. Department of Justice, Bureau of Justice Statistics.

Schneider, B.E. (1993). "Put Up and Shut Up: Workplace Sexual Assaults." In P.B. Bart & E.G. Moran (eds.) *Violence Against Women: The Bloody Footprints*. Newbury Park, CA: Sage.

Schofield, D.L. (1990). "Personal Liability: The Qualified Immunity Defense." *FBI Law Enforcement Bulletin*, 59:26-32.

Scogin, F. & S.L. Brodsky (1991). "Fear of Litigation Among Law Enforcement Officers." *American Journal of Police*, 4:197-202.

Schulz, D. (2002). "Law Enforcement Leaders: A Survey of Women Police Chiefs in the United States." *Police Chief*, 69(3):25-28.

Schulz, D. (1993). "Policewomen in the 1950s: Paving the Way for Patrol." *Women & Criminal Justice*, 4(2):5-30.

Stanish, H., T. Wood & P. Campagna (1999). "Prediction of Performance on the RCMP Physical Ability Requirement Evaluation." *Journal of Occupational and Environmental Medicine*, 41(8):669-677

Searle, J. (1998). *Mind, Language, and Society: Philosophy in the Real World*. New York, NY: Basic Books.

Stunz, W. J. (2002). "Local Policing After the Terror," *Yale Law Journal*, 111(8):2137-2194.

Stuntz, W.J. (2001). "Terrorism, Federalism, and Police Misconduct." *Harvard Journal of Law and Public Policy*, 25(2):665-679.

Stunz, W.J. (2001). "O.J. Simpson, Bill Clinton, and the Transsubstantive Fourth Amendment," *Harvard Law Review*, 114(3):842-876.

Swanson, C.R., L. Territo & R.W. Taylor (2001). *Police Administration: Structures, Processes and Behavior*. Upper Saddle River, NJ: Prentice-Hall.

Sykes, R. & E. Brent (1980). "The Regulation of Interaction by the Police: A Systems View of Taking Charge." *Criminology*, 18:182-97.

Tanner, R. (2002). "Central Park Case Puts Focus on Confessions," *Austin American Statesman*, Dec. 7, 2002: A9.

Tennenbaum, A.N. (1994). "Influence of the Garner Decision on Police Use of Deadly Force." *Journal of Criminal Law and Criminology*, 85(1):241-260.

Texas Department of Public Safety (2001). Traffic Stop Data Report: June 2001 Supplement [Online]. Available: http://www.txdps.state.tx.us/director_staff/public_information/indextrafstop.htm [2002, January 24].

Thompson, A.C. (1999). "Stopping the Usual Suspects: Race and the Fourth Amendment." *New York University Law Review*, 74(4):956-1013.

Thurman, Q., J. Zhao & A. Giacomazzi (2001). *Community Policing in A Community Era: An Introduction*. Los Angeles, CA: Roxbery Publishing Co.

Title 42, U.S. Code Section 1983.

Trostle, L.C. (1990). "Force Continuum: From Lethal to Less-Than Lethal Force." *Journal of Contemporary Criminal Justice*, 6(1):23-36.

Tyler, T.R. (2002). "Trust and Law Abidingness: A Proactive Model of Social Regulation," *Boston University Law Review*, 81:361-406; also citing Mastrofski, et al., "Compliance on Demand." *Journal of Research in Crime & Delinquency*, 33:272 (discussing that skill in handling rebellious and disgruntled persons is the street officer's performance litmus test).

Uelman, G. (1973). "Varieties of Police Policy: A Study of Police Policy Regarding the Use of Deadly Force in Los Angeles County." *Loyola-Los Angeles Law Review*, 6:1-61.

United Press International (1991). "Chief Apologizes, Says Award Shouldn't Have Been Given." (March 20).

Shanahan, P. (2000). "Police Culture and the Learning Organization: A Relationship?" Paper presented at the annual meeting of the Australian Vocational Education and Training Research Association.

Shaw, C. & H. McKay (1972). *Juvenile Delinquency and Urban Areas*, Third Edition. Chicago, IL: University of Chicago Press.

Shelden, R.G. (2001). *Controlling the Dangerous Classes: A Critical Introduction to the History of Criminal Justice*. Needham Heights, MA: Allyn & Bacon.

Sherman, L. (1985). "Becoming Bent: Moral Careers of Corrupt Policemen." In F. Elliston & M. Feldberg (eds.) *Moral Issues in Police Work*, pp. 253-273. Totawa, NJ: Rowman & Allanheld.

Sherman, L. (1983). "Reducing Police Gun Use: Critical Events, Administrative Policy and Organizational Change." In M. Punch (ed.) *Control in the Police Organization*. Cambridge, MA: MIT Press.

Sherman, L. & R. Langworthy (1979). "Measuring Homicide by Police Officers." *Journal of Criminal Law and Criminology*, 70(4):546-60.

Shweder, R. (1991). *Thinking Through Cultures: Expeditions in Cultural Psychology*. Cambridge, MA: Harvard University Press.

Silver, I. (1996). *Police Civil Liability*. New York, NY: Matthew Bender.

Silverman, E.B. (1999). *NYPD Battles Crime*. Boston, MA: Northeastern University Press.

Skogan, W.G. & S. Hartnett (1997). *Community Policing Chicago Style*. New York, NY: Oxford University Press.

Skolnick, J. (1966). *Justice without Trial: Law Enforcement in a Democratic Society*. New York, NY: John Wiley and Sons.

Skolnick, J. & J. Fyfe (1994). *Above the Law: Police and the Excessive Use of Force*. New York, NY: Free Press.

Smith, M.R. & M. Petrocelli (2001). "Racial Profiling? A Multivariate Analysis of Police Traffic Stop Data." *Police Quarterly*, 4(1):4-27.

Spitzer, E. (1999). *The New York City Police Department's "Stop and Frisk" Practices*. New York, NY: Attorney General of New York.

Stafford, A.R. (1986). "Lawsuits against the Police: Reasons for the Proliferation of Litigation in the Past Decade." *Journal of Police and Criminal Psychology*, 2(1):30-34.

Uniting and Strengthening America by Providing Appropriate Tools Required to Intercept and Obstruct Terrorism Act (USA PATRIOT ACT) of 2001, Pub. L. No. 107-56, 115 Stat. 272.

U.S. Census Bureau (2003). Statistical *Abstract of the United States*. Washington, DC.

U.S. Department of Justice (2002). Federal Bureau of Investigation. *Crime in the United States*. Uniform Crime Reports.

U.S. Department of Justice (2001). *Principles for Promoting Police Integrity*. Washington DC: Government Printing Office.

U.S. Department of Justice (2001). Federal Bureau of Investigation. *Crime in the United States*. Uniform Crime Reports.

U.S. Department of Justice (2000). Federal Bureau of Investigation. *Crime in the United States*. Uniform Crime Reports.

U.S. Department of Justice (1990). Federal Bureau of Investigation. *Crime in the United States*. Uniform Crime Reports.

U.S. National Advisory Commission on Civil Disorders (1968). *Commission Final Report*. New York, NY: Bantam.

U.S. National Advisory Commission on Criminal Justice Standards and Goals (1973). *The Police*. Washington, DC: Government Printing Office.

U.S. President's Commission on Law Enforcement and Administration of Justice (1968). *Report on Law Enforcement and Administration of Justice: The Challenge of Crime in a Free Society*. Washington, DC: U.S. Government Printing Office.

U.S. President's Commission on Law Enforcement and Administration of Justice (1968). *Report on Law Enforcement and Administration of Justice: The Challenge of Crime in a Free Society*. Washington, DC: U.S. Government Printing Office.

VanMaanen, J. (1978). "The Asshole." In P.K Manning & J. VanMaanen (eds.) *A View From the Street*, pp. 221-238. Santa Monica, CA: Goodyear Press.

Vaughn, M.S. (1999). "Police Sexual Violence: Civil Liability under State Tort Law." *Crime & Delinquency*, 45(3):334-357.

Vaughn, M.S. (1994). "Police Civil Liability for Abandonment in High Crime Areas and Other High Risk Situations." *Journal of Criminal Justice*, 22(5):407-424.

Vaughn, M.S. & L.F. Coomes (1995). "Police Civil Liability under Section 1983: When do Police Officers Act Under Color of Law?" *Journal of Criminal Justice*, 23(5):395-415.

Vela, S. (2001). "Officer Shoots, Kills Suspect." *Cincinnati Enquirer*, (April 8).

Verniero, P. & P.H. Zoubek (1999). *Interim Report of The State Police Review Team Regarding Allegations of Racial Profiling*. Trenton, NJ: New Jersey Attorney General's Office.

Vitullo, L.P. & S.J. Peters (1981). "Intergovernmental Cooperation and the Municipal Insurance Crisis." *De Paul Law Review*, 30:325-345.

Waddington, P. (1999). "Police (Canteen) Sub-Culture: An Appreciation." *British Journal of Criminology*, 39(2):287-309.

Wagner, A.E. & S.H. Decker (1997). "Evaluating Citizen Complaints Against the Police." In R.G. Dunham & G.P Alpert (eds.) *Critical Issues in Policing: Contemporary Readings*, Third Edition, pp. 302-318. Prospect Heights, IL: Waveland.

Walker, S. (2001). "Searching for the Denominator: Problems with Police Traffic Stop Data and an Early Warning System Solution." *Justice Research and Policy*, 3(1):63-95.

Walker, S. (2001). *Police Accountability: The Role of Citizen Oversight*. Belmont, CA: Wadsworth.

Walker, S. (1999). *The Police in America*. Boston, MA: McGraw-Hill College.

Walker, S. (1985). "Racial Minority and Female Employment in Policing: The Implications of 'Glacial Change.'" *Crime & Delinquency*, 31:565-572.

Walker, S. (1985). "Racial Minority and Female Employment in Policing: The Implications of 'Glacial Change.'" *Crime & Delinquency*, 31:565-572.

Walker, S. (1977). *A Critical History of Police Reform*. Lexington, MA: DC Health and Company.

Walker, S. & D. Irlbeck (2002). *"Driving While Female": A National Problem in Police Misconduct*. Omaha, NE: University of Nebraska at Omaha.

Walker, S. & B. Kreisel (1997). "Varieties of Citizen Review: The Relationship of Mission, Structure, and Procedures to Police Accountability." In R. G. Dunham & G.P. Alpert (eds.), *Critical Issues in Policing: Contemporary Readings*, Third Edition. Prospect Heights, IL: Waveland Press.

Wallerstein, I. & The Gulbenkian Commission (1996). *Open the Social Sciences: report of the Gulbenkian Commission on the Restructuring of the Social Sciences*. Stanford. CA: Stanford University Press.

Warner, C. (1992). *The Last Word: A Treasury of Women's Quotes*. Englewood Cliffs, NJ: Prentice Hall Direct.

Warnke, G. (1993). *Justice and Interpretation*. Cambridge, MA: The MIT Press.

Weiss, J.A. (2000). "A Road Not Taken." *Seton Hall Legislative Journal*, 26(2):415-458.

Weitzer, R. & S.A. Tuch (2002). "Perceptions of Racial Profiling: Race, Class, and Personal Experience." *Criminology*, 40(2):435-456.

Wells, H.G. (1895). *The Time Machine*. New York, NY: Signet Classics, Reprint Edition, 1984.

West, C. & D. Zimmerman (1998). "Doing Gender." In J. Lorber, *Gender Inequality: Feminist Theories and Politics*, pp. 161-166. Los Angeles, CA: Roxbury.

White, J. (2002). "Honored Trooper Charged in Bribery," *Washington Post*, (April 4).

Williams, M. & S. Emling (2002). "Experts Disagree on Degree of Success in America's New War." *Austin American-Statesman/Washington Bureau*, (September 8).

Wilson, J.Q. & G.L. Kelling (1982). "Broken Windows: Police and Neighborhood Safety." *Atlantic Monthly*, 249(3):29-38.

Wilson, O.W. (1950). *Police Administration*. New York, NY: McGraw-Hill.

Wood, D.P. (2003). "The Rule to Law in Times of Stress." *University of Chicago Law Review*, 70(1):459-463.

Wood, J. (1997). *Royal Commissioner into the New South Wales Police Department, Final Report*, Volume 1: Corruption, NSW Department.

Worrall, J.L. (2001). "Culpability Standards in Section 1983 Litigation Against Criminal Justice Officials: When and Why Mental State Matters." *Crime & Delinquency*, 47(1):28-59.

Worrall, J.L. (2001). "The Reasonably Unreasonable Police Officer: A Paradox in Police Civil Liability Jurisprudence." *Policing: An International Journal of Police Strategies and Management*, 24(4):449-469

Worrall, J.L. & R.S. Gutierrez (1999). "Potential Consequences of Community-Oriented Policing for Civil Liability: Is There a Dark Side to Employee Empowerment?" *Review of Public Personnel Administration*, 19(2):61-70.

Zalman, M. & L. Siegel (1991). *Criminal Procedure: Constitution and Society*. St. Paul, MN: West Publishing.

Zhao, J., M. Scheider & Q. Thurman (2002). "Community Policing and Crime: A National Assessment of the Effects of COPS Grants on Crime." *Criminology and Public Policy*, 2(1):7-32.

Zhao, J., L. Herbst & N. Lovrich (2001). "Race, Ethnicity and the Female Cop: Differential Patterns of Representation." *Journal of Urban Affairs*, 33:3-4, 243-257.

Zhao, J., N. Lovrich & Q. Thurman (1999). "The Status of Community Oriented Policing in American Cities: Revisiting Facilitators and Impediments after Three Years." *Policing: An International Journal of Police Strategies and Management*, 22(1):74-92.

Zhap, J., M.C. Scheider & Q. Thurman (2002). "Funding Community Policing To Reduce Crime: Have COPS Grants Made a Difference?" *Criminology and Police Policy*, 2(1):11-13.

Zingraff, M.T., H.M. Mason, W.R. Smith, D. Tomaskovic-Devey, P. Warren, H.L. McMurray & C.R. Fenlon (2000). Evaluating North Carolina State Highway Patrol Data: Citations, Warnings, and Searches in 1998 [Online]. Available: http://www.nccrimecontrol.org/shp/ncshpreport.htm [2002, January 24]

Cases Cited

Atwater v. City of Lago Vista, 532 U.S. 318 (2001).

Bivens v. Six Unknown Federal Narcotics Agents, 403 U.S. 388, 91 S. Ct. 1999 (1971).

City of Canton v. Harris, 389 U.S. 378, 103 L. Ed. 412, 109 S. Ct 1197 (1989).

Lanning v. Southeastern Pennsylvania Transportation Authority, 308 F. 3d 286 (3d Cir. 2002).

Colston v. Barnhart, 130 F.3d 96, 99 (5th Cir. 1997).

Deorle v. Rutherford, (9th Cir. 2001).

Garza v. United States, 881 F. Supp. 1099 (S.D. Texas 1997).

Graham v. Conner, U.S. 109, S. Ct. 1865 (1989).

Heitschmidt v. City of Houston, 161 F.3d 834, 839 (5th Cir. 1998).

Illinois v. Gates, 462 U.S. 312 (1983).

Illinois v. Wardlow, 528 U.S. 119 (2000).

King v. Chide, 974 F.2d 653 (5th Cir. 1992).

Lanning v. Southeastern Pennsylvania Transportation Authority, 308 F.3d 286 (3d Cir. 2002).

Monroe v. Pape, 365 U.S. 167, 81 S. Ct. 473 (1961).

Peer v. City of Newark, 71 NJ Super. 12, 176A.2nd 249 (1961).

Popow v. City of Margate, 476 F. Supp. 1237 (1979).

Riggs v. City of Pearland, 177 F.R.D. 395, 407 (S.D.Texas 1997).

Snyder v. Trepagnier, 142 F.3d 791 (5th Cir. 1998).

Spann v. Rainey, 987 F.2d 1110, 1115 (5th Cir. 1993).

Tennessee v. Garner, 471 U.S. 1, 20 (1985).

Terry v. Ohio, 392 U.S. 1 (1968).

U.S. v. Arviza, 122 S. Ct. 744 (2002).

U.S. v. Jordan, 232 F.3d 447 (5th Cir. 2000).

U.S. v. Lanier, 117 S. Ct. 1219 (1997)

Whren v. U.S. 517 U.S. 806 (1996).

Contributors' Biographical Information

Andra J. Katz-Bannister (Ph.D., Michigan State University) is Director of the federally funded (COPS) Regional Community Policing Institute (RCPI) at Wichita State University and Associate Professor of Criminal Justice at WSU. She is the author of numerous articles, chapters, and papers on community policing, organized crime, computer crime, and police policy issues. She has conducted extensive research in Europe and Asia, has provided training on computer crime and community policing to the Royal Thai Police, and provided training and technical assistance to a wide range of police agencies, notably in Kansas and Nebraska which are the service areas of the RCPI. A former sworn reserve officer with the Wichita Police Department, Dr. Bannister works closely with the POST commissions in Kansas and Nebraska and the Office of Community Oriented Policing Services, U.S. Department of Justice.

Anthony V. Bouza is a former Minneapolis police chief and Bronx police commander. His years of experience allow his readers an unabashed inside look at the state of American policing. In addition, he is the author of eight books, including, *The Decline and Fall of the American Empire: Corruption, Decadence, and the American Dream, Police Intelligence: The Operations of an Investigative Unit, How to Stop Crime, Police Administration: Organization and Performance, Police Unbound: Corruption, Abuse, and Heroism by the Boys in Blue, Bronx Beat: Reflections of a Police Commander,* and the critically acclaimed *The Police Mystique.*

David L. Carter is a Professor in the School of Criminal Justice at Michigan State University. A former Kansas City, Missouri police officer, Dr. Carter was Chairman of the Department of Criminal Justice at the University of Texas-Pan American prior to his appointment at Michigan State in 1985. He has served as a trainer, consultant, and advisor to law enforcement agencies throughout the U.S. and abroad on a variety of policing matters. In addition, he has presented training sessions at the FBI National Academy, the FBI Law Enforcement Executive Development Seminar (LEEDS), police "command colleges" of Texas, Florida, Ohio, Massachusetts, and Kentucky; and served at the FBI Academy's Behavioral Science Services Unit on the first academic faculty exchange. Internationally, he has been an invited lec-

189

turer for the International Law Enforcement Academy (Budapest), Hong Kong
Police, Royal Thai Police, Norwegian Police, Thames Valley Police (UK),
Staffordshire Police (UK), the United Nations Asia Far East Institute (Tokyo)
and others. In addition, Dr. Carter is Director of the MSU Criminal Justice
Study Abroad Program to England. He is the author or co-author of five books
and numerous articles and monographs on policing issues and is a member
of the Editorial Boards of various professional publications. His most recent
book is the seventh edition of *The Police and Community*. Since the late
1980s, Dr. Carter has conducted research on law enforcement intelligence
and international organized crime. His work includes not only teaching an
academic course on the subject, but also providing extensive training to law
enforcement agencies and authoring a 500 page monograph on the subject
used in training and by agencies for developing their units. Since 9/11 Dr.
Carter has conducted training on homeland security/terrorism issues at the
FBI Academy, for USDoJ COPS Institutes in several states, the USDoJ BJA State
and Local Anti-Terrorism Training (SLATT), and the Ohio Association of Chiefs
of Police. He is currently co-authoring two books: (1) *Homeland Security
for State and Local Police* (with Richard Holden) and (2) *Computer Crime:
Policy Issues for Police Administrators* (with Andra Katz-Bannister).

John P. Crank is an Associate Professor of Criminal Justice at Florida
Atlantic University's Treasure Coast Campus. Crank received his PhD. in sociology at the University of Colorado in 1987. His articles have appeared in
such journals as *Justice Quarterly*, *Criminal Justice and Behavior*, and *Journal of Criminal Justice*. He has authored several books including *Imagining
Justice*, *Understanding Police Culture*, and co-authored *Counter-Terrorism
After 9/11: Justice, Security and Ethics Reconsidered* (with Patricia E. Gre-
gor) and *Police Ethics: The Corruption of Noble Cause* (with Michael A.
Caldero). Crank's research interests include attitudes and behavior of the
police, institutional theory of organizations, and organizational cultures. Professor Crank was the recipient of the Academy of Criminal Justice Sciences' 2004 Outstanding Book Award for *Imagining Justice*.

Karen J. Finkenbinder has been in the criminal justice field for 28 years.
She began her career as a military policewoman in the mid 1970's. She com-
pleted her bachelor's degree in Criminal Justice from Missouri-Western
State College and was commissioned as a second lieutenant in the United
States Army. She taught criminal justice courses as an adjunct professor for
Central Texas College and served as Director of Training for the University
of South Carolina Division of Law Enforcement and Safety. She was activated
by the Army Reserves and served in Saudi Arabia as the Intelligence and Security Officer of a prisoner of war camp during Operations Desert Storm and
Shield. She returned to spend more than a decade at the Carlisle Police
Department. There, she served as a patrol supervisor until she resigned to
accept a position as a police training education specialist with the Penn-

sylvania Municipal Police Officers Education and Training Commission. Ms. Finkenbinder has a Masters of Public Administration and is a doctoral candidate in public administration, where she focuses her interests and research in the areas of criminal justice policy and management.

Andrew L. Giacomazzi is an Associate Professor of Criminal Justice Administration at Boise State University. Giacomazzi received his Ph.D. in political science at Washington State University in 1995. His articles have appeared in such journals as *Crime & Delinquency, Justice Quarterly*, and *Police Quarterly*. He is co-author of *Community Policing in a Community Era: An Introduction and Exploration* (with Quint Thurman and Jihong Zhao). Giacomazzi's research interests include community policing, organizational change, and family violence.

Donna C. Hale is Professor of Criminal Justice at Shippensburg University of Pennsylvania. She is a Past President of the Academy of Criminal Justice Sciences. Professor Hale is the Editor of *Women & Criminal Justice*. She is the co-author (with Frankie Y. Bailey) of *Blood on Her Hands: The Social Construction of Women, Sexuality, and Murder*. She is the author/co-author of several articles on women police. She received her Ph.D. from Michigan State University, School of Criminal Justice. She was the Associate Director of the Flint Foot Patrol Project.

Victor E. Kappeler is a Professor of Criminal Justice and Police Studies in the College of Justice and Safety at Eastern Kentucky University. He has written extensively in the areas of policing and criminal justice.

John Liederbach received his Ph.D. in Criminal Justice from the University of Cincinnati in 2002. His primary research interests are the study of police behavior across different types of community contexts and white-collar and professional crime. His work has appeared in *Justice Quarterly* and the *American Journal of Criminal Justice*.

David B. Perkins is an Associate Professor of Criminal Justice at Texas State University–San Marcos. He has experience in both municipal prosecution and criminal defense roles, and for the past 27 years he has been a municipal court judge and magistrate. His teaching experience includes both undergraduate and graduate courses in criminal law and procedure, and in police systems and practices. His research interests and publications involve constitutional law, police tactical unit management, police civil liability issues, and substantive and procedural law and practices in the lower courts.

Joycelyn M. Pollock is a professor at Texas State University–San Marcos (formerly Southwest Texas State). She received her Ph.D. in Criminal Justice at the State University of New York at Albany. She also obtained a J.D. at the University of Houston, and passed the Texas Bar in 1991. Dr. Pollock has published numerous books including, *Ethics in Crime and Justice: Dilemmas and Decisions* was published (2003, 4th ed.), *Prisons and Prison Life: Costs and Consequences* (2003), *Women, Prison and Crime* (2002, 2nd ed.), *Sex and Supervision: Guarding Male and Female Inmates* (1986), *Counseling Women Prisoners* (1999), *Criminal Women* (2000), *Prison: An American Institution* (editor) (1997), and is co-editor with Alida Merlo of *Women, Law and Social Control*, 2nd ed. (2004). In addition to be an author and teaching at Texas State University (formerly Southwest Texas State University), she has delivered training to police officers, probation officers, parole officers, constables, and other groups in the areas of sexual harassment, ethics, criminology, and other subjects. She has taught at the Houston Police Academy, the Bill Blackwood Law Enforcement Management Institute, and has been a guest speaker for the International Association of Policewomen, the Texas Juvenile Justice Association, and the Southwest Legal Institute, among other groups. In 1998 she was awarded a Fulbright Teaching Fellowship to Turku School of Law in Turku, Finland. She has served as President of the Southwest Association of Criminal Justice and is currently a Trustee-at-Large for the Academy of Criminal Justice Sciences.

Karen S. Miller-Potter is an Assistant Professor of Sociology at Eastern Kentucky University. She received a Ph.D. in Sociology from the University of Kentucky. Her major scholarly interest is capital punishment as public policy. Her work has focused on innocence cases and the intersection of race and class as they relate to capital prosecutions, sentencing, and executions. She has also published in the areas of juvenile justice, white-collar crime, and reproductive privacy.

Matthew C. Scheider, Ph.D. is currently an Acting Assistant Director with the U.S. Department of Justice, Office of Community Oriented Policing Services in Washington D.C. The division he supervises is responsible for providing internal policy support, evaluating national community policing programs, and advancing the knowledge of community policing through pilot programs and publications designed specifically for the law enforcement field. His areas of research interest include commuting policing, Federal government program evaluation, criminological theory, and fear of crime.

Robert W. Taylor, Ph.D. is currently Professor and Chair of the Department of Criminal Justice at the University of North Texas in Denton, Texas. Dr. Taylor has an extensive background in academic and professional criminal justice, having taught at four major universities and serving as a sworn police officer and major crimes detective (in Portland, Oregon) for over six years.

He has authored or co-authored over one hundred articles, books, and manuscripts focusing on police administration, international and domestic terrorism, drug trafficking, computer fraud, and criminal justice policy. Dr. Taylor has been the recipient of over $10 million in external grants and is an active consultant to various U.S. and international criminal justice agencies. He is active member of the Academy of Criminal Justice Sciences where he currently serves as the elected Chair of the Police Section. Dr. Taylor is a graduate of Michigan State University (Master of Science-1973) and Portland State University (Doctor of Philosophy-1981).

Quint C. Thurman is Professor of Criminal Justice and Department Chairperson at Texas State University–San Marcos. He received a Ph.D. in Sociology from the University at Massachusetts (Amherst) in 1987. His publications include five books and more than 30 refereed articles that have appeared in such journals as the *American Behavioral Scientist, Crime and Delinquency, Criminology and Public Policy, Social Science Quarterly, Justice Quarterly, Police Quarterly*, and the *Journal of Quantitative Criminology*. Books published in 2003 include a second edition of *Community Policing in a Rural Setting* (with co-author Edmund McGarrell). In 2004 Dr. Thurman co-edited an anthology, *Contemporary Policing: Controversies, Challenges, and Solutions* (with Jihong Zhao), and *Police Problem Solving* (with J.D. Jamieson).

John L. Worrall is an Associate Professor in the Department of Criminal Justice at California State University, San Bernardino. He received his Ph.D. in Political Science from Washington State University in 1999. His research interests are legal issues in policing and crime control policy. Dr. Worrall is the author of five books, including Criminal Evidence: An Introduction (Roxbury, 2004—with Craig Hemmens) and Criminal Procedure: From First Contact to Appeal (Allyn and Bacon, 2003). His work has also appeared in *Crime & Delinquency, Evaluation Review*, the *Journal of Criminal Justice, Police Quarterly*, and the *Security Journal*, among other journals. He is currently a paid consultant with the American Prosecutors Research Institute and a Fellow with the California Institute for County Government.

Jihong "Solomon" Zhao, Ph.D. is an Associate Professor at the University of Nebraska–Omaha. His areas of interest include police reform, organizational assessment and change, and individual values and stress in the workplace. He has written or co-written numerous scholarly articles and books, including *Community Policing in a Community Era: An Introduction and Exploration* (with co-authors Quint C. Thurman and Andrew Giacomazzi), and *Why Police Organizations Change*.

Index

CPSIA information can be obtained at www.ICGtesting.com
Printed in the USA
BVOW080232190112

280914BV00004B/7/P